WHEN THE PRESS FAILS

Studies in Communication, Media, and Public Opinion

A SERIES EDITED BY SUSAN HERBST AND BENJAMIN I. PAGE

WHEN THE PRESS FAILS

Political Power and the News Media from Iraq to Katrina

W. LANCE BENNETT,

REGINA G. LAWRENCE,

AND

STEVEN LIVINGSTON

THE UNIVERSITY OF CHICAGO PRESS · CHICAGO AND LONDON

W. *Lance Bennett* is the Ruddick C. Lawrence Professor of Communication and professor of political science at the University of Washington. His previous books include *News: The Politics of Illusion* and, coedited with David Paletz, *Taken by Storm*, the latter published by the University of Chicago Press.

Regina G. Lawrence is associate professor and chair of the Division of Political Science in the Hatfield School of Government at Portland State University. She is the author of *The Politics of Force* and numerous journal articles.

Steven Livingston is associate professor in the School of Media and Public Affairs as well as associate professor of international affairs in the Elliott School of International Affairs at The George Washington University. In addition to journal articles and book chapters, his previous publications include *The Terrorism Spectacle*.

The University of Chicago Press, Chicago 60637
The University of Chicago Press, Ltd., London
© 2007 by The University of Chicago
All rights reserved. Published 2007
Printed in the United States of America

16 15 14 13 12 11 10 09 08 07   2 3 4 5

ISBN-13: 978-0-226-04284-8 (cloth)

ISBN-10: 0-226-04284-7 (cloth)

Library of Congress Cataloging-in-Publication Data

Bennett, W. Lance.
   When the press fails : political power and the news media from Iraq to Katrina / W. Lance Bennett, Regina G. Lawrence, and Steven Livingston.
      p.   cm. — (Studies in communication, media, and public opinion)
   Includes bibliographical references and index.
   ISBN-13: 978-0-226-04284-8 (hardcover : alk. paper)
   ISBN-10: 0-226-04284-7 (hardcover : alk. paper)
      1. Government and the press—United States—History—21st century.
   2. Press and politics—United States—History—21st century.
   3. Journalism—Objectivity—United States—History—21st century.
   I. Lawrence, Regina G., 1961–   II. Livingston, Steven.   III. Title.
   PN4738.B37   2007
   071'.30905—dc22

                                                        2006034501

♾ The paper used in this publication meets the minimum requirements of the American National Standard for Information Sciences—Permanence of Paper for Printed Library Materials, ANSI Z39.48-1992.

For Tim Cook

INSPIRING COLLEAGUE AND DEAR FRIEND

CONTENTS

PREFACE

There are no hereditary kings in America and no powers not created by the
Constitution.

A FEDERAL JUDGE, IN RULING AGAINST A DOMESTIC
EAVESDROPPING PROGRAM BEGUN BY THE BUSH ADMINISTRATION
AFTER THE 9/11 ATTACKS

Historians are likely to have a field day with the Bush administration and
its War on Terror. Few will be arguing that fighting terror was a bad or
unsupportable idea. But many will be wondering how that fight was conducted so clumsily, with so little insight or learning, and with such hubris. They will ponder how the outpouring of goodwill and support from
so many nations following 9/11 could be squandered so quickly, as polls
registered growing numbers who regarded the United States as a greater
threat to world security than the Islamic extremists it was battling.

From the view of social science, it seems clear that much of the planning inside the Bush administration occurred under the influence of
groupthink—from the rationale for invading Iraq to the hapless conviction
that democracy would flower there spontaneously. In his classic study of
the Kennedy administration's Bay of Pigs fiasco, psychologist Irving Janis
described groupthink as a condition in which dominant personalities (of
which there were many in the Bush camp) are so sure of themselves that
they wall off the decision-making process from outside scrutiny and critical information, and punish those who would question their convictions.

The signs of groupthink persisted throughout the Bush years, deflect-
ing many opportunities for learning. For example, long after many scholars and experts had observed it, the president's own National Intelligence
Estimate (based on the consensus of sixteen intelligence agencies) concluded that the conduct of the Iraq war had become a global recruiting
boon for extremists, and thus contributed to the terrorism threat that

it was supposed to help resolve. The response from the White House was not to rethink its policies, but to send the president on the offensive against opponents concerned about the findings from his own intelligence agencies. Mr. Bush delivered a blistering speech attacking the patriotism of his critics and asking how anyone could believe that fighting terrorism could contribute to the problem.

In the end, as at the beginning, the administration persisted in trying to define reality by the sheer force of its ideas. What is perhaps most interesting about this process is how long the press remained a silent if often uncomfortable partner to this reality-bending exercise. A free and independent press is generally considered essential for democracy, both to raise timely questions about debatable government policies and to report challenges to those policies when they fail. The ideal of press independence does not mean that the resulting open public debate will necessarily shape or improve the course of policy. However, balancing the spin of prominent officials with reasonable challenges can hold government up to the bright light of public accountability—which sometimes does help make policies more intelligent and effective. At the very least, publicizing credible challenges to dubious policies may give large numbers of citizens more timely information. And when those citizens hear their private and sometimes ill-defined concerns aired and clarified in the legitimating space of the mainstream press, they may begin to act as a public, instead of suffering in isolation with their own shock and awe as events unravel before their very eyes.

Perhaps most important, an independent press may spare people from learning too late that they have been deceived or misled, not just by their leaders, but by the press itself, caught up in the web of political power and spin. It seems to be no accident that public confidence in the press in recent decades has followed closely the spiral of declining trust in the executive and legislative branches of government that generate most of the daily news.

This book examines why leading news organizations continued to emphasize the Bush administration's scripting when covering situations that had other, often more plausible sides to them. Despite the availability of credible sources to challenge administration spin, the press often reported those challenges in small fragments buried in the back pages simply for the record. Such diminutive examples of press independence may serve as face-saving gestures for news organizations whose reporters often knew far more about situations than their organizations' heated pursuit of powerful sources enabled them to say. This imbalance of truth and power is small comfort to democracy, however.

Of course, all of this might have been different if the Democrats had behaved as an opposition party and challenged the administration. Through the Bush years they displayed little capacity to generate ideas or leadership, and they were further handicapped by the low power index implicitly assigned to them by the press. The vicious circle of the news game meant that the Democrats were less newsworthy as a party out of power, with consequently fewer institutional levers to pull to advance news stories. But the question, where were the Democrats? begs a more important one: where was the press?

This book explores the reasons why the press reported reality during the Iraq years largely as the Bush administration had scripted it, even when that script seemed bizarrely out of line with observable events. We trace the operating practices of American journalism as they have grown entwined with power and officials. The core concern here is with why the press fails when democracy needs it the most—that is, when the government fails to consider important alternatives and challenges to crucial courses of action.

The refreshingly independent coverage of Hurricane Katrina (whose aftermath was not unlike Iraq in revealing administrative ineptitude) is the exception that proves the rule. Reporters entered a no-spin zone because the administration was caught off guard during the vacations of several key officials. Officials were suddenly challenged and held publicly accountable. And for a moment, journalistic back channels buzzed with talk about a resurgence of press independence. Soon thereafter, however, the news returned to its daily routines of reporting the scripts of the officials in power.

In addition to explaining why the press fails when democracy most needs the independent public viewpoints it could provide, we also explore how news organizations might think about restoring the tradition of "watchdog" journalism. It is important that as America faces a crisis of leadership in a time of global challenge, we restore confidence in what may be our most important democratic institution: a free press.

ACKNOWLEDGMENTS

In the course of researching and writing this book, we have accumulated many intellectual debts. First, we would like to acknowledge the help of our research assistants: Tim Jones, Carolyn Lee, Chuck Rowling, John Werbin, and Christian Breunig. The comments of readers and reviewers have been tremendously helpful also. We particularly want to thank Ben Page and Robert Entman.

Our deepest thanks go to the editorial team at the University of Chicago Press that produced this book. John Tryneski has the uncanny ability to grasp core ideas and give just the right signals about how to develop and sharpen them. He has been involved at just the right times and in just the right ways to make this a better book. And Rodney Powell was an amazing source of timely input and quick answers to questions about the myriad details that can frustrate even the most detail-oriented writers.

Finally, we thank our dear colleague and friend, Tim Cook, to whom this book is dedicated, and whose spirit lives on in these pages.

Introduction

The Press and Power

The American press is in crisis. The symptoms are widely known and much lamented among journalists, academics, and the general public: diminishing levels of public confidence, dwindling audiences, ratcheting profit pressures, shrinking resources, and increasing negativity, sensationalism, and soft news. To top it off, younger demographics—the future market for news—are rejecting conventional journalism in alarming numbers compared with their cohorts in past generations. Those market segments are also the future citizens in our democracy.

This book seeks to identify the core practices that may account for journalism's uneven performance and the resulting decline in the public's faith and following. The short story here is that the press has grown too close to the sources of power in this nation, making it largely the communication mechanism of the government, not the people. This state of affairs is not intentional, and would be denied vigorously by most members of the press corps, who often see themselves as embattled, frequently fighting officials for small bits of information to distinguish their stories from the others. In the end, this daily struggle for small differences is part of the problem. Reporting that steers its course so closely to the leads of officialdom results in stunningly homogeneous outcomes across the majority of mainstream media outlets. This is an odd situation in what may well be the freest press system in the world.

Now is the time to discuss and embrace standards of public accountability that would enable journalists to resist the relentless political spin from their sources better, and to produce authentic and worthwhile news. Fortunately, some hallowed standards already exist, and may simply need to be revisited and refashioned to suit present-day political and journalistic realities. For example, the notion of the press as a public watchdog has long been idealized in the lore of journalism, and is still alive in occasional bursts of reportorial independence. Yet the practical definition and sure

1

application of such standards have been pushed out of daily consideration by relentless pressure from the business side of the news media and the tendency of Washington insiders (including members of the elite press) to conflate power with political reality. These trends are at their most alarming when those in government, business, or other powerful social institutions are bent on deception in order to exercise their will—and hints, telltale signs, or, in the case of the war in Iraq, substantial evidence of those deceptions go unchallenged by the press. At these moments, the decisions made by news organizations to showcase official versions of events, rather than challenging them, can undermine public involvement, discourage opponents within government from stepping forward, and, more generally, fail to set a higher standard of public discourse that officials would be obliged to respect.

This book shows how and why the press provided such an uncritical public context for what turned out to be such a disastrous adventure in Iraq. The cases that we analyze are not accidental or isolated incidents. To the contrary, the unfolding of the Iraq war reflects systematic problems within the U.S. press that will happen again—unless we have a vigorous and responsible public debate about the democratic responsibilities of those who bring us our daily media realities.

Thinking squarely about the democratic role of the press would surely be easier if most mainstream news organizations were not embedded in large corporations that are more concerned about representing shareholder interests than embracing public-interest standards that might better serve democracy. Yet standards of corporate public responsibility have been established in the past, and they can be established again. We are not thinking immediately here about government regulation, although public-interest standards are codified in many nations and still exist in vestigial form in the United States. More important is to begin a healthy public discussion about public responsibilities of the press and the corresponding social responsibilities of the companies who own and operate news organizations. As with most standards of social behavior, the emergence and maintenance of manners, customs, and responsibilities begin and end with some level of everyday awareness, observance, and commitment.

In the absence of much attention to these higher concerns (beyond the occasional mea culpa from a news organization that got a story wrong), the U.S. press system is adrift. The result is that the daily media reality experienced by most Americans is left to be defined by a combination of forces, ranging from the distant economic pressures of corporate owners to the more immediate daily journalistic experience of spin, insider buzz, and the powerful attraction to so-called inside, high-level, or official sources. Those sources often control the terms of journalistic access, along with the allotment of information upon which the careers of journalists and the political success of the officials themselves converge. Consequently, the daily news that reaches most Americans reflects the strange mutual dependencies (punctuated by occasional bursts of antagonism) between reporters and officials. The symbiotic relationships between press and government are similar to the uneasy, mutually necessary balances struck by competitors in a natural ecology.

Journalists' propensity to fashion the news to the realities of power as defined by the officials they cover becomes a problem for democracy if and when the resulting news stories exclude or contradict substantial evidence to the contrary. This is the big story about so many of the examples from the Iraq years that animate this book. When these credibility gaps occur, journalists are often hard pressed to highlight and reconcile them, unless the government itself somehow becomes engaged in policing its own violations of truth, law, or democratic principle. Finding the independent journalistic standpoints from which to speak truth to power—or at least to balance the talk of high-status officials with reasonable challenges— is difficult in an information environment muddled by the conditions that increasingly define the U.S. public communication system:

- *The rise of a dominant class of communication professionals who manage most high-level political situations.* The formulas developed by pollsters, image shapers, marketers, handlers, and spin doctors now shape nearly all aspects of our public communication. This means, among other things, that journalists struggle for nuance in ever more controlled public settings while being kept at arm's length from the newsmakers themselves.
- *The decline of public debate on the democratic responsibilities of the media.* Government regulation of public-responsibility standards for broadcast license holders once provided broader discussion of public accountability norms while encouraging media organizations to regard political reporting as something of a public trust. Subsequent

government deregulation and the rise of huge media conglomerates have relegated news to the same bottom-line demands as entertainment content—meaning fewer resources for investigative journalism, more infotainment and soft features, and a play-it-safe mentality favoring authorized content over more challenging fare. As a result, there is more debate on the air and in print about the lyrics in teen music, the language of radio shock jocks, or an exposed breast during a Super Bowl halftime show than about how to improve the quality of the democratic information environment.

• *The spiral of public disconnection with and antagonism toward both politicians and the press.* Even as news audiences dwindle and confidence levels decline, attempts at serious independent journalism are often met with an orchestrated public chorus chanting about bias, distortion, or negativity. The result is that journalists and news organizations are buffeted by condemnation in the media echo chamber. In this environment, sustained commitments to independent reporting that challenges individuals and institutions in power seem risky in the absence of demands from citizens and media owners, or government standards to support them.

This communication system loops quickly back on itself. When it focuses on political news, the thread that connects those in the journalistic mainstream—starting with the elite newspapers and flowing through thousands of daily local print and broadcast outlets—is that they report much the same stories in much the same terms, because they track the inside power game of Washington politics so closely. In the end, the U.S. mainstream press has trouble with information that has not passed through some government source for its seal of approval. In the case of long-running and divisive conflicts, such as fights over abortion or teaching creationism in the schools, the sides and the issues have become well-enough established that journalists can write the narratives without continuing to consult official sources for their license. However, many foreign policy conflicts such as the Iraq war involve new conditions and high national security stakes that may give officials considerable room to define reality as they see fit, particularly when they go largely unopposed by other powerful actors inside government, as happened through much of the Iraq crisis.

On the positive side, this means that the mainstream press generally reports the public record of decisive government action in a timely fashion. The democratic breakdown occurs when independently obtained information differing from that offered by officials puts news organizations in the uncomfortable position of deciding whether and how strongly to challenge official claims. If, at these critical moments, strong political challengers from inside government emerge to balance the dominant perspectives in the news, the results can be timely, revealing, and salutary. The world still remembers the reporting of the *Washington Post* during the Watergate crisis as a shining example of a democratic press. We now know that the famous Deep Throat, whose information often drove the news story ahead of public government activities, was a highly placed, confidential official source: the second in command at the FBI. His accounts helped advance government challenges to the corrupted Nixon presidency and gave the press an important role in the public accountability process. Yet, as we describe later in the book, a different result often occurs when current or former officials take a stand without the backdrop of ongoing executive branch investigations, court cases, or congressional hearings to support and sustain their versions of reality in the news. Those brave challengers often meet a nasty reception, and learn that political power in Washington can be brutal. Their time in the news spotlight often turns out to be short.

The mutual dependence of journalists and officials does not necessarily mean that the press and government are in bed with each other—although the "embed" experience in covering the war in Iraq indicates that the news collaboration sometimes becomes too cozy. Most of the time, on the surface at least, there is plenty of antagonism between reporters and the officials who try to feed them. The derision shared by politicians and the press has peaked in the past few presidencies; even a casual observer of the press briefings and interactions through the Clinton and Bush years could not miss the often palpable hostility. But the daily rituals of feeding "the beast" (as the White House press corps is known to those who handle press relations) tend to be relatively bloodless affairs in which there is much ado about nothing—rather like the posturings of wary adversaries who recognize their respective niches in the curious ecology of Washington politics.

And so, even as tensions grow, the professional management of contact between reporters and officials has evolved to the point that very little spontaneous public exchange is left in U.S. political life. The strange arm's-length dance between journalists and politicians often produces a dull brand of politics, refreshed only with reports of scandals or snipes at the public gaffes of candidates or leaders who manage the press poorly or dare to speak from the heart.

This alternation between the managed and the sensational in news content has turned off most of the public, leaving most people with a healthy skepticism about government and the press, largely because most people do not have confidence in either what politicians say or how the press delivers their messages. Indeed, the general consensus is that journalists have become political insiders hovering on the edges of power, amplifying the chatter and spin that alternately enhances or damages the images of those at the political center.

The Importance of an Independent Press

The danger in the narrow scope of Washington journalism is simple: information that may be crucial for understanding and evaluating the stories in the headlines often goes unreported or woefully underreported, because it simply is not sanctioned by the powerful sources that drive the news. The heart of our concern in this book is why information that may challenge and even undermine official accounts of events is so often screened out of mainstream news unless there is an opposing official to be the champion who brings it into the story. We saw this pattern in the events leading up to the U.S. invasion of Iraq, with the downplaying of objections to claims made by the Bush administration about the presence of weapons of mass destruction in Iraq and a link between that country and 9/11. We saw it again in coverage of the gruesome story of detainee treatment in the Abu Ghraib prison and elsewhere. After first negotiating a delay with CBS in releasing the damning photos, the White House and the Pentagon mounted a series of heroic news management operations and dominated congressional hearings into the matter in ways that soon contained it in terms of the administration's claims that it was a regrettable case of low-level abuse. Despite continuing reports of detainee deaths and secret prisons, the news perspective on prisoner treatment did not change substantially until Senator John McCain (R-AZ), an official with both credibility on the issue (he had been a POW during the Vietnam War) and the capacity to mobilize

Senate votes, much later called it torture and led a successful political fight to hold the administration accountable to the law. The difference between low-level abuse and government violation of national and international laws against torture is the sort of reality gap that publics in a democracy might at least be invited to consider without waiting for official endorsement. Sometimes official recognition of sensitive political issues comes too little, too late, or not at all.

In their defense, journalists note that they cannot simply advance a story on their own without appearing to be crusading for a cause. This is partly true, although it does not account for when news organizations permit themselves to advance some stories—usually those of less real consequence for the public—through rumor and speculation, and why they regard similar behavior in advancing more consequential types of stories as crusading. There is reason to think that important stories with serious political consequences light the lamp of caution, while rollicking good scandals and sensation get the green light of press independence. Rumor-driven news about the notorious stained blue dress filled the gaps between reports from the special prosecutor during the Clinton-Lewinsky sex scandal. A similar pattern appeared in 2006 as the press pack unilaterally clamored for an accounting of why the national press was not briefed immediately following a hunting accident in which Dick Cheney, the vice president, shot one of his friends.

Unfortunately, when the yellow cautionary lamp is lit in more consequential stories, the press is often unable to bring in credible sources outside the official circles of power to confront dubious official claims. Even if outside sources are introduced, it is difficult to keep their challenges going if high-level U.S. officials dismiss or otherwise fail to engage with them. As a result, in days leading to the war in Iraq, it was simply impossible for the mainstream press to sustain challenges to the Bush administration's hyperbolic stories on Iraq. The irony, of course, is that those war stories, replete with mushroom-cloud imagery, acquired their illusion of credibility largely because they so dominated the media stage, far overshadowing the cautions of United Nations officials and prominent U.S. allies, and the few publicly expressed doubts of domestic opponents.

And so the military might of the United States defied the will of much of the rest of the world. Once the bombs began to fall, public support predictably rallied, the press predictably joined the patriotic circle, and few were the wiser until the policy misadventure spiraled into insurgency, civil conflict, and regional crisis with no clear resolution or exit option in sight. More vigorous public inspection of the thin premise for war given by the administration might not have prevented the invasion, but it might have endowed the nation—government officials, potential opposition voices, and the people themselves—with a temporizing sense of the limits imposed on leaders in a democracy. In the process, a fuller public accounting might have established clearer points of acknowledged public concern, and those benchmarks might have provided starting points for open debate, electoral accountability, and more effective policies.

Challenges to the pronouncements of the powerful did, of course, come from the hundreds of smaller news outlets, magazines, journals, and Web sites often known as the alternative press—what we also refer to as the nonestablishment media. But these media have very small (though often devoted) audiences, are easily dismissed by various sides as partisan, and branded as even more biased than the mainstream media. This leaves the bulk of the national public dialogue to emanate from the offices of power, flowing down through the national press corps and on through the megaphones of mainstream talk radio and the pundits of cable television. In this process, the news that matters the most and that still reaches the most people is also the most likely to miss crucial elements of important stories—unless and until government itself brings them into the picture.

The ironic result is that the U.S. press system works best when government is already working well—debating alternatives, responding to challenges from citizen interest groups—and when elected opponents publicly hold each other accountable. But these are not the times when we need an independent press the most. The democratic role of the press is defined historically, and continues to be defined in the minds of many journalists and citizens, by those moments when government deception or incompetence compels journalists to find and bring credible challenges to public attention and hold rulers accountable. This, after all, is the great lesson learned from the Watergate scandal. This accountability function of the U.S. press has been weakened in the contemporary era, and its standing is sorely in need of greater examination.

The puzzling question, of course, is why does the mainstream press mainly transmit official performances and pronouncements rather than act more as independent watchdogs of our political, social, and economic institutions? Filtering daily political reality through the prism of power may be expedient for maintaining access to inside sources and harvesting large volumes of news efficiently, but it ultimately does not serve the press or democracy well. It is our hope that illuminating this situation will point to some new directions that journalism can take—even within the current constraints imposed by corporate ownership and the often discouraging levels of press-bashing by publics and pundits. Indeed, liberating the press from its self-imposed dependence on officially sanctioned information might diminish the censorial force of officials who bash the press with the aim of actively controlling, and thereby limiting, the flow of information in public life.

Scope of the Book

We explore this tendency of the press to record rather than critically examine the official pronouncements of government by following the arc of George W. Bush's presidency from the aftermath of the terrorist attacks of 2001 through the midpoint of his second term, when officials finally acknowledged the magnitude of the insurgency in Iraq and U.S. generals began to signal Congress that civil war might be imminent there. Though the patterns and problems of press dependence on official definitions of reality are not unique to the Bush years, they appear to have reached new heights (or depths) in the post-9/11 era. Our focus is to identify these by pointing to key moments that show how the press has become trapped in reporting rules of its own making. Most readers are familiar with the post-9/11 period of a patriotic, intimidated, and compliant press. Indeed, leading newspapers have since apologized for being too uncritical of administration spin leading up to the war in Iraq. Yet when we move our focus to the next major series of world-shaking events following the onset of that war—the U.S. treatment of its prisoners at Abu Ghraib and elsewhere—we discover that the mainstream press, once again, failed to challenge forcefully the administration's claims that those gruesome photographs represented only an isolated case of abuse by low-level soldiers. Although early news coverage contained hints that the administration may have developed a covert policy of torturing detainees, the issue quickly faded from the headlines despite the availability of sources and evidence (outside government power circles) to support those reports.

The issue here is not that the press should summarily decide the question of whether the administration chose to employ torture in gathering intelligence—far from it. *The issue is whether the press should have shrunk from a two-sided story in favor of a one-sided official account just because telling the other side required looking beyond government for sources and evidence.* What concerns us—and what our data show—is that when other officials inside circles of power (for example, congressional Democrats) fail to speak out against prevailing government claims (in this case, from the Bush administration), there is no engine to drive critical news coverage. The result of this pattern, from events leading up to the war in Iraq to the Abu Ghraib story, and in other cases documented in this book, is that the government is left to police itself on crucial issues.

More than a year after the Abu Ghraib controversy came to light, powerful officials did begin to raise questions about appropriate intelligence-gathering methods and a host of other issues, and *torture* became a prominent term in the headlines. Most of the information finally produced by Senator McCain and others had been available to reporters earlier, but it simply had not been officially sanctioned. Similar to the weapons of mass destruction episode that triggered the U.S. invasion of Iraq, questions about the administration's bending (if not breaking) laws against torture could have been addressed more prominently and in a more timely fashion by the media, but for the lack of high-level officials and other inside sources to sponsor them. It is as though issues appear and disappear in the news depending on which official wand is waved at them.

The invisible barrier holding back volumes of challenging news accounts finally broke in the aftermath of Hurricane Katrina. Suddenly, the news became filled with more critical examinations of a government whose image-making prowess seemed contradicted by its inaction and inattention during a natural disaster. Indeed, Katrina is the exception that proves the rule of the press being largely dependent on the government to filter, define, and accent the news. At that time, the press entered the eye of a no-spin zone, as many White House officials were away on vacation. Reporters on the scene saw for themselves a natural disaster and national tragedy that was exacerbated by a disorganized government response and the absence of a normally masterful image-control operation from the White House. Only under those exceptional conditions were journalists able to offer independent perspectives that challenged government officials to account for what the nation witnessed. Interestingly, the absence of the usual press dependence on government was not lost on many journalists. Reporters who interviewed each other during the aftermath of Hurricane Katrina noted how liberating it was to be able to cover an event directly as they saw it, without having to accommodate the incessant spin of officials. Indeed, the tables were so turned in this situation that top officials were informed by television journalists of the magnitude of the disaster and the lack of effective government response. If, as in the case of Katrina, the mainstream media still have the capacity to see beyond the spin of government, why do they not use it more often? It seems to take a devastating hurricane drowning or displacing most of the (largely black and poor) population of an entire city, along with many Washington leaders being out of town, for the press to look fully and clearly at events.

The main story in this book involves how the same press system produced such night-and-day differences in its coverage of successive, highly consequential events over such a relatively short period of time. We believe that the Bush presidency reveals more about what needs to be fixed in our democratic press than any other period in modern history. At every point in this story of the U.S. press and the Bush administration, the keys to determining press independence from government spin are the degree to which that spin was one-sided (the lead-up to the war in Iraq, the "mission accomplished" moment, the battle over defining the meaning of the photos from Abu Ghraib); two-sided (reflecting later divisions inside the government over torture, secret prisons, and spying on Americans); or on vacation, with image-making operations shut down and reporters consequently able to access news events directly (Hurricane Katrina).

After we review the recent history of the press's poor performance in chapter 1, we discuss the general conditions that create its dependence on government in chapter 2, which introduces a simple model of why the press routinely fails at those moments when its role in the American democracy is most crucial. The workings of this model of press-government dependence—the binding nature of the Washington press game—are assessed in our analysis of the national news coverage of the Abu Ghraib affair in chapter 3. The consequences of limiting the framing of important national policy stories, both for citizens and for the quality of government policy, are explored in chapter 4, where we look at what was left out of mainstream news coverage of the dark side of the war due to the reporting choices implicitly agreed upon by the press. Those choices arguably widened the perceptual gaps between Americans and the rest of the world. In chapter 5 we examine the ways in which these and many other information choices were structured for journalists by the Bush administration's aggressive news management tactics. In order to understand how spin works, it is also necessary to grasp the constraints on political imagination experienced by journalists who live and work within the Washington power consensus. We attempt to illuminate this subtle but important part of the news-gathering process through interviews with individuals operating inside the Washington news environment. We conclude in chapter 6 by exploring the dilemmas of decision making that have hamstrung the press and limited its independence, and the consequences of the press-government dependence for the functioning of democracy. This chapter also examines different historical and contemporary models of press performance, such as the ideal of "watchdog" reporting, in order to put current press practices in perspective and point toward a new news standard.

The degree of self-imposed press restraint documented in this book seems ill suited to matters that have raised an international uproar, seriously damaged U.S. credibility in Iraq and around the world, and spawned a legacy of policy problems both nationally and internationally that seem daunting at best. As a thought experiment, we wonder what might have happened if different voices and viewpoints had produced a more balanced account of the news in these fateful national moments. Might there have been fuller public debates or more critical responses from citizens? Would intimidated government officials have been encouraged to join the public conversation sooner? Would knowledgeable former officials who eventually spoke out against torture have stepped forward sooner, when it might have mattered more?

We hope that this book stimulates discussion about the press's responsibility to free itself of its self-imposed yoke to government leaders so that it may report credible challenges to questionable official activities in a more timely fashion. Serious questions still exist about the role of the press in American democracy, and we hope to illuminate them further. Many critics have accused the press of aggressively—and inappropriately—setting the political agenda. Others say that the press is largely the lapdog of government. We hope to clarify this seemingly endless debate.

1

Press Politics in America

The Case of the Iraq War

In August 2002, Rumsfeld told Tom Brokaw on NBC News that "there are al-Qaeda in Iraq." On September 26, 2002, he said that the government had "bulletproof" confirmation of links between Iraq and al-Qaeda members. . . . In an October 11, 2002, speech, President Bush said "Some al-Qaeda leaders who fled Afghanistan went to Iraq." . . . [But] There was no evidence of actual links between Saddam and Osama bin Laden, a point often made by the CIA, and such cooperation would in any case have been implausible given Osama's religious commitments and Saddam's ruthlessly secular regime.

CHALMERS JOHNSON, *The Sorrows of Empire*

We now know that officials in the Bush administration built a case for the U.S. invasion of Iraq that was open to serious challenge. We also know that evidence disputing ongoing official claims about the war was often available to the mainstream press in a timely fashion. Yet the recurrent pattern, even years into the conflict, was for the official government line to trump evidence to the contrary in the news produced by mainstream news outlets reaching the preponderance of the people. Several years into the conflict, public opinion finally began to reflect the reality of a disintegrating Iraq heading toward civil war, with American troops caught in the middle. But that reckoning came several years too late to head off a disaster that historians may well deem far worse than Vietnam.

There is little doubt that reporting which challenges the public pronouncements of those in power is difficult when anything deviating from authorized versions of reality is met with intimidating charges of bias. Out of fairness, the press generally reports those charges, which in turn reverberate through the echo chambers of talk radio and pundit TV, with the ironic result that the media contribute to their own credibility problem. Yet it is precisely the lack of clear standards of press accountability (particularly guidelines for holding officials accountable) that opens the

mainstream news to charges of bias from all sides. In short, the absence
of much agreement on what the press should be doing makes it all the
more difficult for news organizations to navigate an independent course
through pressurized political situations.

The key question is, can the American press as it is currently constituted offer critical, independent reporting when democracy needs it
most? In particular, this book examines whether the press is capable of
offering viewpoints independent of government spin at two key moments
when democracy would most benefit: (1) when government's own public
inquiry mechanisms fail to question potentially flawed or contentious
policy initiatives, and (2) when credible sources outside government who
might illuminate those policies are available to mainstream news organizations. It may seem obvious that the press should contest dubious policies under these circumstances, but our research indicates otherwise. The
great irony of the U.S. press system is that it generally performs well—
presenting competing views and vigorous debate—when government is
already weighing competing initiatives in its various legal, legislative, or
executive settings. Unfortunately, quite a different press often shows up
when policy decisions of dubious wisdom go unchallenged within government arenas.

The Iraq Story as Told by the Unwritten Rules
of Washington Journalism

Our story begins with the post-9/11 publicity given to the Bush administration's claims that Iraqi dictator Saddam Hussein possessed weapons of
mass destruction (the now infamous WMDs), and had connections to the
terrorists who attacked the United States. Leading news organizations so
emphasized those claims over available information to the contrary that
two prestigious newspapers later issued apologies to their readers for having gotten so caught up in the inner workings of power in an administration determined to go to war that they lost focus on other voices and other
views. Here are excerpts from a now legendary *New York Times* report
from the editors to their readers:

> We have found a number of instances of coverage that was not as rigor-
> ous as it should have been. In some cases, information that was contro-

versial then, and seems questionable now, was insufficiently qualified or allowed to stand unchallenged. Looking back, we wish we had been more aggressive in re-examining the claims as new evidence emerged— or failed to emerge.

The problematic articles varied in authorship and subject matter, but many shared a common feature. They depended at least in part on information from a circle of Iraqi informants, defectors and exiles bent on "regime change" in Iraq, people whose credibility has come under increasing public debate in recent weeks. . . . Complicating matters for journalists, the accounts of these exiles were often eagerly confirmed by United States officials convinced of the need to intervene in Iraq. . . .

Some critics of our coverage during that time have focused blame on individual reporters. Our examination, however, indicates that the problem was more complicated. Editors at several levels who should have been challenging reporters and pressing for more skepticism were perhaps too intent on rushing scoops into the paper. . . . Articles based on dire claims about Iraq tended to get prominent display, while follow-up articles that called the original ones into question were sometimes buried. In some cases, there was no follow-up at all.[1]

Despite this introspection, much the same pattern of deferring to officials and underreporting available challenges to their claims would soon repeat itself—beginning the very month in which this critical self-assessment appeared—in reporting on the treatment of prisoners in U.S. military detention centers in Iraq and elsewhere. The importance of the Abu Ghraib story for understanding the close dependence of the press on government spin is developed more fully in chapter 3. For now, the point is that this pattern of calibrating political reality in the news to the inner circles of Washington power will go on, despite occasional moments of self-examination by the press, unless leading news organizations and the journalism profession somehow resolve (and develop a standard) to temper their preoccupation with the powerful officials whose communication experts often manage them so well.

Part of the reason the Iraq story was written much as the Bush administration told it is that nearly every installment was well staged and fed expertly to reporters. It also helped that during the events leading up to the war and much of its aftermath, the stories spun by the Bush team were pretty much the only sustained official versions in town—thanks in part to the particularly hard-hitting style of news management practiced by the administration (discussed in chapter 5). As indicated below, plenty of other sources and bodies of evidence outside official Washington power circles could have been elevated to challenge the administration's stories, but those challenges either did not emerge aggressively or were reported only in passing—again, because of the administration's tactics and the unwritten rules followed by the mainstream press for selecting, emphasizing, and sustaining stories. And so, from the WMD story that sold the war to the "mission accomplished" Hollywood ending (which, of course, did not mark the "end" of the war), the unwritten rule of favoring prepackaged, officially sanctioned news events reveals why the ideal of a watchdog press is in trouble.

Mission Accomplished

Consider for a moment that day in May of 2003, when President Bush, wearing a Top Gun flight suit, gave his "Mission Accomplished" speech on an aircraft carrier staged as a big-screen movie set. Nearly every major U. S. news organization reported the story just as it had been scripted. The result was the sort of public relations coup that occurs only when the news can be managed on such a scale.[2] (We believe that the idea originated with a public relations consultant, and was then staged with the considerable resources of the White House communication office and the U.S. military.)

Beyond the irony of a president with a dubious military service record playing Top Gun, the message channeled through the news turned out to be disastrously wrong. But such details were no match for the Hollywood moments that the administration regularly rolled out with the help of Hollywood set directors and Washington PR firms. The news had become something of a reality TV program, replete with dramatic stories from top organizations such as the *Washington Post*, which published the following:

> When the Viking carrying Bush made its tailhook landing on the aircraft carrier *USS Abraham Lincoln* off California yesterday, the scene brought presidential imagery to a whole new level. Bush emerged from the cockpit in a full olive flight suit and combat boots, his helmet tucked jauntily under his left arm. As he exchanged salutes with the

sailors, his ejection harness, hugging him tightly between the legs, gave him the bowlegged swagger of a top gun.[3]

The fact that all of this was known to have been staged just for this effect did not detract from the amount and prominence of news coverage the media lavished on the event. To the contrary, the orchestration of the event fit perfectly with the unwritten rules of mainstream journalism in the United States, and thus helped make the coverage what it was: dramatic, unchallenged, triumphant, and resonant throughout the media. Beyond this staging, the implicit journalistic preoccupation with political power in Washington shaped the plotline of Mr. Bush's Top Gun episode. As a result, most of the coverage of the "mission accomplished" moment was not about whether the war was really over (it wasn't), or even if there was reason to think that things in Iraq were going particularly well (they weren't). The story was about power in Washington, and in particular, Mr. Bush's mastery of the imagery of success—which, at that moment, seemed to make him the odds-on favorite in the 2004 election.

The fascinating aspect of such recurrent reporting patterns is that the news itself is the completing link in the image creation process. Reporting stories according to a calculus of government power and dramatic production values often makes the news reality emanating from Washington an insular, circular, and self-fulfilling operation. News and politics loop quickly back on each other because of the press's preoccupation with how well powerful officials manage their desired images in the news. Thus, in early Iraq coverage, potentially important contextual details such as the dubious reasons and evidence given in support of the war became incidental to the fascination with whether the Bush administration had the image-shaping capacity and the political clout to pull it off.

The Selling of the Iraq War

Consider, along these lines, another important aspect of the lead-up to the Iraq invasion. Much as the Hollywood staging of the carrier landing made for a great news event, the campaign to sell the war was designed to help the press make the administration's story far sharper and more dramatic than the evidence on which it was based. More than a year after a seemingly manufactured case for war had been presented to the public, Senator Ted Kennedy (D-MA) attempted to redefine the political debate by making a speech with this bold claim: "The administration capitalized on the fear created by 9/11 and put a spin on the intelligence and a spin on the truth to justify a war that could well be one of the worst blunders in more than two centuries of American foreign policy." He charged that the war was marketed like a "political product" to help elect Republicans, and that "if Congress and the American People knew the whole truth, America would never have gone to war."[4] Kennedy was quickly dismissed by the Republican rapid-response network as a traitorous liberal throwback. House Majority Leader Tom DeLay (R-TX) said that "[Kennedy's] hateful attack against the commander in chief would be disgusting if it were not so sad," adding that Kennedy had "insulted the president's patriotism." The story was immediately reduced to the Washington news formula of "he said/he said," and the larger issue about selling the war based on false advertising was lost in a story about partisan sniping. Even without the vociferous Republican counterattack, Kennedy was not likely to be a decisive player in mobilizing congressional opposition to the war, and thus did not constitute a news source with enough power to sustain another side to the story.

Equally important, Senator Kennedy's assertion that the Bush administration had marketed the war as a partisan political product came as no news to journalists and other political insiders. A good piece of investigative reporting (characteristically not followed up by the *Post* or other news organizations) had already been produced six months before, establishing independent evidence for Kennedy's charges. Two journalists for the *Washington Post* described a systematic media campaign that had begun in August 2002 with the formation of the White House Iraq Group (WHIG), aimed at rolling out a communication strategy for the coming war. WHIG's "strategic communications" task force planned publicity and news events for a campaign that would start in September, after most Americans (and Congress) had returned from their summer vacations. The *Post* story quoted White House Chief of Staff Andrew Card, from an interview that had appeared in the *New York Times* nearly a year earlier, on why the campaign had been launched in September: "From a marketing point of view, you don't introduce new products in August."[5] This strong signal that the war was being promoted via a concerted communication campaign was in the news fully one and a half years before Kennedy's assertion.

The important question is, why didn't this journalistic "common knowledge" about the selling of the war become big news at the time it was first reported, when there was still time to debate the U.S. invasion of Iraq in public? To the contrary, when it was launched in September 2002, the administration's sales campaign was quickly translated into the news code of the mainstream press and told as a story about how power works in Washington. The fact that the administration was selling the war as a political campaign was noted for the record and then, like much of the its image management operation, passed on to the American public according to plan: prominently featured throughout the news, and unimpeded by serious journalistic investigation of either the sales operation or its veracity. As independent journalist Michael Massing later observed, "Most investigative energy was directed at stories that supported, rather than challenged, the administration's case."[6] The result is that the public was saturated with the sales pitch, which was delivered loud and clear throughout the news media.

The nation's talk shows on the weekend after Labor Day 2002 were filled with Bush administration officials staying on message and reading from a script that pumped fear through the media echo chamber.[7] On NBC's *Meet the Press*, Vice President Cheney raised the specter that Saddam's arsenal of nuclear, chemical, and biological weapons presented an immediate danger to the United States. Secretary of State Condoleezza Rice acknowledged on CNN's *Late Edition* that solid evidence was scarce, but that waiting only increased the risk. Her punch line: "We don't want the smoking gun to be a mushroom cloud." And Defense Secretary Donald Rumsfeld warned on CBS's *Face the Nation*: "Imagine a September 11 with weapons of mass destruction. It's not 3,000, it's tens of thousands of innocent men, women, and children."[8]

In short, a war being promoted through a sales campaign was not the story the news highlighted. The focus of the story was on power—the effectiveness of the campaign in pressuring Congress (and the United Nations) to support the war initiative—not the truth or the propriety of the effort. Here is the *New York Times'* account of the opening weekend of the campaign:

WASHINGTON, Sept. 8—Led by Vice President Dick Cheney, who warned grimly that "time is not on our side," President Bush's

top national security officials said nearly in unison today that
Saddam Hussein's efforts to build an arsenal of immensely destruc-
tive weapons left the United States little choice but to act against
Iraq.

"There shouldn't be any doubt in anybody's mind that this president
is absolutely bound and determined to deal with this threat, and to do
whatever is necessary to make certain that we do so," Mr. Cheney said.
He said that Iraq was sparing no effort to revive its nuclear weapon
program and that in light of the terror attacks of last Sept. 11, its history with nuclear, biological and chemical weapons programs directly
threatened the United States.

In almost identical language that signaled a carefully coordinated
campaign to move Congress and the United Nations in their direction, Mr. Bush's other top national security officials said on television
news programs today that the president would seek support from Congress and the United Nations for action, including a possible military
strike. . . .

It was Mr. Cheney, in a nearly hour-long interview on "Meet the
Press," who outlined the darkest picture of Iraq's potential threat, not
only of Mr. Hussein's efforts to acquire nuclear weapons but of his
possible connections to Al Qaeda and other terrorist groups.

Mr. Cheney cited what he called a credible but unconfirmed intelligence report that Mohamed Atta, one of the Sept. 11 hijackers, had
met at least once in Prague with a senior Iraqi intelligence official a
few months before the attacks.

Of Mr. Hussein's efforts to develop nuclear weapons, Mr. Cheney
said, "All of the experience we have points in the direction that, in the
past, we've underestimated the extent of his program." He added that
he hoped more intelligence about such efforts could soon be made
public, without compromising sources, to help persuade allies, Congress, and the public of the need for action.

"One of the real concerns about Saddam Hussein, as well," he
said, "is his biological weapons capability, the fact that he may at some
point try to use smallpox, anthrax, plague, some other kind of biological agent against other nations, possibly including even the United
States. So this is not just a one-dimensional threat."[9]

These allegations were sufficiently vague and unsupported to warrant serious questioning, yet they passed through their talk-show conduits into mainstream news reports largely as scripted. Why? For starters, the story was being told by the vice president of the United States himself—the kind of source to which journalists typically show deference in matters of national security. It also helped that this was the most dramatic story of the new millennium. More important, as noted above, the implicit journalistic logic of following the trail of government power drove the media's own storytelling: the Bush administration was on a course to war, and the issue in the news was not whether the grounds for war were reasonable or honestly presented, but whether they would be opposed and thus derailed by Congress. The eventual failure to win support from the UN was insufficient to introduce serious challenges into the story, because the UN did not have, or was not perceived to have, the power to stop the administration from attacking Iraq.

As it turned out, there was no decisive domestic political opposition sufficient to block the path to war. There was, of course, significant opposition among European publics, but, like the UN resistance, those opponents lacked the perceived power to derail the administration's war plans. The underreporting of numerous possible challenges to the war campaign effort boiled down to the simple fact that the administration's claims were largely unopposed by the kinds of powerful officials or decisive institutional actors (the opposition party or key administration defectors) who might have rated another side in the news as it is constructed in the United States.

Journalists, of course, may point to a scattering of investigative reports as evidence that they entered independent concerns into the public record. While this may be strictly true, it does not address the larger issue of why the stories that attempt to hold officials accountable for gaps and outright deceptions often get such small play compared to the stories containing the gaps and deceptions. Unless the press reports sustained challenges to inadequate or deceptive government actions, several important democratic dynamics are unlikely to occur: (1) public opinion will not become meaningfully engaged in deliberation about important competing political considerations; (2) knowledgeable insiders may be reluctant to be whistleblowers absent the protective context of ongoing critical coverage; and (3) ill-considered policies formed and defended by "group-think" operating inside the circles of power are unlikely to receive critical reexamination. As a result, key claims in the Bush administration's sales campaign were repeated in the news time and again, with notable effects on public opinion, despite little supporting evidence. The two most notable claims are addressed in the next section.

WMDs and the Al Qaeda Connection

Perhaps the central example that illustrates the press's having limited capacity to challenge potentially questionable, but dominant, official accounts involves the allegation of links between the international terrorist organization Al Qaeda and Saddam Hussein, and between Saddam and 9/11. Those claims, like the charges that Saddam possessed WMDs, were asserted repeatedly by high administration officials including President Bush and Vice President Cheney, but little solid evidence was ever presented. To the contrary, there was ample evidence that Al Qaeda leader Osama bin Laden had condemned Saddam's government as a secular threat to Islamic fundamentalism, and that Saddam feared an Islamic threat to his rule. Indeed, after Saddam's capture, documents were found in his possession ordering Iraqi resistance fighters to refuse to cooperate with any Islamic fundamentalists who entered Iraq, suggesting that Al Qaeda, while sharing an antagonism toward the United States, was also seen as a threat to stir Islamic revolution in Iraq.[10]

Despite the available challenges to this core rationale for the war promoted by the Bush administration, the durability of the Saddam–Al Qaeda connection in public opinion polls continued years into the conflict. Just the right dose of reinforcements from high administration sources continued to receive publicity from news organizations that were curiously ill equipped to balance the spurious claims. Indeed, the underlying ethos of "we report (what officials say), you decide (if it is true)" results in the odd problem of balancing erroneous claims. It might make sense to worry more about whether such claims should be reported so decorously at all. In any event, a poll conducted in July 2006, more than three years after the U.S. invasion of Iraq, found that 64% of Americans still believed that Saddam Hussein's regime had strong ties with Al Qaeda—even though volumes of contrary information circulated just beyond, and sometimes even found its way into, the mainstream press.[11]

There was similarly little evidence presented to support the alleged existence of WMDs—particularly nuclear weapons capacity—that was offered as the imminent threat to U.S. national security that justified the war. The slim evidence put forward by government officials was overplayed in the news, as indicated in the published apologies of both the *Times* and the *Post*. Weaknesses in the accounts and challenges to claimed evidence were either buried deep in the newspapers' inside pages or not examined much at all. Here is how the *Times'* editorial apology to its readers assessed the paper's reporting on an intelligence finding about the aluminum tubes alleged to be part of Saddam's hidden operation to manufacture nuclear materials:

> On Sept. 8, 2002, the lead article of the paper was headlined "U.S. Says Hussein Intensified Quest for A-Bomb Parts." That report concerned the aluminum tubes that the administration advertised insistently as components for the manufacture of nuclear weapons fuel. The claim came not from defectors but from the best American intelligence sources available at the time. Still, it should have been presented more cautiously. There were hints that the usefulness of the tubes in making nuclear fuel was not a sure thing, but the hints were buried deep, 1,700 words into a 3,600-word article. Administration officials were allowed to hold forth at length on why this evidence of Iraq's nuclear intentions demanded that Saddam Hussein be dislodged from power: "The first sign of a 'smoking gun,'" they argue, "may be a mushroom cloud."
>
> Five days later, the *Times* reporters learned that the tubes were in fact a subject of debate among intelligence agencies. The misgivings appeared deep in an article on Page A13, under a headline that gave no inkling that we were revising our earlier view ("White House Lists Iraq Steps to Build Banned Weapons"). The *Times* gave voice to skeptics of the tubes on Jan. 9, when the key piece of evidence was challenged by the International Atomic Energy Agency. That challenge was reported on Page A10; it might well have belonged on Page A1.[12]

Other evidence being pushed by the Bush administration to support its case for war was similarly disputed within government intelligence circles, but effective management of a compliant press kept the lid on the story. For example, intelligence analysts suspected that the document underlying the administration's charges that Saddam tried to purchase bomb-grade uranium in Africa was a fabrication. In fact, the Central Intelligence Agency asked that the claim be removed from a Bush speech during the fall 2002 campaign to raise support for the war. The CIA again pushed successfully for removing the charge from the U.S. ambassador's speech to the UN Security Council later in December. Yet the uranium charge reappeared at White House insistence in the president's 2003 State of the Union address that signaled the coming war.[13] Months after it was discredited, the charge continued to be spread in news interviews and speeches by other administration officials, who simply attributed the claim to British intelligence reports that also proved to be groundless. The repetition of the dubious charge by nearly every top official in the coming weeks was part of the "strategic coordination" of the administration's message, as described by White House communications director Dan Bartlett.[14]

When Joseph Wilson, a well-respected retired U.S. diplomat, was moved by the administration's inaccuracy to explain publicly in an editorial that the nuclear weapons charge had been discredited, the White House retaliated by leaking the identity of his wife, the now well-known Valerie Plame, who was working undercover for the CIA. This bit of hardball led to a special prosecutor investigation of the White House's breach of national security law, and ironically dragged journalists into the awkward position of protecting the very sources who had tried to use them to dissemble public information. As discussed further below, the close news-making ties between key administration figures and prominent reporters like Judith Miller, formerly of the *New York Times*, who wittingly or unwittingly helped the administration to damage Wilson and manage the news, are the all-important backstory that explains much of the front-page coverage of the lead-up to the war. We explore the Wilson-Plame incident as one of many examples of the administration's bare-knuckle news management tactics in chapter 5.

The Intelligence Fiasco

The press's now familiar inability to create better balance independently in its news stories occurred again after the invasion of Iraq, when reporting turned to the particulars of the intelligence that was presented as cause for the war. Once again, the issue is not whether another side to the Bush administration's story ever appeared in the news; it did. But once again, it came and went without leaving much of a trace on public opinion[15] or gaining the prominence needed to provide a safe and inviting public context for other government opponents to speak out.

Perhaps the Iraq story that had the greatest potential effects on public comprehension and government debate was the issue of the faulty intelligence that led to the war. Was the intelligence failure a product of poorly organized and ill-qualified intelligence agencies, as the administration and many in Congress offered as their version of the story? Or was it more the case, as a lesser told version of the story had it, that the desire for war at the highest levels of the administration essentially forced intelligence agencies to certify and promote internally contested and knowingly weak intelligence? It is ironic that this important alternative version of the intelligence story—one with the potential to unravel many other claims by the administration—had such trouble gaining traction in the news despite a stream of former officials who came and went in the front pages, echoing similar versions of these stark challenges to the administration's preferred story.

Impressive as those sources were, they simply operated with a news deficit given their status as past officials who no longer had the mechanisms of office and power to advance their stories. Yet their stories were enormously important, and largely consistent with one another in corroborating firsthand knowledge that high-level administration officials may have pressured intelligence agencies for information to support a preordained war. These charges were lodged in various forms by former treasury secretary Paul O'Neill, former security adviser Richard Clarke, and first-term secretary of state Colin Powell's then chief of staff, Lawrence Wilkerson, among others, who simply could not compete with the administration's news-making capacity to beat them back.

Consider, for example, the news moment surrounding O'Neill, who claimed that discussions about overthrowing Saddam Hussein were held from the earliest cabinet meetings of the Bush administration, long before the attacks of 9/11. In the book *The Price of Loyalty*, O'Neill charged that 9/11 merely provided the pretext for a war that was already on the agendas of Vice President Cheney, Defense Secretary Rumsfeld, and the president, among others. According to O'Neill, who had been a trusted Bush political ally, the administration's belief was that regime change in Iraq would provide a model for democracy that would transform the rest of the region. The main question, he claimed, was how to justify going to war, and the president set a tone of "Fine. Go find me a way to do this."[16] Both Bush and Rumsfeld issued strong denials after the book came out, and the White House retaliated by calling for an investigation of whether O'Neill had broken governmental secrecy laws in providing the author with official documents to back up his claims.

Such reports came and went in the news, with the stories taking on a "he said/they said" quality. In such stories, the advantage quickly tilted to administration officials with better news access and the inclination to challenge ferociously the patriotism and credibility of anyone who might question their preferred script. And so the charges that the administration had pressed for intelligence to support the war also came and went as sporadic news backdrop—sustained mainly as long as the sources were able to promote their books on cable and late-night television shows. Even Colin Powell's former chief of staff Lawrence Wilkerson received little news traction for his charge that the war was pushed through the administration by a "cabal" of Rumsfeld and Dick Cheney.[17]

The parade of former Washington insiders—former government officials and lower-level agency technicians and bureaucrats—pointing out the spurious origins of the war in Iraq came and went, with most of them quickly dropping from the news. Even though, as long-time government insiders, they enjoyed considerable credibility among journalists, as mere *former* officials they lacked the daily story-advancing mechanisms attached to their former offices, leaving them few of the institutional processes that might keep their side of the story in the news, such as daily press briefings, hearings, official trips, investigations, litigation, legislative initiatives, and other news-making activities. As we explain further in chapter 5, some of these critics had somewhat greater success in sustaining media attention than others, depending in large part on their own public relations resources and their personal vulnerability to intimidation by the administration.

What about those potential storytellers who did have access to the institutional mechanisms that drive stories—members of Congress in particular? They were effectively held hostage to their earlier acceptance of the administration spin that filled the public sphere. Since the climate of press debate about the grounds for war was so stifling that most Democrats ended up voting for the U.S. invasion of Iraq and publicly accepting the dubious intelligence as grounds for military action (which, of course, further stifled news coverage), there was little room for them to stake out a subsequent antiwar position when the early rationale proved unfounded. Cries of deception were quickly deflected by administration officials who said that the Democrats had seen the same intelligence reports that the administration saw, and that everyone then believed that Iraq presented an imminent security threat. Latter-day critics, the administration charged, were exercising convenient hindsight.

All of this may seem strange to an outsider who, when presented with the facts, might simply reason that since intelligence may have been cooked to pave the way for an unwarranted war, the opposition would have reason to cry foul, and to use this as a key issue in upcoming election campaigns. Yet the capacity of the Bush administration to promote its news story of intelligence failure and reform over considerable evidence to the contrary made it difficult for the Democrats to formulate and publicize possible objections, particularly when confronted with equally blaring news featuring the administration's charges of waffling and lack of patriotism among the opposition. Once again, the absence of an institutional power platform from which to press their case left the Democrats in a defensive position of denying the administration's smear charges, at least as the press chose to construct the story.

So ingrained is this press calibration of the relative power and status of the available sources when constructing balance, plot, and viewpoint in news stories that even the revelation of "smoking gun"—type evidence about the administration's intelligence fixing was similarly marginalized. On April 30, 2005, the *Times* of London published minutes of a secret meeting between Tony Blair, the British prime minister, and top British military and intelligence officials. The minutes showed that a core topic was constructing a legal cover for going to war in light of documents from a high British intelligence official who had attended prewar meetings in Washington, at which time it was made clear that 9/11 was being used as a pretext for removing Saddam Hussein from power. As his report put it, the "facts were being fixed around the policy."[18]

Yet when the so-called Downing Street Memo was disclosed soon thereafter in the United States, it was largely treated either as old news or as a British politics story (an election problem for Blair). Even the huge surge of blogging activity aimed at getting the mainstream media to take up the story was largely ineffective.[19] One of our interviewed sources revealed that the pesky bloggers squeezed only one grudging front-page story out of the *Washington Post*.

The importance of power calculations in the making of a political news story was further evidenced by how the *Washington Post* constructed the attempt of Representative John Conyers (D-MI) to publicize the implications of the memo by holding a House informational hearing. That hearing was held in the political context of Republican dominance of the House, and the continuing muddle among Democrats about making an election issue out of being deceived on the war. Given this context, the hearing was unlikely to result either in a shift in Democratic position or in any direct political repercussions for the Bush administration. The degree to which these power considerations by the press trumped (indeed defined) the implications of the document is shown in a telling story by *Washington Post* reporter-analyst Dana Milbank which began with the headline "Democrats Play House to Rally against the War." The lead sentence was even more revealing about the power calculus underlying news construction: "In the Capitol basement yesterday, long suffering House Democrats took a trip to the land of make-believe."[20]

For some news organizations, the lack of coverage became a larger story than the story itself, suggesting that many journalists knew they were looking at something important, but simply could not imagine how to fashion a big sustainable story out of it. And so they blinked. In an NPR commentary, Daniel Schorr called it the biggest "under-covered story of the year."[21]

The Unwritten Rules of Washington Reporting

Beneath the surface of all these curious reporting patterns are a few core working principles that both drive and limit the mainstream news system. Above all, the practice of filtering political stories through the perceived power alignments in government makes it difficult for mainstream news reporting to sustain credible challenges that come from sources outside those spheres of power. This is largely because outsiders, including former government officials, as well as lower-ranking officials such as agency technicians and bureaucrats, lack the built-in advantages of high office and institutional processes to sustain stories. As explained earlier, these processes include press briefings, hearings, official trips, investigations, court cases, legislative debates, and other government news levers.

The occasional exceptions to this practice also tend to demonstrate the rule of official power. For example, when the UN debated a resolution to end the military conflict between Israel and the radical Islamic movement Hezbollah in Lebanon in August of 2006, various foreign challenges (for example, from France and Russia) to the U.S. position were reported in some detail, because those challengers had the power to block the desired American policy path. On the other hand, when it was clear several years earlier that the United States could wage war on Iraq with or without UN approval, the objections of other nations and even the claims of weapons inspectors and other UN officials were not incorporated as centrally into the news.

Understanding these basic reporting principles of power and process suggests that the press failings of the Iraq-Bush years will likely happen again, and again, under similar circumstances, with or without the added embellishment of a crisis such as 9/11. The tendency of the press to defer to the best-packaged officially advanced political story will go on, until we—citizens, journalism faculty, scholars, teachers, news executives, and working journalists—take a clear look at the self-imposed limits that the journalism profession has helped place on political coverage, and have a serious national conversation about the role of the press in today's highly managed, public relations–driven democracy.

In understanding the unwritten rules of the Washington news game, then, it is important to recognize that what carries a story is not necessarily its truth or importance, but whether it is driven by dominant officials within institutional decision-making arenas such as executive policy circles, or legislative or judicial processes. The advantage generally goes to those officials with the greatest perceived power to affect the issues or events at hand, the greatest capacity to use the levers of office to advance their news narratives on a regular basis, and the best communication operations to spin their preferred narratives well. In the next chapter, we expand and clarify these power cues that help journalists decide how to play stories. For now, the point is that voices of dissent such as Senator Kennedy's were heard infrequently because Kennedy was a lone voice and, though an influential member of Congress, hardly represented a serious national political threat to President Bush or his war policies. The critiques by former officials, such as Richard Clarke, were heard more prominently, but they too dropped out of the news relatively quickly. Meanwhile, the chorus of congressional Republicans and Bush administration officials voicing and echoing the administration's story helped keep it dominant in the news.

In short, the American mainstream news code favors those who wield the greatest power, even when what they say is subject to serious challenge. As noted in earlier, this propensity for stenographic reporting can even extend to cases in which official claims are clearly not true. A telling example of the diminished capacity of the press to challenge untruths came following the vice presidential debate in the 2004 election. On his *MSNBC Hardball* program, Chris Matthews noted that Vice President Cheney had made several incorrect claims during the debate—including a denial that he had linked Iraq to 9/11—and the press seemed unable or uninterested in challenging them. Matthews asserted that Cheney had swaggered to a victory in the debate, but asked his guest, CBS reporter and anchor Bob Schieffer (who was to moderate the upcoming final presidential debate), what journalists could do in the face of claims by officials that were factually incorrect. Schieffer averred that dramatic-performance qualities were probably more important to the voting public than factual accuracy in such situations. When Matthews persisted about the responsibility of journalists to set the record straight, the veteran journalist seemed stumped and puzzled by the issue, and they both eventually laughed off the awkward moment.[22]

From before the war until long after the invasion of Iraq had turned from its "mission accomplished" moment into a protracted guerilla insurrection, the continuing dependence of mainstream journalism on the story lines fed them by powerful officials was not due to some aberration, but to the routine rules of the news game. The expertly sold prewar buildup and the planned Hollywood ending were not isolated incidents of the press reporting the official line. Long before Mr. Bush landed on the *Abraham Lincoln*, the leading U.S. news organizations had effectively become government communications channels. This was surely not intentional—at least as most news organizations saw it—but good intentions do not always make for good outcomes. The lead-up to war was paved by ferocious government spin, against which the mainstream press proved no match. In addition, many journalists convinced themselves that their embedding with the military would somehow tell the real story of the war and not, as it turned out, just give those select reporters personal war stories to tell.

What about 9/11?

In thinking about the performance of the press during the Bush years, we do not want to minimize or ignore the backlash received by journalists and news organizations in the aftermath of 9/11. The public front in the Bush administration's battle for the hearts and minds of Americans was a ceaseless barrage of fear and patriotism. Those images were amplified by conservative media networks that echoed searing denunciations of any opponent—including other news organizations—bold enough to raise questions about the goals and plans of the administration. Yet news organizations with a stronger sense of independence from government sources—and less inclination to look over their shoulders and worry when they are not all reporting the same story—might be less likely to cave in to that sort of political pressure. Lacking such firewalls, the safe course for the mainstream press is to stick to what officials say and do—and bring outside sources in when they fit within the bounds of official debate. The problem is that this turns political reporting into an insider game suitable for political junkies, but tedious and uninformative for the majority of average citizens who are left perpetually on the outside.

And so, in the most important story since the end of the cold war, the front pages of the newspapers and the lead stories of the newscasts continued to be filled with administration spin, while other sides to the administration's story line were consistently screened out by the unwritten journalistic rule system. Much as with the earlier dramatic tales of WMDs and 9/11 conspiracies between Iraq and Al Qaeda, the press dutifully reported the ongoing backpedaling about a war going off script, as delivered regularly by administration sources. Thus, the administration line about "would you rather fight them here or over there?" drowned out another side to the story supported by experts (most of whom were not current officials) concerned that the war was creating far larger numbers of "them" than ever existed before.

Even as the war dragged on with bloody images and reports of poor planning and mismanagement, the storytelling edge continued to go to the Bush administration. Ironically, this was due in part to the fact that the situation had so deteriorated that many reporters on the scene found it too dangerous to venture out of the fortified Green Zone in Baghdad.[23] The war soon fell into a pattern of daily reports of bombings and uprisings balanced by periodic hopeful moments such as the Iraqi elections and Washington visits from newly empowered Iraqi officials who spoke fluent English, wore appropriate business attire, and indeed, walked right out of what was left of the administration script.

What about the Democrats?

Clearly the most obvious reason for the systematic underreporting of other sides to these historic events is that the Democrats so often failed to offer another side. Yet even if they had been more rhetorically coherent or bold, there remains a question of how effectively they could have used government decision-making processes to keep their story going, given that they had such slim purchase on any branch of government. As an outnumbered minority in government lacking much real institutional power—and lacking political incentives, in the post-9/11 environment, to be a serious challenge to the administration—Democrats could not gain control of the news narrative.

Indeed, the failures of the press in recent years are linked to the depletion of the Democrats as an opposition party. Beyond their reluctance to stand out against the climate of fear and patriotism created after 9/11, the Democrats were as removed from governing power after the election of 2000 as the Republicans appeared to be in the mid-1960s following the disastrous defeat of Barry Goldwater in the 1964 presidential race. Such diminished institutional positions offer fewer levers of government with which to advance an opposition position in the news, even if there is one to offer. An obvious opportunity to regain political power (and to make the news) presented itself in the 2004 presidential campaign. But the party's candidate, Senator John Kerry of Massachusetts, was seriously compromised, as were virtually all Democratic members of Congress, by a series of consistently narrow strategic political calculations that cautioned against challenging an initially popular president who had wrapped himself and his war in the flag and every other high patriotic symbol. With few exceptions, party leaders and serious presidential candidates (with the notable exception of former governor Howard Dean's [D-VT] moment during the 2004 primaries) hedged their bets on the war so thoroughly that when cracks in the administration's popularity and credibility finally appeared, there was little left to say that didn't sound duplicitous or hypocritical. Thus, the Democrats were easily contained and displaced by administration spin reminding everyone that they too had bought the "faulty" intelligence about WMDs. The Democrats thus remained largely silent—and silenced—on the larger issues about culpability for the war and its conduct.

These dynamics resulted in the press settling time and again on the widely shared official political story that nearly everyone at the start of the war believed that Saddam had weapons, and that what needed fixing was the intelligence process that produced such bad information. The irony, of course, is that news along those lines became an important linchpin in securing that generally accepted version of events. The faulty-intelligence cover story enabled both Democrats and Republicans to save face, but at the public cost of a better accounting of what may have actually produced the disaster in Iraq. Our larger point here, as illustrated in the cases we analyze in later chapters, is that a press system dedicated to telling "both sides of the story" so often reported only one. That failure stemmed not from the lack of credible sources or evidence to support another side, but largely from the inability or reluctance of leading institutionally placed sources to offer a counterstory.

In other words, the press's failures to present a full and balanced picture are often caused by failures of other political institutions to provide the kinds of checks and balances that cue the press toward more critical and inclusive coverage. Blaming press performance on the long-running existential dilemma of the Democrats, however, begs a larger question. Why must the press wait for the other side of a story to emerge from official and powerful (that is, potentially decisive) government sources such as an opposition party that can use its institutional position to challenge a dominant president or party? We can understand the incentives of political decision makers to promote a one-sided cover story, but it is less clear why a democratic press would help write it just because the configurations of power in government deny them the easy pegs they normally rely on for reporting the other side. *The big question for us is why the press clings to a set of rules of its own choosing that make it hard to report—and nearly impossible to sustain—opposing stories unless sources with power in government choose to tell them.*

The Self-Imposed Dilemma of American Journalism

At some level, leading news organizations seemed aware of their daily entanglement with power even as they told the stories that helped to sell the war, yet they also seemed unable to disentangle themselves. As noted earlier, the chief signs of this awareness came in the form of apologies from the *New York Times* and the *Washington Post* about their previous deference to the Bush administration's efforts to promote the invasion of Iraq. Editors at these prestigious organizations admitted that they had been spun badly (or well, depending on how one looks at it) in their quest for scoops and inside access to information.

In one of the more insightful pieces of journalism about the news decision-making process during the lead-up to war, Howard Kurtz noted that the editors of his own paper, the *Washington Post*, had decided early on that the war was inevitable. As a result, journalists who dug up stories that challenged the administration's rationales were discouraged. The following excerpts from Kurtz's report illustrate both this editorial-level participation in the Washington power consensus and its effects on news decisions:

> Days before the Iraq war began, veteran *Washington Post* reporter Walter Pincus put together a story questioning whether the Bush administration had proof that Saddam Hussein was hiding weapons of mass destruction.
>
> But he ran into resistance from the paper's editors, and his piece ran only after assistant managing editor Bob Woodward, who was researching a book about the drive toward war, "helped sell the story," Pincus recalled. "Without him, it would have had a tough time getting into the paper." Even so, the article was relegated to Page A17. . . .
>
> "The paper was not front-paging stuff," said Pentagon correspondent Thomas Ricks. "Administration assertions were on the front page. Things that challenged the administration were on A18 on Sunday or A24 on Monday. There was an attitude among editors: Look, we're going to war, why do we even worry about all this contrary stuff?"
>
> "In retrospect, said Executive Editor Leonard Downie Jr., "we were so focused on trying to figure out what the administration was doing that we were not giving the same play to people who said it wouldn't be a good idea to go to war and were questioning the administration's

rationale. Not enough of those stories were put on the front page. That was a mistake on my part." . . .

From August 2002 through the March 19, 2003, launch of the war, the *Post* ran more than 140 front-page stories that focused heavily on administration rhetoric against Iraq. Some examples: "Cheney Says Iraqi Strike Is Justified"; "War Cabinet Argues for Iraq Attack"; "Bush Tells United Nations It Must Stand Up to Hussein or U.S. Will"; "Bush Cites Urgent Iraqi Threat"; "Bush Tells Troops: Prepare for War." . . .

"People who were opposed to the war from the beginning and have been critical of the media's coverage in the period before the war have this belief that somehow the media should have crusaded against the war," Downie said. "They have the mistaken impression that somehow if the media's coverage had been different, there wouldn't have been a war."[24]

It is revealing that Downie so missed the point about why it mattered to tell another side of the story. The point of covering both sides of the story is not to be "crusading" in an effort to prevent a war, but to get something closer to the whole story—not just the part of it that resides closest to the center of Washington power. Informing people about compelling alternative viewpoints would also, perhaps, encourage opponents in government to break through the feelings of vulnerability produced when one side dominates public discourse, thereby reversing the spiral of single-sided storytelling. Downie's closing remarks indicate that even after recognizing at some level that he got the story wrong, he continued to look at his decisions through the lens of implicit judgments about policy outcomes and power, thus missing the reasons why covering other opinions might matter. Elite news executives tend to worry that departing from reporting the record of government activity moves them dangerously close to being "crusaders," which is a negative term in mainstream journalism today. More significantly, the basic news rule of focusing on politics through the prism of power leads to news decisions based on which side of the story has superior political momentum.

In the end, the responsibility for the content of the news lies with the news executives who choose how to report the stories. In this case, news organizations repeatedly decided to apply the unwritten rule that without some government mechanism such as a congressional hearing or a serious election challenge from the Democrats, there was nothing to sustain that second side to the story about the fabrication of the cause for war, or the exaggeration of intelligence findings, or any number of other sides to other stories. And so these ripe topics would be left for historians, who are just recently putting the finishing touches on the parallel account of how we got into the Vietnam War. What interests us about these scenarios is that this press problem with handling challenges to power (unless they come from others in power) results mainly from a set of unwritten rules of the press's own making.

The above sketch of the logic behind news-content decisions resonates with a general principle from our previous research on how the press works, and when it fails: *In news about most government policy issues, the absence of credible and potentially decisive opposition from inside government itself leaves the mainstream press generally unable to build and sustain counterstories.*[25] This is true even when credible sources outside government can offer evidence to the contrary, and, for the most part, even if opposition exists from domestic public opinion or foreign governments. This process is so regular that it has been referred to by one of the authors as "indexing" the range of news content to the degree of institutional conflict noted by journalists.[26] There are some nuances to this rule that will be introduced in the next chapter, and like all generalizations about social behavior it does not explain everything all the time. We offer it as a useful starting point for thinking about the behavioral tendencies of the press in U.S. politics, particularly when covering foreign policy and war.

For now, let's explore the implications of a news system driven more by perceptions of power than independent judgments about the credibility of various stories. One obvious implication in the case of Iraq is that many of the sources who were available before the war to support a stronger challenge to the Bush administration's story appear to have been far more credible in terms of expertise and political motivations than the sources offered up by the administration. Contrast, for example, Mohamed Al Baradei, frequent administration foil, head of the UN International Atomic Energy Agency, and subsequent winner of a Nobel Prize, with favored official source Ahmad Chalabi, whose self-serving fabrications about WMDs and other conditions in Iraq eventually embarrassed even his own supporters in the administration.

It was nearly two years after the administration owned the front pages during the lead-up to war before top *New York Times* reporter Judith Miller was finally disgraced for uncritically buying what her sources— most notably, Mr. Chalabi—were selling (though that story was overshadowed by the parallel one of her imprisonment for refusing to disclose her administration sources in the Valerie Plame leak case—a story in which she played the ironic role of First Amendment heroine). She defended her discredited reporting on Iraq by saying that "if your sources are wrong, you are wrong." Perhaps most tellingly, she revealed: "My job isn't to assess the government's information and be an independent intelligence analyst myself. My job is to tell readers of *The New York Times* what the government thought about Iraq's arsenal."[27] To this, *Times* columnist Maureen Dowd broke ranks with her former colleague and responded in her column: "investigative reporting is not stenography." Hearing of Miller's desire to return to the *Times* to cover national security threats, Dowd warned readers that if that happened, "the institution most in danger would be the newspaper in your hands."[28]

Unfortunately, the problem with the loss of press perspective was larger than Judith Miller and her editors at the *Times*. To return to the above observations by Leonard Downie at the *Post*, the problem was that the nation's leading news organizations had in effect become caught up in the Washington consensus that the war was inevitable, and decided to put the news focus overwhelmingly on the insider politics and the pronouncements of those determined to wage it. As media scholar Daniel Hallin has observed, this practice of mainstream journalism following the Washington consensus (or, as he puts it, "the sphere of legitimate controversy") is at least as old as the U.S. involvement in the Vietnam War.[29] This propensity of the press to stick to official scripts makes it far more an instrument of the government's public opinion management than an institution dedicated to holding government accountable.[30]

The result of this repeated pattern of the establishment press living up to its name is that the national story about the war in Iraq did not include a well-developed account from its challengers, who bore the burden of being outside Washington power circles—or, like Senator Kennedy, lacking the political support to mount a serious opposition to the Bush administration's policies and hence its dominance of the news. Their challenges may continue to echo, however, in the minds of those who pay close attention to the broader spectrum of the news offered by nonestablishment media. Perhaps they echo all the more loudly because they soon seemed so prescient: that the war was based on false premises; that it reflected a hidden political agenda opportunistically tied to 9/11; that it was less likely to lead to the spread of democracy than to regional unrest; that it was a distraction from the administration's War on Terror policy or, worse, it would create more terrorists than before; that it would damage the goodwill the United States had won following 9/11; and so on. All of these concerns appeared sporadically in the mainstream press, but like the earlier example of those who charged the administration with cherry picking (if not ordering up) the intelligence that supported the cause for war, they were mostly a backdrop to the mesmerizing administration spin that, with the help of the press, forged the Washington political consensus.

Ultimately, despite the momentary recognition that it somehow blew the real story, the mainstream press still seems to have overlooked the larger possibility that it missed precisely because of following its own unwritten but binding reporting principles. When challenged on these matters, journalists generally invoke those principles and point, often in frustration, back to government itself. In one of many public forums about the performance of the media after 9/11, *Washington Post* reporter Dana Priest was asked by one of the authors why the press did not give more play to the doubts expressed by many experts and former government officials about the Bush administration's case for the war. Her revealing answer was that a few pieces did appear, but they produced no public reaction from Democrats in Congress, so the counterstory had little to keep it going. At the same forum, *New York Times* Washington bureau chief Philip Taubman was asked about Abu Ghraib: Given the chain of evidence and credible sources such as Red Cross reports that all pointed to administration policies skirting laws against torture and "taking the gloves off" in dealing with detainees, why was the story allowed to be driven by administration spin and congressional hearings that ultimately framed it as a case of regrettable but isolated abuse? His reply was simply that without government investigations pointing to a policy of torture, the press simply lacked the "flywheel" it needed to sustain or advance another side to the story.[31] In both cases, government failed to feed another side to the story, and so the press alone could not sustain it.[32]

When journalists cannot imagine how to keep a story going without the flywheel of government to advance it, the press becomes more a government mouthpiece than an accountability mechanism. During much of the Iraq story, the problem seemed to be simply that neither the right sources nor the right story-advancing mechanisms existed to develop other sides fully. And so the news echoed the Washington consensus. Indeed, the mainstream press not only reported the consensus, but in the reporting helped to create it.

At the core of this scenario of a failing watchdog press is a fundamental journalistic pattern that existed long before 9/11, and continues to this day. The U.S. journalism establishment has developed a largely self-imposed idea of what qualifies as legitimate political news—a standard that makes it difficult for the press to exercise its constitutionally protected independence from government at the very times democracy most needs it. The reigning press standard favors news that consists of simple, dramatic narratives told from the standpoint of those in power. When the powerful are challenged by other players deemed able to influence government decisions or election outcomes, the news includes the alternative perspectives of the challengers. Following this standard, it becomes nearly impossible for editors and reporters to pass up big stories that exude Hollywood drama (WMDs, Osama-Saddam conspiracies), particularly when their plots confirm editors' and reporters' perceptions about where the political action is heading in Washington power circles. Without changing its basic operating procedure, there was little chance that the news media would not blow the story on the war. And until the unwritten rules change, it will happen again.

When the Press Succeeds: The Press and Iraq in Perspective

Our point is not to claim that the press in the United States is failing all or even most of the time. In fact, it functions fairly well much of the time. But there is a catch: the press system tends to work well when the political system is already doing its job of debating and giving public scrutiny to policies that affect the general welfare and security of its electorate. To cite just one example, the U.S. press seem to have outperformed its German counterpart on the issue of abortion, which has generated lively public media debate for decades now in the United States.[33] When covering such issues, journalists can write stories that are relatively rich with competing viewpoints and policy frameworks simply by reporting on the divisions and battles within courts, legislatures, or executive agencies. When prominent officials or institutions are in public conflict over an issue, the news gates of the mainstream American press typically open to admit a wider range of voices and viewpoints from society, including advocacy groups, interest organizations, policy experts, and members of communities.

The contrast drawn here between relatively open and closed news coverage is not just between foreign and domestic policy, although even if it were, it would be serious enough to warrant concern given the high stakes of foreign misadventure. Domestic issues may also suffer from narrow press scrutiny if they are not subject to vigorous government policy debate. For example, the AIDS crisis in the United States during the 1980s suffered nearly a decade of shrouded and painfully limited press coverage due primarily to the success of the Reagan administration in defining and dominating official debate about the disease as a moral issue.[34] And so the general news tone was set, despite efforts by advocacy groups to introduce scientific evidence and international trends to expand public understanding and focus attention on remedies beyond moral judgment.

The general rule remains that when opponents within governing institutions clash, the press reports what they and their echoing advocacy groups in society say and do, and the public generally gets two sides (and sometimes more) of a story.[35] Probing and clarifying different sides of a story often produces well-developed perspectives to help citizens simplify, organize, weigh, and summarize information. Media scholars call such organizing schemes *frames*.[36] Strong, competitive framing of political situations may produce better understandings not just for citizens, but also for decision makers, who become accountable for addressing challenges raised by media scrutiny.[37]

On controversies such as abortion, gun control, prayer in schools, and other enduring social-policy battles that have rolled through institutional settings for years, news stories may begin to take on lives of their own, freeing reporters somewhat from locking the range of news debate to just what happens in government during the latest present episode. Yet even in these cases, government decision-making processes remain the touchstone for framing, continuously tuning the competing political frames for news narratives. Political coverage seldom finds journalists straying far from official cueing about whom to call for comments and what adjustments to make to the shifting political boundaries of an issue.

As a result of the issues in public life that trigger open conflict in the courts, legislatures, and executive agencies of the land, there are plenty of stories in which the press offers a range of contrasting viewpoints over long-enough periods so that something resembling public deliberation can occur.[38] Thus, we can give the press solid marks in these areas, along with high grades for the occasional investigative series that alerts policy makers and citizens to scandalous conditions in nursing homes or the false conviction of prisoners, or warnings that the levees of New Orleans would not withstand the likes of Hurricane Katrina.[39] The *New York Times'* revelation of the National Security Agency's domestic surveillance program, and *USA Today's* follow-up story revealing the scope of the program and the extent of cooperation between major telecommunications companies and the NSA, also reminds us that essential investigative reporting is still alive (although in the former case, the *Times* held its story for over a year, at least in part out of deference to a request by the Bush administration).[40] If the citizens and their elected representatives ignore these news alarms, the press cannot be blamed for failure to sound them.

However, on major policy questions like going war against Iraq, more seems required than an occasional alarm bell. And while government officials in the minority party (in this case, the Democrats) certainly bear responsibility for raising alarms, waiting for the Democrats or for some other powerful official opponent to emerge does not satisfy our concern about whether the press can gain enough independence from its own journalistic code to hold government accountable when powerful officials are not doing that on their own.

Why the Press Depends on Government Sources

The democratic dilemma we raise in this book involves cases in which poorly conceived policies fail to receive careful public scrutiny by either government or the press. These moments in history are not as rare as we would like to think. The U.S. commitment to escalate its involvement in the Vietnam War was based on a largely fabricated naval incident in the Gulf of Tonkin that led Congress and the press to rubber-stamp President Lyndon Johnson's desire to wage full-scale war in Southeast Asia.

Funding for Ronald Reagan's proxy wars with armies of mercenaries in Central America was secured when the White House ran scathing election ad campaigns questioning the patriotism of vulnerable Democrats in a closely divided House of Representatives. Even though the national press covered the opposition of those Democrats in their defeat of earlier requests by the administration to fund the proxy armies, the same press fell silent when congressional opposition was silenced, even though there continued to be plenty of experts and interest groups available to provide news organizations with credible alternatives to the administration's claims.[41]

The lesson from Vietnam, to the Iran-Contra affair that capped the Central American escapades of the 1980s, to the Iraq crisis of the new millennium is that lack of public scrutiny often, and perhaps usually, results in bad policies that undermine American values and public confidence in the core democratic institutions of government and the press. Countering this argument are observers who point to the curiously American traits of public indifference and disinterest in politics (in particular, the unpleasant matters of managing the empire). Since most of the public doesn't pay much attention to politics or news, this argument goes, what does it matter that the news is strikingly homogeneous, or that it becomes an extension of governance at precisely those times when government is operating unchecked?

We see a vicious circle here. When the press becomes an echo chamber for well-managed but misleading information, the result is only likely to deepen the spiral of cynicism and distrust among the public. To turn the argument around and recall the idealized role of the press in democracy: an independent and constructively critical press is the only wake-up call that may reach large numbers of citizens. When important events, from wars to welfare reforms, reach general publics, those audiences receive most of their impressions from repeated exposure to the mainstream media. Even if those impressions are filtered thorough the patter of late-night comedians, their material generally comes from mainstream news outlets. And even as the much-discussed Fox News may bend the uniformity principle of mainstream journalism a bit to the right, it does so not by sampling outside official versions of events, but by sampling even more narrowly within them.

The point here is that while attention is sparse, some messages do reach the citizenry, and they tend to be the ones most repeated by the officials who are given the prime share of news space.[42] The unchallenged framing of the key arguments for the war by the Bush administration, outlined above, created strong public support at the outset of the invasion, and enduring public misapprehension of the situation far into the conflict. For example, the much-heralded claims about WMDs and Al Qaeda connections were still believed by substantial numbers of people even after credible sources had shown them to be groundless. A strong majority of nearly 70% continued to believe the ongoing official insinuations that Saddam had assisted the 9/11 terrorists, even when credible (but less prominently reported) challenges emerged within months of the invasion.[43] As noted earlier, this popular misperception did not recede appreciably even as the war dragged on, and evidence to the contrary mounted.

There were, of course, some differences in levels of misinformation corresponding to news sources, suggesting that the media did not uniformly constitute a propaganda arm of the government. But the preponderance of mainstream audiences suffered considerable short-circuiting due to their high exposure to administration spin. Not surprisingly, belief in various unsupported rationales for the war ran to over 80% of viewers of Fox News, but hit levels of 71% among those who watched CBS, 61% at ABC, 55% at NBC and CNN, and 47% for the average print-news reader.[44] These opinion trends should not be surprising in light of the messages that dominated the news. For example, of the 414 stories on the buildup to and rationale for the war told by ABC, CBS, and NBC from September through February 2003, only 34 originated outside the White House.[45]

Beyond the public-opinion effects of press dependence on official spin, the news greatly impacts the perceived power and strategic positioning among Washington elites themselves. Officials look to the daily news as though it were the very mirror of public opinion and accountability.[46] And, in a way, it is. After all, political power, or at least its commanding illusion, is partly established through news-making prowess. Spin is aimed at shaping the news strategically for those who are paying attention. Politicians tend to associate with those who have spun a situation well, and to dissociate from those suffering spin problems. Even journalists tend to give grudging respect to those who spin them well, while finding (or echoing rumored) vulnerabilities in politicians foolish enough to address the public spontaneously without professional scripting and staging (ask Howard Dean). One implication of this maxim is that an intimidating wall of spin can silence potential critical voices from inside government. Another implication is that poor news management, perhaps compounded by an untimely turn of events, can result in those unpleasant press feeding frenzies that shrink the once powerful back to normal size.

Beyond the issues of how press coverage affects the maintenance of political power in Washington or public involvement in the policy-making process, there is another potential consequence of its capacity to challenge the claims of the powerful: helping to prevent groupthink among the policy elite. We suspect that as the Democrats contemplated the spectacle of a well-spun media against the backdrop of a nation whipped to a patriotic frenzy, the impulse to raise critical questions or challenges to the impending war may have seemed politically suicidal. However, the absence of critical voices, in turn, required even less public accountability from those making the policy. This could only have added to the hubris of a Bush administration already displaying the classic symptoms of groupthink as described by the psychologist Irving Janis in his analysis of such earlier foreign-policy disasters as the Bay of Pigs invasion of Cuba: closing decision circles, discounting evidence to the contrary, denigrating critics, projecting fantasy images (cakewalks, open-armed greetings, and the immaculate birth of democracy), and resisting learning from policy failures when these improbable visions failed to materialize).[47] The absence of public accountability pressures in the media can only reinforce such potentially disastrous policy-making conditions. And yet the spiral of awkward public discussion of the war continued for years as the Democrats remained trapped in their initial public display of support for the war, which the press reinforced by continuing to construct them as relatively powerless.

All of this meant that the loudest public voice that continued to be heard, even as it lost public favor, was the official cadre of the Bush administration claiming, improbably, that its policies were aiding in the birth of a new, freedom-loving Middle East, albeit with a few birth pangs along the way. Despite the growing gap between these official news claims and the palpable evidence to the contrary in daily reports of chaos and carnage (spun as press negativity by the administration), the relationship between the press and government generally maintained the fundamental pattern outlined here. The press channeled the images manufactured by high government offices outward to intermittently attentive citizens, and back to perhaps the most important audience of all: those other officials arrayed down the hierarchy of power reinforced by this communication process. We expand on the democratic implications of these press-government relations in the rest of the book.

2

The Semi-Independent Press

A Theory of News and Democracy

We all know the abiding paradox of newsmaking: News professes to be fresh, novel, and unexpected, but is actually remarkably patterned across news outlets and over time. Rather than providing an unpredictable and startling array of happenings, the content of news is similar from day to day, not only in featuring familiar personages and familiar locales, but also in the kinds of stories set forth and the morals these stories are supposed to tell.

TIMOTHY COOK, *Governing with the News*

The picture of the mainstream press that emerged during the Iraq war is one of journalists generally knowing more about the story than they could report. The news output was sorely restricted by the curious self-imposed constraints that have developed in American journalism. Even when intrepid reporters and editors occasionally overcame those limits and placed solid investigative stories on the front pages, they were met with unresponsiveness or angry denunciations from a government apparently more concerned with avoiding culpability and shoring up electoral fortunes than investigating possible incompetence and wrongdoing on its part. Without what *New York Times* Washington bureau chief Philip Taubman termed the "flywheel" of government activities to advance them, important stories kept falling out of the news even when they raised substantial, well-documented challenges to government claims. Some stories, such as the one about the National Security Agency's domestic eavesdropping, continued to pop up, but they were typically bent to the institutional power context in which they appeared: whether Congress would investigate; whether Congress would pass retroactive legislation authorizing what the president did, despite not really knowing what he did; or whether the eavesdropping program would affect the outcome of hearings on the president's appointee for CIA director, who formerly oversaw the NSA operation. What was lost due to the close referencing of story lines

to the shifting institutional power contexts was a sustained emphasis on
political accountability questions: whether there was reason to think that
the law may have been broken; whether anyone in government was likely to
take a hard look at that possibility; and, even if some officials regarded the
program as illegal, whether anyone cared enough to try to enforce the
law. The tenuous status of such accountability issues in the news raises
even more disturbing questions: If democracy failed, how would we know?
Would the media provide a supportive context for citizens or isolated
officials who tried to raise this question?

One way of thinking about the oddly dependent relationships between
the press, public officials, and government news "flywheels" is that they
may rest on an idealized belief in the open flow of public information
and a shared commitment by elected officials to democratic values. Indeed, most journalists, like most Americans, probably want to believe
that these articles of democratic faith underlie their government. It seems
almost unthinkable, not to mention somehow paralyzing, to contemplate
the possibility that those granted disproportionate power over our lives
and the fate of the world might have a diminished sense of accountability
to the law or to higher democratic values. The lack of clear press accountability guidelines beyond following the trail of power may help explain
the press's avoidance of serious public discussion (until Senator McCain's
eventual efforts to reassert the law) about whether there was high-level
authorization of torture in U.S. detention facilities overseas, and if so,
what should be done about it. Similarly uneven attention was given to
the issue of whether intelligence manipulation by the executive branch
paved the way for war in the first place, and if so, what should be done
about that.

Perhaps the implicit democratic compact between officials, the people,
and the press has generally been honored in the past, or as in the case of
the Nixon administration, a little help from the press enabled a more willing government to correct its accountability problem. But in the Bush era,
unlike the Nixon years, government power was not divided between the
parties. The reluctance of the ruling party during the Bush years to initiate investigations that might undermine its own power left open many
uncomfortable questions of democratic values and competence to govern,
including intelligence distortion; war planning; motives for targeting Iraq;
conduct of the reconstruction efforts there; assignment and oversight of

contracts; the torture and questionable legal status of detainees; large-scale domestic spying without authorization or oversight; and a host of concerns regarding national preparedness, cronyism, and bureaucratic competence raised by Hurricane Katrina.

The various conclusions that might be drawn about these and other matters are not the point here. There are surely differences of opinion and remedy that would emerge. The point is that these issues rose and fell in the news tightly tethered to the actions of those in government with the capacity and interest to affect policy about them. Since the government was solidly in control of one party that sought to avoid more than a modicum of self-investigation, the news seldom focused on any given issue long enough to cultivate informed public opinion or pressure for remedies. When government does not examine its own democratic commitments and policy effectiveness, it becomes reasonable to ask: where was the Fourth Estate when democratic ideals were so challenged?

A Theory of the Press and Politics

The general pattern discussed in this book is that when all parties to the public information system are operating in reasonably good faith, the public receives a generally good accounting of its important issues. However, this process becomes embattled when powerful parties are playing hardball, intimidating opponents or pushing them out of decision making. Democratic accountability is similarly embattled when narrow political calculations or intense ideological preferences bend the facts in the service of poorly examined policies, and there is no opposition within government with enough power or courage to challenge that course of policy. What is puzzling yet important to understand is that because of its dependence on power blocs in government to correct the democratic balance, the press is shut out from the political accountability process, and becomes increasingly subject to manipulation. Such self-imposed journalistic rules that rely on government to self-correct make it difficult in many cases for the press to bring outside information and sources into play in an effort to establish an independent public accounting. This chapter explores how this rule system operates, while pointing to occasional conditions under which journalists may achieve some greater margins of independence from their official handlers.

The core principle of the mainstream press system in the United States appears to be this: the mainstream news generally stays within the sphere of official consensus and conflict displayed in the public statements of the key government officials who manage the policy areas and decision-making processes that make the news.[1] Journalists calibrate the news based on this dynamic power sphere. The process is simplified by focusing on key policies that are in play (for example, subject to decision or challenge); the perceived power of the factions that are lined up for or against the dominant options; and whether any reputedly viable institutional initiative or action might change the course of policy or the outcome of a decision, and then faithfully recording the spin operations of the most powerful players. Tangential narratives may, of course, enliven the news with fewer restrictions on content when political contestants engage in personal attacks and other skullduggery.

This ongoing, implicit calibration process conducted by the press corps creates a weighting system for what gets into the news, what prominence it receives, how long it gets covered, and who gets a voice in the stories. The implicit weighting of these key story elements according to the positioning of power blocs at key decision points along news beats is so regularized that it has been called *indexing* by Bennett.[2] This process is similar to the mechanics of opening and closing the news gates. The press gatekeepers (that is, the news executives) open the gates wider or close them more tightly as they perceive potentially decisive challenges or a lack of challenges to the most powerful institutional players and their agendas.

Shifting periods of elite consensus in the policy-making process become punctuation points in news coverage as political forces line up for or against particular initiatives.[3] The press monitors these power formations, and reports them in insider terms of strength of support or opposition for the leading initiative or the contending initiatives, resulting in something of a scorecard that updates political junkies on the winners and losers in the game.[4] Indexing the news to points of institutional decision conflict sets the broad terms of press narratives, within which various news sources are sorted primarily in terms of their ability to affect the political process and to spin the media most aggressively and effectively.[5] Most of the time, both of these factors—political power and spin capacity—accrue to highly placed officials in the White House and (to a lesser extent) Congress, though occasionally lower-level sources gain temporary ability to shape the news.[6] Resulting stories focus on who won and who lost a vote, a court case, a struggle over the budget, or a decision to go to war. And those stories generally stick to the language and political limits set by the officials involved, especially with regard to fundamental decisions about foreign policy and war.[7] Whether gleaned from the officials' public statements or from their background spin operations, the story lines of the news tend to track closely with journalists' perceptions of power in government institutions.[8] News accounts remain fairly stable after policy decisions are taken (or in the case of the lead-up to the war in Iraq, when a decision seemed inevitable), until the next decisive moment occurs, in which case the Washington consensus and news accounts may shift again.

Perhaps the most important dynamic in this Washington conversation about power is that judgments about the credibility or truth of many dominant news positions do not seem to be central aspects of news reporting. The prominence of various perspectives in the news does not have so much to do with whether they are supported by available facts, but whether they have powerful champions, and whether they go unchallenged (or survive challenges) by other powerful players. Pegged in this way, news invites the sort of character assassination that emerges whenever a credible source steps forward to challenge the official administration line. Rather than engage in a consideration of facts, news often degenerates into an examination of personal motives, questioned credentials, and personal innuendo. Indeed, this sort of behavior rests at the heart of the Washington power dynamic we describe in chapter 5. Pegging the news to power seems to be the basis of *Washington Post* executive editor Leonard Downie Jr.'s reasoning about why the *Post* missed the other side of the story about the grounds for war. The truth was not the issue, power was. In this odd universe, the focus is on telling the story of power, and it becomes difficult to report anything else, including facts that get in the way and simply don't fit.[9] Thus, it was not until after the Iraq war had spun well off course, beyond the bounds that the Bush administration's media spin could fully control, that the *Post* and the *Times* admitted to underplaying important challenges to the administration's story that had sold the cause for going to war.

The dilemma facing mainstream news organizations is that knowledgeable sources who could tell other sides of the story were known to exist when the administration was spinning its Iraq war rationale, and they existed in the ensuing episodes as well. What would it take to make the press change its sourcing decisions or its lack of emphasis on challenging perspectives, even after such a poignant moment of self-reflection? By its own self-defined rules, the mainstream press ordinarily does not foreground sources that fall outside the scope of the Washington power calculus. And even when less powerful news sources succeed at staging news events—as in the embodiment of antiwar sentiment by Cindy Sheehan, whose son died in the war, in her protests at the Bush ranch in Crawford, Texas—they typically lack access to the institutional processes that make it possible to stay in the news spotlight. Thus, in the lead-up to war, the United Nations weapons inspectors' disclaimers about weapons of mass destruction were reported for the record, but they simply lacked enough political standing in the rudimentary press model of U.S. politics to serve as major news makers. And the series of retired generals and other former officials who have since woven their way through the news with pained confessions of disagreement with their former commander in chief have lacked engagement with the "flywheels" of institutions—or the capacity for major spin operations—to give their perspectives sustained emphasis in the news.[10] And so, when the next case came along that might have enabled the press to redeem its mea culpa, we anticipated that it would ultimately not be able to do so unless assisted by powerful players inside government itself.

Case in Point: The Tortured Path of Torture

As shown in the next chapter, the shifting patterns of elite discourse associated with actors in key decision-making processes of institutions (a.k.a. news "flywheels") explain the tortured path taken by journalists in covering the scandal at Abu Ghraib and other U.S. military detention and interrogation facilities. Our evidence shows that news story frames changed markedly with the shifting punctuation points of Washington power alignments over prisoner treatment in the War on Terror. In the early stages of the story, following the release of horrifying photos from the Abu Ghraib prison, the available evidence supporting a deeper discussion about torture policy simply did not have powerful government champions capable of challenging the Pentagon or the White House, and so the story was written as the Bush White House and Pentagon would have

it: a case of isolated, if regrettable, low-level *abuse*. The now iconic formu-
lation is "Animal House on the night shift."[11]

Later, when Senator John McCain, a powerful opponent in government (indeed, within President Bush's own party), had mobilized enough
Senate votes to force the president to accept a legislative admonition
against torture, the news changed its language accordingly, using the
term *torture* much more prominently to talk about high-level tactics in
the War on Terror. (We detail these patterns more fully in chapter 3.)
Yet even in this phase of the story, the news was framed as a political
contest between Congress and the White House in which Congress held
sway. Since a Republican Congress was careful to avoid questions of presidential legal culpability for past behavior, the news largely avoided those
questions as well.

This simple theory of indexing thus explains why, even when it entered
the story, the language about torture continued to be severed neatly from
legal questions that might otherwise have been addressed to high officers
of the Bush administration, including the attorney general, the president,
the vice president, and the secretary of defense. (Chapter 4 suggests
that the elite press remained interested in these questions, but seldom
pushed them beyond the official bounds set by congressional investigations.) In the end, the news failed to address a prominent question: why
was there need for a legislative provision commanding the administration
to obey the law if there was not concern that it had broken it? As a result of this indexing or calibration of the daily story line to power, there
are often two realities existing in tension around important political stories: a documented outside reality about the situation and a Washington
political reality about the situation, and the U.S. press generally allows
the latter to define the former—even when the two are known to be far
apart.

Not only does this rule keep the press closely tethered to government,
but it also renders much of the world outside the United States largely
irrelevant, although the better news organizations report high-level official positions of other nations for the record. These positions tend to
become a critical factor in domestic U.S. news stories only when key political policy decisions drift into international institutions such as the United
Nations, or into joint international operations in which other nations
share in the decision making, such as in the bombing of Libya in 1986, the

bombing of Kosovo in 1999,[12] or the UN effort to draft a resolution to stop the fighting between Israel and Hezbollah in Lebanon in 2006.

Once the Washington story becomes set, other sides of the story become more easily excluded by the mainstream press, even when there are reputable sources outside government that could introduce and support them. And so the Washington consensus reigns, with the press acting alternately as filter, amplifier, echo chamber, and adjustment mechanism. As we explain in chapter 5, the conventional wisdom and daily perceptions of Washington power politics that hold these shifting news decisions together is reinforced by the professional and social ties among Washington players—including leading journalists—and by often aggressive news-management techniques employed by the White House and its public-relations minions. Tipping points may be reached when new official opponents emerge, and talk begins to recast the script: who's up, who's down, who's in, who's out, and what daunting uncertainties confront players in the game of power politics.[13]

How Do We Know It Works like This?

A critical reader might think that we have got this theory of the news backwards. After all, the majority of Americans believe journalists are biased, and books about the media's alleged partisan bias have become bestsellers.[14] How can a system commonly thought to be politically biased produce such regular patterns of reporting in lockstep with whatever the prevailing balance of political power happens to be? The ongoing calibration of news content to power balances on policy issues often results in shifts in content and sources that may seem arbitrary and politically motivated to audiences not aware of the underlying mechanics of mainstream journalism.[15] Indeed, the rise of the Republican right from the ashes of the mid-1960s amidst charges of liberal bias in the press contained the proverbial grain of truth: since the Democrats held the balance of political power in all three branches of government following the disastrous Republican presidential election defeats of 1960 and 1964, the news undoubtedly favored Democratic Party views and those of their social constituents more than the Republicans, who until Nixon's political resurrection in 1968 had little decisive input into national policy. But that favoritism stemmed from press deference to power, not some pervasive liberal bias in the press.

Forty years later, the political tables had turned, and the Democrats found themselves in roughly the same political position the Republicans were during that earlier era. The difference was that the Republicans had learned the value of keeping the press disciplined by continuing their charges of liberal bias, which became an effective publicity tool to extract an added measure of caution from the practitioners of an already unpopular profession. Along the way, the Republicans had also assembled a dense national communication network of talk radio and cable news pundits that served to echo the party line, air differences, and maintain the monitoring and disciplining of the press.[16]

These broad patterns notwithstanding, the popular perception of an arbitrary and biased press remains so strong that we feel compelled to address the lingering question: what makes us suspect that journalists are not selecting their preferred sources according to political partisanship, or to other standards such as a simple appetite for drama? An even more audacious explanation of the news might be that the much touted agenda-setting capacity of the press is so strong that public figures read the daily currents in the *New York Times* and the *Washington Post,* and begin to drift in line with them—that politicians respond to the press, rather than the other way around. While it is clear that the way the news covers issues often affects what people think about and even how they think about it—that the news agenda sets the public's agenda[17]—in most matters of public policy, the news agenda itself is set by those in power. In order to establish the likelihood that the press is not setting the national agenda according to simple partisanship or some other standard, it is important to find some measures of political power and source positions independent of those reported in the news itself, and see if they accurately predict what journalists do.

Over the years, a number of scholars have submitted the indexing theory to such tests, and generally found that the press faithfully tries to read the power balances among elites within policy decision circles and shape their reporting accordingly.[18] The most impressive such study was done by Zaller and Chiu, who looked at thirty-nine cases of foreign policy crises spanning the years 1945–91. They created two independent measures of official division of policy opinion based on legislative vote splits and speeches about the crises entered into the *Congressional Record.* They then coded the content of major newsmagazines in terms of the balance of hawks and doves, that is, the reporting slant on whether sentiment in Washington favored or opposed military intervention in the crisis. They found impressive correlations ranging between .63 and .70 between the direction of congressional political sentiment and the corresponding press slant.[19] Next they broke the data down into different time periods, different regions, and different types of conflict, and found similarly strong relationships, suggesting that the direction of causality is from government cues to press narratives, not the other way around, concluding that "the relationship between congressional opinion and press slant reflects a broad tendency within the data set as a whole."[20]

A similar conclusion was drawn by Jonathan Mermin, who examined television and newspaper coverage of post-Vietnam U.S. interventions in Haiti, Panama, Grenada, Libya, and the Gulf War of 1991. He concluded that in every case, press story lines closely followed the degree of public debate in government power circles, and seldom included other sources that held views outside the conventional Washington wisdom.[21] These findings parallel Daniel Hallin's earlier conclusion about the dynamics of press coverage during the Vietnam era, which conformed closely to the official (and often highly suspect) versions of the war when officialdom was lined up behind those stories, but included greater criticism of the war when that consensus broke down in the late 1960s.[22]

This systematic information flow from the circles of power to the portrayal of political realities in the news also explains another important aspect of the U.S. press system that remains significant for our national politics. Only the existence of a widely shared news construction norm such as indexing can account for a free press system in which the thousands of organizations making up the mainstream press generally end up running much the same news every day, with much the same emphasis, despite often fierce competition for stories and "scoops."[23] Our simple rule helps explain the irony of how the core press system in the United States, which may be the world's freest from government regulation, censorship, and other forms of constraint, produces such a remarkably uniform set of content.[24] It is this uniformity that helps demarcate the mainstream press from alternative news outlets, while serving as a wall that blocks most information from alternative sources from entering the mainstream.

What about the Alternative Press? Why the Mainstream Press Matters

An important "So what?" question at this point involves why we put so much of the focus here on the mainstream press when there are lively flows of diverse information just beyond in the nonestablishment press. With so many alternative news sources beyond the mainstream, people can get just about any perspective they want. Why worry about self-imposed limits of the mainstream press?

First of all, it helps to think of the mainstream press as producing the default reality option—a highly visible and focused version of events in the midst of a sea of chaotically competing alternative accounts. Despite all the jostling and scooping, the explosion of the Internet and the blogosphere, and the persistence of hard-nosed independent journals of opinion, the bulk of the nation's news media still ends up with much the same daily result across the vast number of papers and programs. As noted earlier, even Fox News simply samples more narrowly from within the prescribed daily official line. This uniformity of content helps demarcate the mainstream press—with its comparatively huge audience—from the alternative, nonestablishment news outlets ranging from long-standing independent magazines such as the *New Yorker* and *Harper's*, to more explicitly ideological outlets like *Mother Jones*, *The Nation*, or the *Weekly Standard*, to the many thousands of blogs and other Internet sites offering everything from well-sourced databases, to impassioned and sometimes insightful political commentary, to raw rumor and humor.

Thus, the mainstream press serves as a wall that at once signals an easy-to-assimilate version of reality (stamped as "official" and "authoritative"), while blocking most alternative information sources from entering the prevailing current of public discourse. Indeed, the perimeter of the mainstream press is maintained with remarkably well-patrolled boundaries. This flow pattern is, of course, reversed on occasion, as in the famous instances of bloggers challenging the CBS News story on President Bush's National Guard record or bringing on the downfall of Senator Trent Lott when his racist remarks at a birthday party for former colleague Strom Thurmond were heavily blogged. However, in matters directly pertaining to government policy, the sources and range of information reported tend to be more difficult to insert from outside the circle of the mainstream press. Recall from the last chapter, for example, the general failure of bloggers to push the Downing Street Memo into the mainstream news. In short, while an occasional report may be admitted from blogs or from publications such as the *New Yorker* or the *National Review,* the thousands of perspective-based public-affairs outlets are generally relegated to the gray zone of "opinion," even when they may contain more investigative reporting than the mainstream.

In this multitiered information system, evidence that challenges a government's argument for going to war, or points to a high-level policy authorizing the torture of detainees, has a hard time traveling from the nonestablishment media tiers into the mainstream. Yet the news agenda of the mainstream press travels easily to the periphery, where it becomes grist for polemics, bloggers, and the lamentably small percentage of Americans who actively seek deeper understandings of events. In the screening of news between mainstream and nonestablishment news outlets, stories are selectively branded according to sources and controversial angles that may veer from establishment positions.

Even when stories in alternative outlets become the basis for mainstream journalists to question or challenge officials, those questions and their sources can be loudly dismissed in official pronouncements as "liberal," unpatriotic, biased, and misinformed. Even veteran investigative reporter Seymour Hersh's detailed reporting on Iraq and Abu Ghraib in the *New Yorker* was dismissed by Pentagon spokespeople as "outlandish" and "conspiratorial." And although Hersh's reports were initially noted in mainstream publications, they were soon beaten back by officials, and did not ignite a second front in the story.[25] In short, the mainstream press sets the tone of national politics, and sources outside it are simply not considered authoritative for most people—including the mainstream media themselves. Because this is so important to grasp, we offer a brief distinction between the mainstream and the nonestablishment press in the next section.

Defining the Mainstream Press

This is a book about the workings of the so-called *mainstream* American press, from the *New York Times,* the *Washington Post,* the *Wall Street Journal,* and a few other leading organizations at the top, to national television news (where many people still monitor their world), to the thousands of daily papers and local TV news operations that struggle to put together what they report about the outer world from wire feeds, chain reporting, and video syndication services. This constellation of news organizations, big and small, constitutes what we call the mainstream press. This is a story about the workings of that core information apparatus which has become so integrated with government.

This sprawling network of mainstream news organizations, from the prestigious newspapers to local TV, has been described by Timothy Cook and others as a single "governing" institution.[26] This view draws our attention beyond the daily scrum of noisy journalists jostling for sound bites and photos, toward seeing a political ecology in which competitors feed from the same sources and generally end up reporting the same stories with minor and nuanced variations. Being the first to get the story is generally far more important than having a different story to tell, and the uniformity of stories can generally be traced to the management of news content by officials. In a very real sense, governing today has become almost synonymous with active and skillful management of the mainstream press.

The symbiotic relationship between government and this institutionalized mainstream press has gone through various changes over the modern era since it was first observed by scholars.[27] Yet one feature remains remarkably constant: for all the diversity of information in America that lies beyond the mainstream, those diverse second and third tiers of media reach only small, factional audiences, and do not speak with the singular, agenda-reinforcing voice that emanates from the top tier. This helps explain the irony of how the United States can be blessed with such an assortment of information channels, yet accept that most of them are removed from the process of shaping mass opinion or reinforcing the policy agendas set by influential members of government and interest networks.

We hope to add here to the work of others who have noted the symbiotic relationship between press and government in several ways: by identifying the specific mechanisms through which journalists and news organizations implicitly hook their narratives to the political processes inside government; by reconciling the pattern of press-government dependence to those event-driven moments in which breaking situations may open up greater independence in reporting; and by explaining why the mainstream press sets the tone for public discourse even though peripheral outlets often contain a diversity of competing and often more encompassing information.

This last point is often the most difficult to grasp. The great irony of public information in the United States is that the entire spectrum of information available to our citizens may be unsurpassed by any other nation, given the profusion of alternative publications, niche cable and radio, and the extraordinarily high rates of broadband and general Internet access. But it is the institutional press that matters most for governance— precisely because it speaks with such a singular voice, and because that voice is, in effect, the voice of government itself. This institutionalized *mainstream press* is defined by the cluster of news organizations, from the prestigious press to local outlets, that

- are regularly fed, monitored, and targeted with spin by influential elites;
- share the same broad network of wire feeds, such as the Associated Press and the *New York Times* news service;
- look to the same leading organizations (the *New York Times,* the *Washington Post,* and the *Wall Street Journal,* among others) for determining the top stories and the organizing plots that help journalists screen information and decide what to emphasize or downplay in their stories;
- assign most of their political reporting staffs to cover the official activities of government—that daily institutional stream of press conferences, briefings, hearings, lawsuits, and policy decisions—all filtered through the insider buzz, from the corridors of power to Washington cocktail parties; and
- maintain an enduring if fraying commitment to the objective of trying to be objective (often euphemized as *fair* or *balanced*), which ironically supports the reliance on officials as surrogates for authoritative information.[28]

And yet, for all of its institutional homogeneity, there are moments (Hurricane Katrina comes to mind) when mainstream journalism can produce unblinking accounts of important events without automatically filtering them through official story lines. Our theory of the press and American democracy must also account for these openings that offer clues about how and when a more independent press can emerge.

When Is the Press More Independent?
Expanding the Theory

There are notable conditions that may lead to sometimes radical adjustments in the nature and content of news stories, and shift the public debate about important national issues; but they seldom come from news organizations suddenly recognizing their failure to report neglected sources outside the closely defined arenas of Washington power. A typical situation that opens the news gates to underreported versions of events involves some shock to the Washington consensus: a catastrophic event or policy failure, a scandal, an electoral realignment, or a building political opposition that changes the power balance within institutional decision-making circles. Sometimes a news event that is cleverly spun by an interest group conveys a sense of public shock or disbelief that penetrates the Beltway. An antiwar protest embodied by the mother of a dead soldier and nicely staged for the press outside the Texas ranch of the president is a case in point. In other cases, an iconic cultural moment may enable journalists to continue interrogating official claims, as Lawrence documents in her study of journalistic uses of the videotaped beating of African-American motorist Rodney King by a group of white Los Angeles Police Department officers.[29] At such pivotal moments, the news may become a more active political agency in examining new voices and views, and in shaping a new consensus around them.

Media scholar Robert Entman refers to information flows in the mainstream press—whether in conventional directions, from highly placed officials downward through the news to society; or the occasional reversal, which pushes alternative perspectives from secondary social or political sources, and even public opinion, upward to government—as cascades.[30] The capacity for mainstream news occasionally to reverse the conventional flow of information suggests that there are limits on news management, even by skilled official communicators. It goes without saying that press dependence on government officials is not an absolute. Within the limits of the core operating principles outlined above, journalists have varying degrees of leeway to narrate and challenge official claims. It is equally important that our emerging theory also includes the conditions that favor greater independence of news judgment about stories that fall farther from the corridors of power.

Looking Critically at the Theory: Other Factors
Affecting News Gatekeeping

If the indexing principle explains why the news is so often dependent on assessments of government power balances on issues, it does not fully explain the tensions that exist within this system, and the conditions under which moments of relative press independence may emerge. In other words, the real world is not as black and white as the core axiom in our theory might suggest. For example, there was clearly an important element of press independence in the simple fact that news organizations broke the story of Abu Ghraib when they came into possession of photographs taken by soldiers on the scene (although CBS held the story for two weeks at the request of the government). Without those photos and the story they sustained, the incident would likely have been buried—at least for American audiences—in far more concealed and easily spun Pentagon investigations and reports. In short, in understanding the interplay between the press and government, we also want to assess the factors that may make the press more dependent or less under different circumstances.

Indeed, it is because the story of the Bush administration and the press is so instructive about the conditions under which varying degrees of press independence may emerge that we want to consider and compare different episodes during those years. For example, as noted above, it seems that the administration's media mastery began to wane, and press independence to rise, with the story of Cindy Sheehan, the grieving mother of a dead American soldier whose weeks-long protest camp at the president's Crawford, Texas, ranch captured the media spotlight in the summer of 2005. The Bush media thrall seemed to disintegrate almost entirely when Hurricane Katrina slammed into the Gulf Coast, leaving painful scenes of devastation and evacuees to be framed by journalists wondering where the government was in time of need. We seek to explain these moments also.

In addition, we want to address the fact that many government decision makers and journalists have come to believe that journalism today is far more independent than ever because news organizations can send reporters directly to the scene of many events, and employ new technologies to report nearly instantly on what they see. There are even those who contend that the capability to produce news in real time may force government policy responses that might have been slower, more considered, and far less public in earlier times. This view has been termed "the CNN effect" for the perceived impact of the first 24/7 cable news operation that covered the world in real time. Though empirical support for the CNN effect is limited,[31] since this perspective remains widely in circulation, we will look at its core idea that *new communication technology enables greater coverage of live events*—and assess the degree to which this capacity helps free the press of its ties to government minders.

Moreover, despite the resource depletion facing journalists in today's business-driven newsroom, enterprising reporting still goes on. *Investigations*, and the *leaks* they often feed upon, may put pressure on governments to operate within the bounds of the law and democratic principles (although, as we detail further below, the leak system itself often becomes a behind-the-scenes governmental news management strategy on which some leading reporters have become deeply dependent). We don't want to overlook the continuing importance of investigative journalism, and the willingness of some officials to leak what they know, often at great personal risk, as additional factors that counter the tendencies of the news simply to amplify the dominant official line. In fact, it was largely due to leaks from within the military and the administration that important stories such as Seymour Hersh's reporting on Abu Ghraib, or the *New York Times'* reporting on the NSA's domestic surveillance program, were able to see the light of day.

Finally, we acknowledge the potential for the news to include sometimes unlikely political stories—even about activists and ordinary citizens—if their sponsors have the publicity skills and resources to package them properly. It may seem to be asking too much of otherwise credible news sources to mount the same level of communication skills that are available to officials and well-financed political candidates in order to get their messages into the news. However, we would be remiss not to consider the possibility that outsider sources with the capacity to package their *counterspin* neatly may sometimes enable journalists to expand the scope of their reporting.

In thinking about what other factors may help fill out our simple theory of press behavior, then, we consider these three added factors of *technology-enabled event-driven news, investigations and leaks,* and *effec-*

Table 2.1: A Model of Press Semi-Independence

Basic axiom: "Indexing": News generally reflects the story lines of those with the:

- Greatest *perceived power* to affect the situation or issue
- Greatest *institutional capacity* to engage government news "flywheels"
- Best *communications operations*

Indexing is reinforced by the *Washington culture of consensus* and the *tactical management of news sources.*

This core indexing dynamic can be modified and press independence enhanced by:

- Event-driven/technology-assisted news
- Leaks/investigative reporting
- Outsider counter-spin

tive outsider spin. These elements may sometimes work against the core tendency of journalistic dependence on official sources. The idea is not to present these variable elements of the news process as though they were separate and somehow competing explanations for how the news comes out. Rather, we see them as potentially balancing and integral elements of a more general understanding of journalistic dependence on and independence from government. Table 2.1 spells out these various dynamics concisely (and alludes to some additional enabling factors that reinforce indexing, described further in chapter 5).

Technology-Enabled Event-Driven Reporting

The technological capacity of journalists to record and transmit information independently of government is surely greater than ever before.[32] In just a few short years, the encampments of satellite feeder trucks that trundled into the conflict zones of Kosovo have given way to portable videophones that reporters can stow in an airplane's overhead bin. This makes it possible for journalists to give publics earlier, more independent views of events before officials begin to spin and frame them.

In the case of Abu Ghraib, the availability of digital images recorded by soldiers in Iraq and passed to reporters surely enabled greater press independence in the early stages of the story. Photos launched the story and kept it going for several weeks, before official information management processes ultimately took over and controlled the framing. This dynamic suggests that, on the positive side, technology may help produce stories that would not have been told—or, at least, told as prominently—without it. On the other hand, those stories do not automatically stand apart from the news management machines of government and powerful politicians, who may seek to reshape, divert, and perhaps dispense with them.

In another important example, technology enabled journalists to run far ahead of the government in response to Hurricane Katrina, and to frame a story about the Bush administration's policy failure that enabled a lively and timely national debate about accountability. The capacity to show viewers unedited live coverage of an event of such magnitude, and to pit inept officials against their incapacity to spin away such a sprawling reality, enabled the press to orchestrate something of a national deliberation. This suggests that, beyond the technology that gave journalists and their audiences more information than came from the officials that they normally cover, aspects of Katrina as both a natural and a political event helped to liberate journalists from the news management syndrome.

When technologies permit covering them, highly dramatic events may contain other properties that embolden news organizations to step, if only briefly, outside government definitions of reality, and report alternative views that can shape national understandings.[33] The case of Hurricane Katrina again comes to mind in this regard, with its high volume of journalistic criticism of the government's failure to get relief to the hundreds of thousands of evacuees from the devastating storm. What enabled this level of press independence? Yes, technology helped, but it operated in relationship to officials and their news management operations—or in the case of Katrina, the lack of them. For more than a week, reporters operated in a rare "no-spin zone," as one reporter labeled it. Journalists beat government officials and press managers to the scene. They had nearly a week to report what they actually saw, which included an apparent lack of governmental preparedness for a human disaster of such scale, compounded by a seemingly unresponsive Bush administration. As a journalist for the *New York Times* told another reporter, "In some ways, it's refreshing in a way to not have the official line, where your only choice is just to see it in front of you. . . . This was the unfiltered experience. It's just the story in front of you." Another said that Katrina presented a situation in which "the press was much, much better than the official government sources you'd want to go to get information."[34]

The government was on vacation during Katrina in more ways than one. Mr. Bush was on his ranch and apparently did not wish to be disturbed until aides assembled a video of news coverage of the disaster and pressed him to watch the highlights. Vice President Cheney was also at his personal retreat. Secretary of State Rice was seen shopping in New York. And Deputy Chief of Staff and senior adviser Karl Rove, the acknowledged master of using news to create political power, was out of communication as well. When the news management operation was finally assembled again and teams of administration officials swarmed the region, it became all too painfully apparent that what the administration did best was to deliver prepackaged news about itself, not competent policy responses to real situations. Thus, Katrina marked a turning point, because the usual rules of the media game were temporarily suspended. Some reporters on the scene, disturbed by what they saw, went on the offensive against the very sources to whom they usually deferred. Americans and the world got an unvarnished look at the kinds of poverty and devastation we normally associate with underdeveloped countries and corrupt regimes.

While Katrina, like some high-profile events before it,[35] clearly revealed the government's policy gaps and failures, it is asking too much to rely on catastrophic events to sustain a large measure of press independence from official spin. For the most part, what we have learned about a good deal of this "event-driven" news is that, just as nature abhors a vacuum, so the press abhors stories that it must advance without the help of officials to move them forward.[36] A study by two of the authors of international stories covered by CNN between 1994 and 2001 showed that while thousands of stories from around the globe initially were driven by events that officials did not control, the vast majority of these stories soon found officials dropped into the middle of their coverage.[37]

Thus, event-driven and technology-assisted coverage seems not so much to present a radical or competing alternative to journalistic dependence on official news filtering as to reflect healthy tensions within the political information system that can yield varying measures of journalistic independence. Much the same dynamic tends to apply to investigations and the inside leaks that so often make them big news.

Investigative Reporting and Leaks

Among the special conditions that may free the press to exercise more independent news judgments are leaks that fuel enterprise journalism. Most leaks come from official sources who wish to remain anonymous, and many are part and parcel of government efforts to manage the news.

But critical leaks are sometimes compelling enough to keep a story going prior to more substantial government engagement. A classic case is the legendary Deep Throat during the Watergate scandal, who turned out to be the second in command at the Federal Bureau of Investigation. A more recent example occurred with the bombshell revelations in late 2005 that President Bush authorized secret spying on American citizens as part of the War on Terror. Both of these stories eventually became entwined with the flywheels of institutional activity, and in important ways they pushed those flywheels to engage, albeit with considerably different results due to the partisanal differences in the respective governments.

On the side of press independence, the New York Times broke its domestic spying story against the wishes of the Bush administration, and did so on the eve of a congressional vote to reauthorize the Patriot Act, thus potentially affecting the government's agenda. However, a number of aspects of the story's development also show that investigative reporting is held in tension against the strong pull of official spin that moves the daily news flow. To begin with, the Times waited for over a year to make the story public, later citing the administration's repeated claims that the program was legal as a reason for withholding the story.[38] Even when the story was published, the paper withheld portions of it at the government's request, indicating that after a year of internal debate about publicizing the most extensive case of government spying on American citizens since the Vietnam era, the Times was unable to fully separate its own judgment of the public interest from that of the government. Also weighing in the decision to publish was the paper's concern over possible legal repercussions, perhaps driven by fear of an administration that had, in the absence of public scrutiny, come to define itself as above the law. Attorney General Alberto Gonzales, formerly known for redefining torture to suit the political needs of his superiors, soon declared that the only laws that had been broken in the spying case were those in connection with the leaking of information to the press. In December 2005, the Justice Department opened a criminal investigation into the disclosure of the NSA eavesdropping program.[39] With explicit reference to the 1917 Espionage Act, which had rarely if ever been used for such a purpose, the Bush administration made the extraordinary threat of possible criminal prosecution of the New York Times for the publication of information about the NSA surveillance program.[40]

These aspects gave the spying story some legs, but the difficulty of independently advancing a story even of such magnitude is revealed by the quick settling in of a familiar "they said/they said" political story formula. The administration claimed to have the authority to eavesdrop on domestic communication without a court order. This position was quickly matched up against congressional critics and civil liberties groups, who disagreed. In the end, the presidential legal-culpability angle to the story began to fizzle as it became driven by institutional processes, such as legislative negotiations over what congressional procedures to pursue to authorize the spying retroactively. In a Republican-controlled government, even powerful critics within the party sought to avoid the larger question of lawbreaking by the executive branch in favor of the political issue of reestablishing at least the appearance of congressional participation in setting policy. Thus, a story that might have become a major constitutional or presidential crisis in a differently aligned government was allowed to take its official political course by the mainstream press. And so a potential blockbuster of a story morphed into a more mundane political fight.

Looking more generally at the trajectory of investigative journalism suggests that it has diminished as a force for political accountability. Most news organizations have cut investigative units and budgets since the heady days following the Watergate reporting of the 1970s.[41] Investigative journalism can also be risky, separating a news organization from the pack on high-stakes stories and further subjecting reporters to withering fire from government or business. In these and other ways, emphasizing official views and inside spin is generally safer from the collective standpoint that everyone reports much the same version of reality, while competing fiercely for occasional "scoops."

Moreover, the staying power of press investigations is often limited. True, there were sporadic investigative reports over the years preceding Hurricane Katrina predicting a levee-breaching disaster waiting to happen. But, like many good stories that pass through the news sporadically, they seemed somehow lost and ineffective in retrospect. One problem of investigative journalism's operating within the indexing system is that unless governments react to the stories (which sometimes happens, and sometimes does not), the so-called agenda-setting capacity of the news is relatively weak. Many important topics, from melting ice caps to chronic levels of youth neglect, tend to come and go in the news, with crises such as flooding or school shootings returning them to our attention. Yet many, and probably most, journalists would reject staying on such stories in the face of government inattention because, according to the prevailing norms of mainstream journalism, that would be crusading.

Outsider Counterspin

Although routine journalism assures regular production of a daily news supply, the results seldom encourage the timely involvement of citizens in their own governance. On occasion, however, those ordinary citizens do make the news in ways that offer journalists other sides to the official story line.

Most of the time, protesters do not receive positive coverage of their messages or movements.[42] They tend to be framed as lawless or disobedient, because their messages usually seem too complex and sound too shrill to present in the fair and balanced centrist world of the mainstream press. This can change, however, when activists package themselves in line with journalistic values and offer up well-prepared spokespeople who provide catchy sound bites to help journalists write simple stories. When those outsiders overcome the next hurdle by somehow keeping their messages in the news, it makes sense to look for signs of professional spin—and political context—to help account for their continued presence.

There is little denying that, whether from officials or from outside opponents, spin's the thing that makes the news go round. Most of the time, the spin is from government leaders feeding the daily line to journalists. But sometimes it comes from timely opponents who offer up a dramatic story to counter an official frame that has begun to clash badly with observable reality. Even the eruptions of political scandals and press feeding frenzies generally result from one side failing, and another side succeeding, in feeding the press.

How did the lone mother of a dead soldier come to represent an entire protest movement (however loosely defined that movement might have been)? Because of the rules of news objectivity and packaging identified above, it is difficult for U.S. journalism to cover complex and contentious things such as entire antiwar movements, and so the movement was distilled into one person. Reducing complex situations to simple plots based on highly personalized framing is a common news pattern.[43] Thus, Cindy Sheehan entered the news as the embodiment of antiwar sentiment in the summer of 2005. It helped, of course, that she operated with the kinds of conditions that favor outsiders making the news: summer is the slow news season, the president was at his ranch on vacation, the press contingent hovering around him had little news to report, and suddenly there was a dramatic story with the potential for episodic developments camped right outside the ranch. Such news conditions may help initiate what Entman refers to as a reverse news cascade, in which lower-level sources suddenly begin to get their perspectives elevated in the news—at times even competing with sources at the top of the information hierarchy.[44]

The Cindy Sheehan episode also reveals the reality that public relations resources are generally required if outsiders are to out-spin more powerful news makers occasionally and gain at least momentary news access on their own terms. Sheehan's success in steering media attention to her cause stemmed in part from the expert public relations help she received from progressive spinmeisters. For example, the *Washington Post* reported that True Majority, an organization founded by Ben Cohen (of Ben & Jerry's ice cream fame) hired the mainline Washington public relations firm Fenton Communications to help plan Sheehan's media campaign. And Joe Trippi, former campaign manager for presidential candidate Howard Dean, helped organize bloggers to echo her messages.[45]

Having professional help does not, of course, guarantee successful news making. Indeed, other conditions must be ripe as well. Consider the context in which Cindy Sheehan made her foray into the news. First and foremost, daily images from Iraq began to chafe against the Bush administration's claims about freedom, democracy, and hope to the point that public opinion supporting the war had plummeted to all-time lows. Such conditions surely primed journalists to the possibility of personalizing the story of public opposition. Also important, as noted above, was the fact that it was summer vacation time, and hence little news to report from official government channels. Journalists became more receptive to stories from other sources during these so-called "slow news" periods. In this context, enter Cindy: camped in a perfect "photo op" just outside the Bush ranch, complete with press briefing materials and new sound-bite messages nearly every day. The convergence of such conditions begins to explain how bottom-up information cascades may occur occasionally, reversing the downward flow of story lines from the top of the power pyramid.

Yet life at center stage of the political news is generally short lived for all but those few players, such as presidents, who have permanent press entourages attached to them, and who have the resources to generate news scripts on a regular basis. The ability of outsiders to successfully counterspin the media depends on a helpful political context. Sheehan's next big media event—an ill-timed bus tour across the country—was quickly displaced from the news by Hurricane Katrina, ending her moment as the icon for antiwar protesters. When she resurfaced at the end of the tour in a large antiwar rally in Washington, she appeared as just one of many faces and flavors of antiwar sentiment. Just as quickly as she entered the news, she faded out—becoming just another protester on a stage with dozens of others. She had suddenly become part of a complex social protest story with ambiguous relationships to power in government that the press often has trouble telling.

Testing Our Expanded Theory

The factors identified above clearly create opportunities for varying degrees of journalistic independence from official news management. Our general question is, what determined the more or less independent development of stories that arose under different conditions throughout the Bush years? The arc of news events from the invasion of Iraq to Hurricane Katrina offers a rich look at a range of press-government relationships that produced varying degrees of press independence: (1) the early, nearly complete press dependence on government pronouncements in the lead-up to war; (2) a somewhat more independent press in the publication of the photographs from Abu Ghraib, with government quickly regaining control of the framing of the story; (3) a nascent press examination of the wisdom and costs of the war, piggybacked on coverage of Cindy Sheehan's vigil; and (4) relatively independent story framing in the weeks following Hurricane Katrina, with sustained challenges to government policies and actions in the aftermath of that disaster. What happens to the news under different combinations of the factors described here? And what can we say in general about the self-imposed limits of press independence from government? These are the questions that guide the remainder of the book.

As noted earlier, the press's first break with its nearly complete mastery by the Bush administration occurred shortly after that unusual moment of self-examination in which leading news organizations admitted that they had not put nearly enough emphasis on the reasonable doubts, the countervailing evidence, and the well-placed questions about the administration's case for war. This led us to set up something of a natural experiment to find out what would happen the next time the press had the chance to tell another side of a major story that ran counter to the dominant government line. That opportunity emerged soon enough in the gruesome images of naked and hooded prisoners in U.S. custody at Abu Ghraib. Our investigation of national press coverage during this period shows that news organizations had not just graphic eyewitness photos but also numerous documents supporting another side of the story—one pointing to a policy of torture and violations of law. Pressure against reporting that side of the story was intense, coming from an administration that used every institutional news lever at its disposal to define the events at Abu Ghraib as regrettable acts of abuse by low-level soldiers.

How this battle for public information turned out reveals a good deal about how independent from government news management the press can be within the current system. Even though some important independence-producing conditions mentioned above existed in the Abu Ghraib story—notably the possession of technological access to events by the press—the suasions of a government determined to write the record of history are considerable. This fascinating battle for public information illustrates why authoritative sources positioned at decision-making points in government institutions are generally required to keep another side of a story going. The higher the stakes and the more expertly managed the official story, the more dependent the press becomes on government itself for telling another side. The case of Abu Ghraib illustrates why it is that in those times when democracy needs it most, the press is least capable of independent reporting.

3

None Dare Call It Torture

Abu Ghraib and the Inner Workings
of Press Dependence

Officials of the Bush administration, who counted on the fact that the public, and much of the press, could be persuaded to focus on the photographs—the garish signboards of the scandal and not the scandal itself—have been proved right. This makes Abu Ghraib a peculiarly contemporary kind of scandal, with most of its plot-lines exposed to view—but with few willing to follow them and fewer still to do much about them. As with other controversies over the Iraq war, the revelations have been made, the behavior exposed, but the moral will to act, or even to debate what action might be warranted, seems mostly lacking.

MARK DANNER, *New York Review of Books*, OCTOBER 2004

When Specialist Joseph Darby arrived at his post at the Abu Ghraib prison in Iraq in November of 2003, he heard about a shooting in Tier 1A. An Iraqi detainee had obtained a gun from an Iraqi prison guard and shot a military police officer. Darby asked the MP in charge of that tier if there were any photographs of the site of the shooting. Specialist Charles Graner gave him two CDs of photos, but they were not what Darby had expected to see. As a *Washington Post* story later put it, those images would soon "become iconic, among them, the naked human pyramid [and] the hooded man standing on a box hooked up to wires."[1]

It is a measure of the photographs' impact that they could be described as "iconic" only three weeks after CBS's *60 Minutes II* made the photos public on April 28, 2004. After Darby turned over his CDs, other pictures began to emerge from soldiers, their families, and their friends—photos snapped on digital cameras, many e-mailed halfway around the world. Ultimately, thousands of photographs accumulated at the offices of CBS News, the *Washington Post,* and the *New Yorker.* They included images of degrading treatment of prisoners, including building pyramids with their naked bodies and leashing them like dogs; sexual humiliation, including simulated sex acts and forced masturbation; and brutality, such as threatening naked prisoners with unmuzzled dogs and posing, grinning, beside a prisoner's corpse. Though these distinctions would rarely be made clear in the news coverage, the photos showed both instances of humiliation for the apparent entertainment of the soldiers present and the use of interrogation techniques that had been approved by higher officials, such as hooding, forced "stress positions" like prolonged squatting, and the use of dogs.[2]

Though it was ready to be broadcast on April 12, CBS withheld its Abu Ghraib story at the request of the Defense Department for two weeks. The network finally aired the story on April 28, citing other journalists who were ready to break it—a reference in particular to Seymour Hersh, who was working his prodigious network of sources for what would become two lengthy investigative articles in the *New Yorker*.[3] When the story finally aired, over four months had passed since the last of the abuses pictured had taken place. In that time, a confidential report on the conditions and treatment of prisoners in Iraq had already been issued inside the Pentagon, and a military investigation had passed almost undetected by the nation's news media. But once aired, the story ignited a political firestorm. As shown in more detail below, national news coverage of the Abu Ghraib story soon exploded.

President Bush, administration officials, and other Republican leaders immediately and emphatically called the events at Abu Ghraib isolated cases of "mistreatment" and "abuse" at the hands of low-level soldiers, rejecting the claims of some commentators that the photos signified a new departure in U.S. foreign policy—the deliberate torture of terror suspects. According to a speech made by President Bush, the photos did not indicate anything more than "disgraceful conduct by a few American troops, who dishonored our country and disregarded our values."[4] Critical questions about whether that was all the photos really showed were quickly consumed by a summer-long information management battle that included congressional hearings; official apologies; high-level trips, investigations, and reports; indictments of low-level soldiers; and heavy administration spin emphasizing poor supervision and low level abuse, which is where the predominance of news coverage left the story by the end of summer 2004.

Abu Ghraib as a Test of Press Independence

Looking back today, *torture* almost seems to have become a household word in the aftermath of the Abu Ghraib scandal. This is because a public debate on torture and terrorism finally occurred in late 2005, led by powerful figures inside government, particularly Senator John McCain (R-AZ), who had himself been tortured as a POW during the Vietnam War. That contest became so heated in the press that the president was moved to proclaim that "we do not torture"—even as he was threatening to veto a Senate bill provision that would prohibit it. What is interesting for our exploration of press independence—the capacity to offer timely and sustained news perspectives that challenge dominant government positions when evidence warrants them—is that such high-level official debate about U.S. torture policy did not break out at the time the press released the searing photos from Abu Ghraib. As a result, and despite considerable evidence pointing to the existence of a torture policy at that time (over one and one half years before the McCain anti-torture amendment), news organizations inside the mainstream daily press could not sustain the Abu Ghraib story as an account of torture policy. Our aim is to explain why.

What is intriguing about the way the Abu Ghraib story was ultimately told is that the press had not only a large volume of photographs to continue its coverage throughout the summer of 2004, but also various credible sources outside government such as the Red Cross and other human-rights nongovernmental organizations who had documented similar practices in other U.S. military detention facilities inside and outside Iraq. Moreover, journalists had access to a series of military reports, none of which overtly labeled the events at Abu Ghraib as *torture*, but most of which suggested that the photographs captured only the tip of the iceberg in terms of conditions in U.S. detention centers. They also had access to a series of government memos that explicitly condoned the use of harshly coercive tactics against terrorism detainees. For the record, and as we show in our data below, some fairly probing stories about torture policy did appear, though they were often buried in the back pages. Often the best that mainstream journalists can do when frustrated by their organization's dependence on official confirmation of sensitive stories is to fight to get critical reporting inserted somewhere just for the record. Being able to claim that challenging information was introduced into the record may preserve journalistic integrity in an embattled information environment. But it surely does not provide the visibility that an alternative perspective needs in order to reach distracted publics, much less to put the heat of public accountability on government information managers who seek control of the headlines as their main political strategy.

Meanwhile, several reporters for organizations outside the establishment press drew on this available evidence to report that the government had elaborated a systematic policy of torture since 9/11. Those reports noted that torture was often known to generate false information, that it probably had been applied to many innocent detainees caught in military sweeps, and all in all had fomented a public relations disaster in the Islamic and Western democratic worlds. Yet the daily mainstream news— that record on which most citizens rely, and to which politicians look as an instant public accounting of their actions—was unable to sustain an independent perspective to challenge the Bush administration's spin. The few early press questions about whether the photos revealed a new torture policy were soon lost in the volume of reported claims by the administration that Abu Ghraib was an isolated case of low-level "abuse." And so spin trumped the publication of horrifying images by the press, and the considerable independent evidence that there was far more to the story than a few soldiers run amok. How did this happen?

The political contest over defining what was going on in those pictures raises serious questions about how much independent evidence the mainstream press needs before it can dispute government claims. In fact, the Abu Ghraib scandal offers a "natural experiment" for testing the limits of press independence—especially given that the nation's leading media had only recently admitted that they had been led astray by the White House's claims about weapons of mass destruction and Al Qaeda connections in Iraq.

Dramatic News Events as Opportunities
for Independent Journalism

A great deal of daily news appears to be "indexed" to the official political agenda, with coverage bounded by the range of public debate in Washington power circles. In short, power talks with the loudest and sometimes the only voice in high-stakes, hard-news stories. But surely there are times when so much evidence and compelling perspective exists within the purview of journalists that they may fashion more challenging accounts. For example, the Abu Ghraib photos could have become a vehicle for journalists to turn to independent and credible sources outside government for asking hard questions about the conduct of the war in Iraq.

Sometimes, dramatic, spontaneous events do embolden the news media to bring challenging questions into mainstream discourse. Events that arise unexpectedly, off the beaten track of established news beats, can support relatively independent and critical news narratives, especially if they produce provocative visual images.[5] When a dramatic event breaks that practically demands media attention, journalists often begin looking for ways to make sense of the event for their audiences, and they may turn to sources off their regular news beats for help in this regard. Such event-driven stories can encourage the news media to draw on sources who present ideas that, absent the event, might seem too politically motivated or otherwise biased for objective journalists to take on.

For example, the news media turned highly publicized and provocative events, such as the 1991 beating of Rodney King or the 1999 shootings at Columbine High School, into opportunities to deliberate about the social problems those events seemed to signify, often casting a wide news net to include a broad array of sources and perspectives. News coverage turned the Columbine shootings into an indicator of the alleged corrosive effects on America's children of widely available guns, a violent popular culture, and a number of other problems.[6] Quite often this expansive, event-driven debate occurs when official explanations of the event seem inadequate to contain and define the imagery people see on their TV screens. The beating of King, an African American, by white police officers triggered an explosive national debate on institutionalized racism that led, among other things, to the ousting of LAPD chief Daryl Gates, who had denied that King had been treated wrongly.

These event-driven news dynamics are often propelled or enhanced by technological developments that make it easier for news organizations and even average citizens to gather news material quickly and independently. The Rodney King beating was famously captured on tape only because one George Holliday happened to train his new video camera on a disturbance outside his apartment window. Examples of this event-driven news pattern in the foreign policy realm include the so-called CNN effect in which the media may draw U.S. policy makers into the foreign fray.[7] Advances in news-gathering technologies, such as videophones, have placed more emphasis on live on-the-scene reports from events occurring outside the United States.[8] Technological innovation has not removed officials from the foreign news picture, but it sometimes gives news organizations the capacity to set the news agenda more independently. The Abu Ghraib photos, captured not by professional photographers but by soldiers on the scene using digital cameras, are yet one more example of this trend.

Given this history of occasional but high-profile event-driven stories, it seems reasonable to assume that the Abu Ghraib photos could have occasioned a cascade of more challenging and independent news coverage that put the events in the larger context of detainee treatment at various sites of the War on Terror and raised critical questions about the war in Iraq. Media scholar Robert Entman proposes that such cascades of coverage that challenge official positions may occur when sources pushing alternative perspectives are readily available to journalists, and when the events being covered are culturally ambiguous—that is, when they are difficult to make sense of in ways that fit easily with the public's widely shared beliefs.[9] So when leading news organizations gained copies of photographs that seemed to show the foreign policy equivalent of the Rodney King beating, there was reason to expect that the story could become a focal point for challenging the Bush administration's claims about the treatment of prisoners—particularly since the incident had become an international flash point.

We will explore further below the question of what sources were available to push such critical questions. But certainly, the photographs were ambiguous enough to invite competing interpretations into the news. Some observers, writing as editorialists or as journalists working outside the daily news mainstream, saw in the photographs reason to question government policies. For example, cultural critic Susan Sontag wrote,

> The issue is not whether the torture was done by individuals (i.e. "not by everybody")—but whether it was systematic. Authorized. Condoned. All acts are done by individuals. The issue is not whether a

majority or a minority of Americans performs such acts but whether
the nature of the policies prosecuted by this administration and the
hierarchies deployed to carry them out make such acts likely.

Considered in this light, the photographs are us.[10]

Some others, notably talk radio's Rush Limbaugh, saw the photos differently, using their media platforms as echo chambers to deliver the
Bush administration's spin to audiences who speak a somewhat different
language:

> This is no different than what happens at the Skull and Bones initia-
> tion, and we're going to ruin people's lives over it, and we're going to
> hamper our military effort, and then we are going to really hammer
> them because they had a good time. You know, these people are being
> fired at every day. I'm talking about people having a good time, these
> people, you ever heard of emotional release? You [ever] heard of need
> to blow some steam off?[11]

Limbaugh's interpretation foreshadowed the one offered by former defense secretary James Schlesinger, who, in releasing his panel's investigation of the Abu Ghraib incidents late that year, described them as "Animal
House on the night shift"—even as his report left dangling threads that
suggested a bigger story.[12]

Moreover, the context in which the Abu Ghraib story broke was ripe
for training public and journalistic attention on what the photos might
signify about the conduct of the war in Iraq. Abu Ghraib came to light at
a time of increasing public unease about the war. The period before the
photos surfaced had been one of the bloodiest of the conflict. Just a month
before the story broke, four Americans working for a security firm in Fal-
luja had been ambushed and killed and their bodies burned, mutilated,
dragged through the streets, and hung from a bridge over the Euphrates
River. That story was covered in the U.S. mainstream press in surprisingly
gory detail, reminiscent of coverage of an incident years earlier involv-
ing an American soldier in Somalia that precipitated the U.S. withdrawal
from a humanitarian relief mission there.

In this context, simply publishing the Abu Ghraib photos represented
significant news content that helped to send public approval of the U.S.

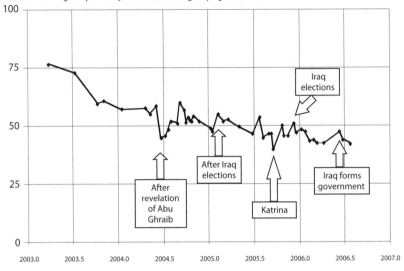

In view of the developments since we first sent our troops to Iraq, do you think the United States made a mistake in sending troops to Iraq, or not? (Percentage saying "no")

Figure 3.1: Public opinion drop following release of Abu Ghraib photos and resurgence of support following administration information management campaign. Comparison of support trends in three wars.

military presence in Iraq plunging downward past support rates for the first time since the war began. As shown in figure 3.1, this was one of the sharpest drops in wartime approval rates in the last half century. What happened next, however, was even more significant as the Bush administration waged a fierce battle to define and limit the meaning of those images in concert with congressional allies and the conservative media echo chamber. The important element of our story concerns the inability of the press to prominently report and sustain alternative perspectives to challenge administration spin, leaving public opinion management and political accountability in the hands of the government itself. The result of this one-sided battle for information was a sharp reversal of the drop in public approval. Indeed, administration spin appears to have produced the sharpest restoration of support yet measured in the Korean, Vietnam, or Iraq conflicts.[13]

A number of other important points are suggested by figure 3.1. The drop in public support of the war following the Abu Ghraib story— greater than any single short-term drop in either the Korean or Vietnam

In view of the developments since we entered the war in Vietnam, do you think the United States made a mistake sending troops to fight in Vietnam? (Percentage saying "no")

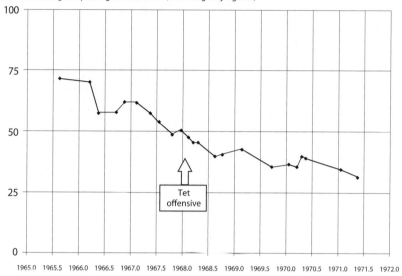

In view of the developments since we entered the fighting in Korea, do you think the United States made a mistake in deciding to defend Korea (South Korea), or not? OR: Do you think the United States made a mistake in going into the war in Korea, or not? (Percentage saying "no")

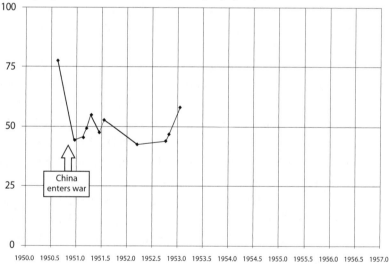

Figure 3.1: (Continued)

conflicts—followed by the acquiescent press coverage we detail below dispels the myth that the press follows public opinion in gauging the boldness of its coverage. The rebound in support for the war to pre–Abu Ghraib levels following the administration's press management campaign was unprecedented in the history of the three relatively comparable wars shown in the figure, with support levels rebounding even more sharply than the surge of public support following the entry of China into the Korean conflict.[14] And the restoration of pre-photo public approval levels following mainstream press conformity to the administration line indicates that the mainstream press, not the often more independent views found in alternative media sources, is the primary media influence on public opinion. In short, Abu Ghraib did not become a vehicle for a full-fledged, bottom-up cascade of critical news, and instead was told largely as a one-sided, top-down story.

Abu Ghraib, the Evidence for Torture, and Why It Mattered

Before providing evidence for this claim, it is necessary to first address the question of whether the term *torture* was even an appropriate label to describe the events at Abu Ghraib. Some may see this as a question only legal experts can answer (as perhaps many journalists believed at the time), or believe that the treatment depicted in the photos did not rise to the level of torture. From that perspective, it would not be surprising or troubling that the media proved to be reluctant to raise a critical debate about torture.

Indeed, one of the difficulties in making sense of the Abu Ghraib photographs is that some of the actions they pictured, such as the use of unmuzzled dogs and the stripping of prisoners, clearly violate the Geneva Convention on Torture, to which the United States is a signatory, while other activities, such as sexual humiliation done purely for the sadistic entertainment of guards, are "cruel, inhumane, and degrading" under international law and merely teeter on the edge of torture.[15] Both torture and cruel and inhumane treatment are prohibited under all circumstances by international law, but torture represents a higher threshold in the public imagination. Therefore, some may assume that *torture* was not an appropriate label for what happened to prisoners at Abu Ghraib—especially if one recalls only the most widely publicized photographs, which showed sexual humiliation of prisoners.[16]

In light of the above considerations, it may make sense to shift the discussion around a bit for those who feel that *torture* was not the right term at all. We note that a quiet battle (that is, largely unreported at the time) raged among legal officers in the Department of Defense and between higher-ups at DOD and the White House over the more generally encompassing issue of cruelty. The human right to be free from cruelty is protected not only in the U.S. Bill of Rights, but also in various laws and treaties prohibiting the U.S. government from inflicting cruelty on prisoners of war.[17] From the viewpoint of those who waged and lost this power struggle, the legal category of cruelty transcends and encompasses torture and offers a more principled legal foundation from which to make and adjudicate policies in the War on Terror. This view was held, among others, by Alberto Mora, the former general counsel of the U.S. Navy. Mora fought an unsuccessful battle to uphold that long-standing legal principle against the cadre of top-level White House and DOD legal staff assembled by Vice President Cheney and Defense Secretary Rumsfeld.

The predominant efforts by the Bush administration to rewrite (and thus break) the law were regarded by Mora as putting U.S. troops in jeopardy of reciprocal treatment, with the policy results leaving troops and the highest civilian officers of the administration also vulnerable to future charges as war criminals. The most disturbing aspect of administration policy, in Mora's view, was not just its use of torture; the authorized practices for interrogating and imprisoning detainees assaulted democracy itself:

> If cruelty is no longer declared unlawful, but instead, is applied as a matter of policy, it alters the fundamental relationship of man to government. It destroys the whole notion of individual rights. The Constitution recognizes that man has an inherent right, not bestowed by the state or laws, to personal dignity, including the right to be free of cruelty. It applies to all human beings, not just in America—even those designated as "unlawful enemy combatants." If you make this exception, the whole Constitution crumbles. It's a transformative issue.[18]

Like the other good soldiers who later came forward and revealed their discontent with the conduct of the war, Mora maintained his proper military posture and did not publicly challenge his superiors at the time. Had he done so, he might have contributed to a reversal of the top-down cascade of news sources and information. However, we suspect that even if Mora had tried to explain publicly why such an innocuous-sounding term as *cruelty* was actually more important in democratic terms than the subordinate category of torture, he would have been swept out of the news with a wave of administration spin and intimidation of the sort we examine in chapter 5.

The more general point here is that beyond those in the government who maintained a code of public silence, there were other sources available to tell another side to the story, but they resided outside the government power hierarchy. Those sources might have framed the photos from Abu Ghraib in ways that would have offered the American public another perspective on U.S. policies and practices in the War on Terror. We contend that seeing the photographs in terms of an evolving U.S. torture policy was a story that could have been told in the comparatively simple terms required by the mainstream news. It was a perspective that not only deserved to be seriously explored at the time, but since then has been verified by later developments.

The evidence we review below, available and known to journalists at the time, strongly suggested that something more than isolated abuse had occurred. The scope of similar incidents at multiple U.S. military detention facilities beyond Abu Ghraib also suggested something more than low-level lapses of judgment. As one legal expert has noted, "A widespread practice in multiple locations implies an institutional policy, not human error."[19] Even one U.S. military investigator publicly conceded that some of the Abu Ghraib abuses rose to the level of torture, while another military report (in its classified version that was leaked to the press) said that the treatment of prisoners at Abu Ghraib had violated the Geneva Conventions.[20] It is also important to remember that most of the many documented injuries and deaths of prisoners in U.S. facilities in Iraq and elsewhere were not pictured in the photographs from Abu Ghraib that were made public, meaning that those photos were not the full story.[21]

Despite the strength of the evidence we review below for *torture* as an appropriate label for events at Abu Ghraib, we do not argue that *torture* was the *only* correct label, but simply that there were adequate grounds for presenting torture policy as a debateworthy perspective. The head-to-head competition of views based on the Bush administration's claims and independent evidence could have illuminated policy questions in a timely fashion to address issues such as damage to the United States' global reputation, possible high-level legal breaches, and the cultural self-understanding of Americans. For example, if policies had been created that separated the Bush administration from both domestic and international laws on torture, then the United States had become a rogue nation, with its troops subject to torture by other nations and its leaders subject to war crimes charges—matters that might warrant public scrutiny.[22] If, on the other hand, the events at Abu Ghraib were isolated cases of prisoner mistreatment, then existing procedures for prosecuting individual soldiers were adequate to contain the problem.

A sustained press debate about torture also could have had domestic political consequences. A survey by the Program on International Policy Attitudes released in July 2004[23] showed 66% of respondents agreeing that "governments should never use physical torture," and 60% agreeing that the United States should extend war treaty rights to unconventional combatants.[24] Large majorities regarded the United States as a "moral leader" that "should not lower itself by engaging in torture or cruel or degrading treatment." Yet only 35% to 55% of respondents knew that the secretary of defense had authorized some practices similar to those depicted in the photos: hooding detainees, using dogs to frighten them, and forcing them to go naked. Among those who knew that these were official policies, 59% said they were less likely to vote to reelect President Bush. As it turned out, however, the opportunity for timely public debate about torture was largely missed.

The Documentary Evidence

Considerable documentary evidence from a variety of sources was available to mainstream news organizations for supporting a challenge to the Bush administration's claim that the Abu Ghraib scandal represented only instances of isolated abuse. These included five U.S. military reports, several sets of leaked military and administration documents, testimony at Senate Armed Services Committee hearings, and reports by three international human rights organizations. (For a summary, see appendix A.) These documents were not unknown to mainstream journalists; indeed, the Washington Post, whose coverage we analyze closely below, drew upon all of these sources in its own reporting. The issue we explore is how those documents were defined and emphasized in that reporting—

and how independently the mainstream press analyzed and utilized their findings.

One of the most influential of these documents was the Taguba report (named for Major General Antonio Taguba, who headed up the investigation), made public shortly after the photographs were first aired. The report found a pattern of "sadistic, blatant, and wanton criminal abuses" at Abu Ghraib[25] and noted that the detention facility had been effectively put under the control of military intelligence (MI) officers, in violation of military rules. Taguba recommended that one of the MI commanders be reprimanded and punished and that the former director of the Joint Interrogation and Debriefing Center be relieved of duty (for either ordering or allowing military police officers who were neither trained nor authorized to interrogate prisoners). As interpreted by investigative journalist Seymour Hersh for the *New Yorker*, Taguba's report concluded that "interrogating prisoners and getting intelligence, including by intimidation and torture, was the priority" at Abu Ghraib.[26] Yet as spun by the administration and reported by much of the news media, the Taguba report seemingly did more to solidify the "isolated abuse" claim than to challenge it.

The Schlesinger report and the Fay report (named for one of the chief investigators, Major General George Fay), released within days of each other in late August 2004, offered a more critical analysis that pointed to higher levels of responsibility. The portions of the Fay report that were unclassified for public release faulted senior military commanders for helping to create the conditions for what happened at Abu Ghraib by conducting overzealous "cordon and capture" missions that brought thousands of detainees of questionable intelligence value into the facility. (As detailed in chapter 4, this story about the wisdom and the fallout of detaining and degrading innocent civilians was rarely explored in the news.) The Fay report also revealed that General Ricardo Sanchez, the former top commander in Iraq, had issued a shifting set of rules for interrogations of detainees, which, the report claimed, caused policy confusion among lower-level soldiers carrying out the interrogations.[27] Classified sections of the report that were leaked to the press contained less ambiguous descriptions of detainee treatment, including the use of dogs to intimidate prisoners, which, according to the report, was "clearly in violation of the Geneva Conventions."[28]

The Schlesinger report traced the lines of responsibility higher, to the office of the Secretary of Defense, Donald Rumsfeld. The report held Rumsfeld's office indirectly responsible for the abuses at Abu Ghraib, by failing to plan for and respond to the Iraqi insurgency and the swelling of the prison population adequately, and by sowing confusion about which interrogation tactics were allowable. According to one panel member, "We found a string of failures that go well beyond an isolated cellblock in Iraq. . . . We found fundamental failures throughout all levels of command, from the soldiers on the ground to the Central Command and to the Pentagon. These failures of leadership helped to set the conditions which allowed for the abusive practice to take place."[29]

More damning to the Bush administration were a series of Pentagon and Justice Department memos that came to light shortly after the Abu Ghraib story broke—government documents that brought the possibility of a high-level torture policy directly into the picture. One was a list of interrogation techniques—some pictured in the photos from Abu Ghraib—approved by Secretary Rumsfeld for use at the U.S. detention camp at Guantanamo Bay, Cuba. The Schlesinger report later cited this memorandum (which the Pentagon later modified) for creating "confusion" among soldiers while pressuring them to use more coercive interrogation techniques. Another was a 2002 memo written by the assistant attorney general in the Justice Department's Office of Legal Counsel, Jay S. Bybee, which made a case for exempting prisoners in the War on Terror from certain U.S. and international legal restraints on torture. The memo suggested that the president could legally authorize an array of coercive interrogation techniques as long as they stopped short of "death, organ failure, or serious impairment of body functions"[30]—a standard much more permissive than that contained in international law against torture. Another, earlier memo written by then White House Counsel (and later U.S. Attorney General) Alberto Gonzales told the president that he could declare members of the Taliban and Al Qaeda outside the protection of the Geneva Conventions in order to allow more coercive interrogation of them, yet protect U.S. officials from prosecution under the federal War Crimes Act of 1996. The *Washington Post* reported Gonzales as advising the president: "In my judgment, this new paradigm [of the war on terrorism] renders obsolete Geneva's strict limitations on questioning of enemy prisoners and renders quaint some of its provisions."[31]

Beyond the government's own documents that seemed to warrant introducing a sustained press challenge to the Bush administration's claims about Abu Ghraib, reports by independent organizations and investigative reporting by a few U.S. journalists provided additional and extensive evidence linking the Abu Ghraib photographs to the possibility that the United States had embarked on a policy of torture. For example, a summary report of 14 investigations of U.S. military detention facilities in Iraq conducted by the International Committee of the Red Cross in 2003, which was used as a background source in several mainstream press stories about Abu Ghraib, charged that military police had repeatedly engaged in "excessive and disproportionate use of force . . . resulting in death or injury" to detainees.[32] One Red Cross visit to a U.S.-run prison in October 2003 had found prisoners being stripped and humiliated—practices that were termed "part of the process" by the military intelligence officer in charge of interrogation. This treatment of prisoners at these U.S. facilities, the ICRC concluded, was "tantamount to torture."[33] Reports by Amnesty International and Human Rights Watch echoed these concerns about conditions at U.S.-run facilities.[34]

Meanwhile, Hersh's two pieces in the *New Yorker*[35] traced a trail of evidence connecting the photos to even more appalling practices documented in the Taguba report (though not widely reported by the mainstream media), and followed a document and informant trail about U.S. interrogation policy through the highest levels of the Defense Department, linking command channels at Abu Ghraib, across Iraq, and at Guantanamo. Later in the year, independent journalist Mark Danner, writing for the *New York Review of Books*, provided an extensive analysis of the gaps and contradictions in the Fay and Schlesinger reports. Both Danner and Hersh then published books linking Abu Ghraib and torture.[36] Danner's work was particularly cogent in connecting the many dots, observing that the various documents and

the photographs themselves, some of which depicted military intelligence soldiers assisting in abuses they supposedly knew nothing about—all strongly suggested that the images were the brutal public face of behavior that involved many more people than the seven military police who were quickly charged. The [Fay and Schlesinger] reports not only decisively prove what was long known, widening the

circle of direct blame for what happened at Abu Ghraib to nearly fifty
people, including military intelligence soldiers and officers—although
subsequent disclosures suggest the number is at least twice that. More
important, the reports suggest how procedures that "violated established interrogation procedures and applicable laws" in fact had their
genesis not in Iraq but in interrogation rooms in Afghanistan and
Guantánamo Bay, Cuba—and ultimately in decisions made by high
officials in Washington.[37]

These various documents and reports, coupled with scores of damning photographs taken by U.S. soldiers themselves, coming in the midst
of growing discomfort with the war and on the heels of leading news organizations acknowledging lapses in their own critical judgment about
the lead-up to the war, would all seem to offer a truly independent press
all the license it needed to question the Bush administration's claims that
Abu Ghraib represented nothing more than a low-level problem of military discipline. While no one photograph, document, or report offered
an irrefutable smoking gun, the various pieces of evidence strongly suggested something more than "Animal House on the night shift" at a single
detention facility—and suggested a connecting thread of high-level policy
decisions about how detainees in the so-called War on Terror should be
handled. As we detail below, the leading news media did raise early questions about what those photos really showed and how high up responsibility for the acts depicted there extended. But our data also demonstrate
that the mainstream press failed to turn those questions into a sustained
and coherent alternative perspective—such as the possible development
of a torture policy—that offered audiences an easy-to-grasp challenge to
the administration's simple story line about Abu Ghraib.

Perhaps the greatest irony is that masthead editorials in both the *New
York Times* and the *Washington Post* charged the government with torture,
using the very same evidence that their news stories hedged. This suggests
that leading journalists clearly saw the possibility of an official torture
policy in those pictures and documents, but the absence of official sanction meant they could more easily raise direct questions in the form of an
editorial viewpoint rather than hard news. (We will see in chapter 4 the
extremely cautious way that the news pages handled questions about, for
example, the role of Donald Rumsfeld in crafting interrogation policies

that were used at Abu Ghraib.) Such insider political dialogue is lost on the general citizenry who, at best, attend only to prominent and repeated messages in news stories that echo through the media landscape on a daily basis. If they were attended to at all by those in power, such editorial views were dismissed by the administration's information managers as unpatriotic and negative attacks on thousands of good soldiers by the liberal media.

News Framing of Abu Ghraib

The news can either promote or inhibit the public's understanding of information and context surrounding news events, thereby helping or hindering an administration's efforts to mold public opinion. In rare cases, the news can even turn simple public exposure into a powerful instrument to hold the government accountable for mistakes and corruption of law or principle. Dominant news perspectives (media scholars call them news *frames*) can produce various results, sometimes arousing public attention by labeling events in ways that evoke moral disapproval, establishing empathy with people who have been harmed or victimized and attributing responsibility for events to particular people or policies that can be held accountable.[38]

In this chapter, we simplify the idea of a news frame and connect it to our larger question about press independence by focusing primarily on the news media's *definition* of events at Abu Ghraib. That is, how were the actions at the detention facility labeled by the press? We also assess whether there was a single dominant definition of Abu Ghraib or if there was robust debate about how to label those events (a phenomenon scholars call a *frame contest* or *counterframing*).

Entman suggests a useful way to measure how independently the news media frame events. Meaningful media independence, he argues, is signaled not merely when the media publish "scattered morsels" of critical information, but only when they present a coherent counterframe "that attains sufficient magnitude to gain wide understanding as a sensible alternative to the White House's interpretation."[39] According to this standard, a productive frame contest exists in the news only when information *independent of* an administration is put on a par with information *obtained from* that administration, and when the media present a coherent counterperspective, not just bits and pieces of alternative perspectives. This is admittedly a high standard, though some studies suggest it is met in U.S. news coverage of social issues like abortion.[40] But if our ultimate concern is with public opinion and democratic accountability, anything less in the daily news stream may constitute a single-message environment that produces a compliant rather than an informed public, and emboldens government officials to pursue ill-considered policies in the absence of public accountability.

To assess the relative strength of various definitions in mainstream press coverage of Abu Ghraib, we tracked four labels that were most prevalent in a preliminary analysis of a sample of national news we examined during the spring and summer of 2004: *mistreatment, abuse, torture,* and *scandal* (together, these labels comprised over 95% of the labels applied to the events at Abu Ghraib in our content analysis of the *Washington Post* coverage). *Scandal* in and of itself connotes little of substance about the actions in question except that they have become controversial. (The term *abuse scandal* became a prominent way of defining Abu Ghraib, but the key term in that combined label was *abuse,* for Abu Ghraib was almost never labeled in the U.S. media as a *torture scandal.*) *Torture* has a stronger connection in both common usage and legal terminology to *intentional* behavior, particularly interrogation policies and practices, than do the terms *mistreatment* and *abuse.*[41] The label *torture* also more readily suggests an alternative account of causality highlighting policy initiatives up the chain of command to the secretary of defense and possibly even the president, who, as described above, reviewed legal briefings advising that domestic and international laws against torture might not apply to unconventional combatants. In other words, to speak of *torture* leads more readily to questions about who ordered or condoned it—that is, to questions of *policy.* The predominant labels assigned to events at Abu Ghraib thus offered broad cues to policy makers and publics about the meaning of those events and how to react to them. Because of the independent evidence detailed earlier, and the unequivocal official denials, torture was the definition that most directly challenged the Bush administration's claims. Taken together, the trends in how and how often these four terms appeared in the news tell us a great deal about the ability or inability of the press to challenge the government when the spin machine is set on high.

We began our analysis with 294 news articles and editorials that focused on the events at Abu Ghraib and were published between January 1 and August 31, 2004, in the *Washington Post*. The *Post* was a lead news organization on the story, as it steadily published from its large cache of photos and assigned considerable reporting resources to the story after CBS aired its initial piece on April 28. The time frame of our analysis begins just before the brief and sketchy reports on the initial Pentagon investigation of Abu Ghraib appeared in the press in mid-January, and ends with the final military investigations and congressional hearings that put the story to an uneasy rest before the 2004 presidential campaign entered its last stage. We added to this study an analysis of the full text of Abu Ghraib pieces aired on the *CBS Evening News* for the same time period. (See appendix B for further methodological details.)

We assessed the prevalence and prominence of the various labels these news outlets used for events at Abu Ghraib by recording the label that appeared first in each story (what we call the "primary label"). We also noted whether that label appeared in the headline or lead paragraphs of the story or appeared later ("primary label placement"), and also noted whether it was a journalist or another kind of news source who applied that label to Abu Ghraib (such as military commanders or members of the Bush administration). To construct a more generous test of media definitions, we recorded which labels (if any) appeared second in each story, and combined these with the primary label data into a single "prominent label" variable.

We also looked beyond the *Washington Post* and CBS by examining a sample of national newspapers, and extended the time period to include the late 2004–early 2005 Senate confirmation hearings for Alberto Gonzales, who had drafted one of the White House policy memos justifying relaxed conventions against torture in the War on Terror. This study involved searching the Nexis news database to ascertain the frequency of the same four labels in a total of 895 news articles and editorials about Abu Ghraib published in ten newspapers from around the country (the *Atlanta Journal Constitution, Boston Globe, Chicago Sun-Times, Los Angeles Times, New York Times, Cleveland Plain Dealer, San Francisco Chronicle, Seattle Times, St. Petersburg Times,* and *USA Today*) between April 2004 and mid-January 2005. For ease of analysis and presentation, and because we

Table 3.1: Primary story labels used to describe Abu Ghraib, by type, *Washington Post*, Apr. 1–Aug. 31, 2004

	Abuse	Torture	Mistreatment	Scandal
News (N = 242)	81% (188)	3% (9)	3% (7)	12% (29)
Editorials (N = 52)	61% (32)	17% (9)	3% (2)	13% (7)

*These data are based on the *first* label used in each article. Numbers in parentheses are the counts for each cell; percentages are not rounded.

discovered that *scandal* so often appeared in conjunction with *abuse* (a standard label for the Abu Ghraib story became *abuse scandal*), *scandal* was dropped from this stage of the analysis.

Defining Abu Ghraib—The Pattern and Volume of Press Perspectives

In the pages of the *Washington Post*, even at the height of the Abu Ghraib story, the most prominent categorization by far was *abuse*, with *torture* barely appearing in the news coverage, and only slightly more often in editorials. Table 3.1 shows the primary-label frequencies in both. The frame imbalance in the news was overwhelming, with just 3% (9) of the stories offering torture as the primary definition of the photos, compared with 81% (188) emphasizing abuse. Adding *mistreatment* and *scandal* accounted for the balance of the primary story lines, meaning that our four terms comprised 99% of the primary framing categories. The editorials were a bit more likely to introduce *torture*, but only 17% led with that term, while 61% led with *abuse*.

Recall that we constructed both tougher and more relaxed standards to assess the strength of different definitions, with the toughest standard based on whether the label appeared in the headline or lead paragraph. By this measure, only 2 of 242 news articles in the *Post* offered *torture* as the strongest cue for reader interpretation. And even in these two articles, close reading of the text reveals that *torture* was literally and figuratively distanced from Abu Ghraib. For example, the opening paragraph of the *Post*'s May 11 article, headlined "The Psychology of Torture," reads: "The U.S. troops who *abused* Iraqis at the Abu Ghraib prison near Baghdad were most likely not pathological sadists but ordinary people who felt they were doing the dirty work needed to win the war, experts in the history and psychology of *torture* say" (emphases added). In other words, even in the rare news piece that mentioned *torture* in the headline or lead, the term was evoked in the abstract, while *abuse* was used to describe events at Abu Ghraib.

Our more forgiving measure of news definitions counted both the first and second label mentioned in each article, regardless of where in the article they appeared, and treated the two as equal (even if one appeared in the headline and the other was buried deep in the story). By this standard, *torture* was still a remote challenger to the *abuse* label. Fully 91% of news articles and 82% of editorials in the *Washington Post* used *abuse* as the first or second label to describe events at Abu Ghraib, compared with 11% and 30%, respectively, that used the term *torture* (see appendix C, table 1). The *Post's* preference for the term *abuse* was most pronounced on the news pages, where it was used ten times more often than *torture*. On the editorial pages, *abuse* was used three times as often as *torture*. A similar pattern prevailed on CBS, where *abuse* was the first or second label in 50 out of 54 stories (92%), compared with 10 (18%) that used *torture* in either the first or second position.

Reading these stories in their entirety also reveals a careful segregation of *torture* and *abuse* that is evident throughout the coverage. For example, the *Post's* thousand-word story about the Gonzales memo on the "quaint" provisions of the Geneva Conventions contextualized quotations from that document with White House claims that the memo did not apply to Abu Ghraib; yet, without noting the apparent contradiction, went on to report that Secretary of State Colin Powell had tried to persuade President Bush not to implement the recommendation. Nonetheless, the word *torture* was used only once in this *Post* story, in an ironic reference to the disclosure that the Gonzales memo caused the Bush administration to postpone a State Department report on the U.S. commitment to international human rights, including fighting the practice of torture.

Linking our source variable with our primary-label data shows that journalists were more reluctant to use the term *torture* independently. Ninety-five percent of the instances of *abuse* in the *Washington Post's* news pages (that is, 179 appearances of that term) were in reporters' own words, contrasted with only 55% of the instances of *torture* (which, given the small number of stories that called the events at Abu Ghraib torture, amounted to only 5). (See appendix C, table 2.) This suggests that once a political pattern emerges on a story within the governing institutions covered by the mainstream news, the story takes on a life of its own, and journalists simply "know" the right defining terms for introducing it. While *abuse* quickly became the freestanding story frame, journalists continued to be more careful about using *torture*, a term more likely to be attributed to an outside source, particularly on the news pages. As the data in table 3.1 show, editorialists spoke a bit more freely of torture than their counterparts on the news pages. Again, in contrast with an independent press that is appropriately skeptical in using terms fed them by official information managers and press handlers, and that reports equally terms gathered from sources independent of government, the semi-independent press in this instance relied most heavily on an officially sanctioned term that quickly became "common sense."

Our sample of newspapers from around the country followed the same general patterns. Out of a total of 895 news articles and editorials about Abu Ghraib, nearly all (97%) of the stories in the sample mentioned one of our three main labels. Fully 60%, however, did not mention the term *torture* at all, and 35% (primarily editorials) used it only in conjunction with one of the other labels. Only 1%—that is, nine articles—in the sample used *torture* standing alone as a primary label in news coverage. The data reveal some variation across the newspapers, but there was far greater variation in volume of coverage than in framing. For example, the *New York Times* published 210 stories about Abu Ghraib during the time period studied, and the *Cleveland Plain Dealer* published only 10. The *Times* also showed the highest proportion of alternative labels, but even so, *torture* stood alone in only five items (2% of its articles), four of which were editorials, while 62% of *Times* news articles and editorials made no reference to torture at all, putting it close to the national averages on both counts. (See appendix C, table 3.)

The Timing of Perspectives: When Did Torture *Appear
and Disappear in the News?*

Analyzing the frequency of the various perspectives given by the press over time allows us to assess the factors that can initiate and sustain independent press perspectives. The results show that not only was torture a rarely offered perspective, it was not even a consistent background element in the ongoing news coverage. In fact, the limited debate about what to call Abu Ghraib wrapped up pretty quickly after it began. *Torture* appeared most prominently in the two weeks after the story broke, and then faded quickly as the initial reportage about the photos became contained or displaced by managed government activities, including a series of military investigations, public appearances by the president and prominent members of the Bush administration and military leadership, and congressional hearings. In the *Washington Post*, 15 out of 28 (54%) appearances of *torture* as either a first or second label occurred during the first two weeks after the photos were revealed, then dropped to 1 the following week, and never exceeded 3 in any week throughout the remainder of the summer. Similarly, on CBS, 8 of the 10 uses of *torture* as either a first or second label appeared between April 29 and May 12. Thereafter, through the end of summer, *torture* was used only twice on the *CBS Evening News* to describe events at Abu Ghraib.

Thus, only in the early weeks did reporters openly, though cautiously, counterframe the story. For example, CBS anchor Dan Rather claimed in the lead-in to a May 3 story that "evidence of mistreatment, even torture of Iraqi prisoners has inflamed many in the Muslim world," and reporter Bill Plante, in the lead-in to a story broadcast May 5, reported that "around the world newspapers and magazines have seized on the torture to pour scorn on American promises of democracy for Iraq." Consistent with other instances of event-driven news, this journalistic license occurred early in the story, before official news management was fully established.

During this early period, but to a very limited degree, *torture* also entered the news through alternative source channels such as former detainees, other foreigners, and human rights organizations such as the ICRC. But once the language of abuse had settled in, it appears, nothing could dislodge it. Any signs of a cascade of alternative definitions of Abu Ghraib suddenly stopped. The resulting stories awkwardly reported evidence that was hard to subsume under the abuse perspective, but journalists lacked a sanctioned vocabulary to illuminate it more fully. For example, the *Post's* own investigative reporting had strongly suggested that the incidents at Abu Ghraib could be linked to a much larger systematic problem, but those reports generally refrained from naming that problem. In a front-page, 3005-word article published May 11 and headlined "Secret World of U.S. Interrogation" reporters Dana Priest and Joe Stephens wrote, "The Abu Ghraib prison in Iraq, where a unit of U.S. soldiers abused prisoners, is just the largest and suddenly most notorious in a worldwide constellation of detention centers—many of them secret and all off-limits to public scrutiny—that the U.S. military and CIA have operated in the name of counterterrorism or counterinsurgency operations since the Sept. 11, 2001, attacks." They reported that according to one military officer who worked closely with CIA interrogators in Afghanistan, "Prisoner abuse is nothing new," and a dozen former and current national security officials, "including several who had witnessed interrogations, defended the use of stressful interrogation tactics and the use of violence against detainees as just and necessary."[42] But what occurred at Abu Ghraib or these other facilities, and the policy decisions these events might signify, was not called torture.

This became a common pattern. Even in the best investigative reports that linked injuries, indignities, and deaths at Abu Ghraib and other U.S.-run prisons in Iraq, Afghanistan, and Guantanamo, *torture* was rarely evoked. A pointed example of leading news organizations' continuing reluctance to apply the term *torture* can be found in the *New York Times'* front-page story of May 20, 2005, which outlined in disturbing detail the violent deaths of two Afghans in U.S. custody at the Bagram detention facility in 2002—shortly after, the article notes, "President Bush's final determination . . . that the [Geneva] Conventions did not apply to the conflict with Al Quaeda and that Taliban fighters would not be accorded the rights of prisoners of war." Yet the article's descriptions of interrogators' acts that surely contributed to the detainees' deaths were carefully circumscribed: "Like a narrative counterpart to the digital images from Abu Ghraib, the Bagram file depicts young, poorly trained soldiers in repeated incidents of *abuse*" (emphasis added), which, the article notes, "went well beyond the two deaths." The only time the word *torture* appeared in the 6,143-word article was in briefly noting that one of the interrogators was known by his colleagues as "The King of Torture."[43]

As the Abu Ghraib story lingered through the summer of 2004, *torture* largely disappeared, except for a brief reemergence—in conjunction with other labels—in August, accompanying the release of the official Fay and Schlesinger investigation reports. These reports occasioned two hard-hitting masthead editorials in the *Post*, one arguing that they "have dragged the Bush administration and Pentagon brass a couple of steps closer to facing the truth about how and why U.S. soldiers and interrogators committed scores of acts of torture and abuse in Iraq and Afghanistan."[44] Notably, even as the editorial pages, which speak largely to other political elites, held forth on torture, the term had been all but purged from the news articles that cue general public opinion.

These findings are displayed graphically in figure 3.2, which shows the results of three distinct searches aimed at capturing the possible dominant story lines about Abu Ghraib in our sample of ten newspapers from around the country. The top line ("no torture") shows all articles (news, opinion pieces, and editorials combined) that mentioned either *mistreatment* or *abuse* but did not mention *torture*. The second line ("other + torture") shows all items that mentioned *torture* but also used the terms *abuse* or *mistreatment*. The bottom line ("torture only") represents all items in which only the label *torture* and none of our other main labels appeared. (For ease of analysis and presentation, and because we discovered that *scandal* so often appeared in conjunction with *abuse*, *scandal* was dropped from this stage of the analysis.)

The "torture only" line shows how rarely the *torture* label stood alone. Even at the height of coverage in early May, the number of items *solely* using the term *torture* was small, and almost all appeared on the editorial pages, not in the news itself. If editorials are excluded from the graph, the "torture only" line literally disappears except for a tiny blip in May, right after the story broke. The predominance of the "other + torture" trend line over the "torture only" line shows that when *torture* did appear, it generally was paired with—and softened by—other labels. If our close analysis of the *Washington Post* and CBS is any guide, stories that mixed *torture* with other labels generally placed *torture* deep within the story—not in the headline or lead, and not as the first descriptive term in the story—and segregated that term from specific discussion of what happened at Abu Ghraib. Overall, our data show, the bulk of stories about Abu Ghraib did not discuss torture at all.

Figure 3.2 also shows that *torture* reentered the national news in December 2004 and January 2005 in conjunction with the Gonzales confirmation hearings, almost always in reference to his infamous "torture memo," as official sources at the congressional hearings, and later reporters, labeled it when it first emerged in May. Yet, even as the memo appeared in coverage of Gonzales's confirmation hearing—prompting an end-of-year uptick in mentions of *torture* in the news, as shown in figure 3.2—the news seldom

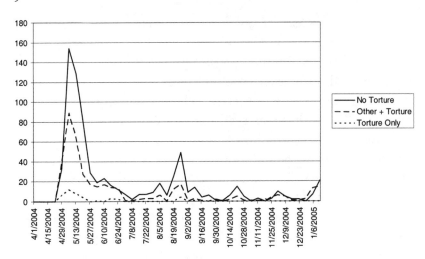

Figure 3.2: Mentions of *torture* and other labels in connection with Abu Ghraib in news and editorial items, national newspaper sample, Apr. 1, 2004–Jan. 19, 2005.

linked the memo or the practice of torture directly to Abu Ghraib. Indeed, an additional Nexis search shows that the *Post* mentioned *Gonzales* and *torture* together in 37 news articles, editorials, or op-eds appearing between mid-December 2004 and January 2005—far more than it prominently used that term in nearly 300 pieces about Abu Ghraib between April and September of 2004. Yet only nine of those items mentioned Abu Ghraib, and only two of those were news stories (each mentioned Abu Ghraib only once, deep within each story). Thus, in much of the coverage, any connection between Gonzales's memo and the scenes depicted in the photos remained unclear.

It is worth reiterating at this point our central working assumption: not that *torture* was the "correct" label for events at Abu Ghraib, but that, particularly given the documentary evidence that continued to emerge throughout the spring and summer after the story broke, the language of *torture* would have presented another side to the story. Having a second side to the story would have been not only conducive to public debate about high-level policies in the War on Terror, but an indicator of substantial press independence as well. Instead, we have found that within two weeks, the photos had been defined decisively, following the Bush administration's lead, as "abuse."

Explaining the Limits on Press Independence

The question of why, given the provocative photographs and the store of documentary evidence, the nation's leading news organizations, along with the daily news mainstream, failed to offer a coherent counterperspective for Abu Ghraib is all the more interesting in light of the fact that editors of two of the top organizations covering the story did not view their framing choices as particularly difficult or even conscious ones. The *New York Times'* public editor Daniel Okrent asked that paper's editors why they settled on *abuse*—a label that Okrent described as "comparatively delicate" given the evidence at hand—rather than *torture*. He reported that the editors "were surprised when I raised the issue." Both denied that the *Times* had a policy one way or another, but acknowledged that "readers may be right" that *torture* was a more appropriate label. One responded simply, "Now that you tell me people are reading things into our not using 'torture' in headlines, I'll pay closer attention."[45] *Washington Post* editor Leonard Downie Jr. held an online chat with readers, and his response to a similar question suggested that his choice was more deliberate: "Abuse is obvious from the information and images we have, and is serious in its own right. Torture is a more loaded term and its use requires more information about whether the abuse constitutes torture."[46]

Downie's formula at first take seems reasonable as a commonsense journalistic guideline. Yet he does not specify just how much or what kind of information he would require, or from which sources, to tip—or in this case, create—the balance in news perspectives. The results in his own newspaper suggest that nothing short of official sanctioning of the *torture* label would do, as in fact happened more than a year later when Republican senators, backed by a chorus of military brass, condemned the Bush administration's torture policies and joined with Senator McCain to restrict them. Downie's rationale is also troubling in that it seems to clash with another commonsense journalistic perspective: the ideal that news organizations generally try to present at least two sides of a story. Support for another side of the Abu Ghraib story was available. By the time Downie made this statement on May 21, much of the documentation reviewed above had already emerged about high-level policy discussions on coercive interrogation procedures, and about implementation of such procedures at Abu Ghraib and other U.S. detention facilities—evidence the *Post* had drawn upon in its own reporting. But the data presented here show that the *Post*'s framing became even more cautious after Downie articulated his reasoning, even as the evidence of a torture problem continued to mount.

If the potent combination of photos, documents, and political context, including the administration's past pattern of successfully spinning the press, was not enough to sustain a critical media counterperspective, what would suffice? Our study suggests that only high-level official dissent would have made the difference, for that was the only critical factor missing from the news context, and that was the factor that did push torture into the news long after public attention to the searing photos from Abu Ghraib had faded. What Downie implies is that the news generally presents multiple sides in such a story when there are multiple official views to report. A more realistic version of this news standard is that when investigative reporting turns up independent evidence that disputes official views, as it sometimes does, those challenging perspectives cannot be sustained unless the voices of those in power take them up and keep them going through what *New York Times* Washington bureau chief Philip Taubman called the "flywheel" of ongoing government action.

These findings from Abu Ghraib, when added to the findings from previous research, suggest that news of provocative events, particularly in the foreign policy realm, is highly constrained by journalistic dependence on government sources and processes to advance perspectives and stories. Yet there is more going on here. Having the digital photos (like so many other contemporary technologies) in their possession enabled journalists to break news of gripping events ahead of authorities. Yet despite the initial independence offered by information technology, the story ended up being turned over quickly to government officials to provide the interpretive perspective. This emerged as a general trend in research by Bennett and Livingston, who examined eight years of international stories on CNN. They found that even though new technologies have allowed ever greater numbers of event-driven stories to appear, officials "seem to be as much a part of the news as ever."[47] Once officials engage with news events, the story frames generated by journalists are then generally "indexed" to the range of sources and viewpoints that reflect levels of official agreement and consensus.

These news dynamics also occur in domestic policy areas, but the presence of sustained conflict over social issues such as abortion may give journalists more license to broaden their sourcing and framing of stories that have taken on lives (and well-established narrative lines) of their own.[48] Journalists may track the circles of power more closely in sensitive national security and foreign policy issues, where stakes are high, debate more constrained, and news organizations more reluctant to probe far beyond the cues offered by inside sources.[49] There are, of course, some chinks in this routine relationship between the government and the press. In foreign policy, some observers point to the weakening of the cold war bipartisan consensus as a possible opening for more independent reporting.[50] Scott Althaus proposes that journalists may exercise greater "discretion in locating and airing oppositional voices," yet his empirical examinations conclude that today's mainstream press does not "produce many bold statements of fundamental criticism" of U.S. foreign policy.[51] Similarly, Entman's case studies of cascading news frames that support or oppose the White House's preferred perspectives reveal that, in practice, the mainstream press generally falls short of consistently offering robust counterframes, even when covering controversial events.[52]

Meanwhile, the "alternative" media may offer counterperspectives more consistently, but they are unlikely to sway mainstream news coverage or public opinion. True, individuals may have informed themselves about the larger story surrounding the Abu Ghraib photos by reading Seymour Hersh in the *New Yorker* or Mark Danner in the *New York Review of Books*. But these are publications with limited reach beyond the corridors of the intellectual elite. Our data challenge the notion that such relatively peripheral sources are likely to trigger a bottom-up cascade of competing views in the information regime absent some official sanctioning that would open mainstream news gates. Although Hersh's reporting may have shaped the inside-Washington conversation about Abu Ghraib, his strongest claim—that the United States had embarked on a new policy of torture in its war on terrorism—was not picked up prominently or consistently by the rest of the national media.[53]

These mainstream news dynamics may look different in an administration less adept at news management—or caught off guard. In fact, they did look different when a devastating hurricane caught this same administration on vacation, with both its news management and disaster relief capacities in disarray. In the case of Abu Ghraib, by contrast, the Bush administration saw its information management problem coming, thanks in part to the two-week reprieve granted by CBS. The White House communications staff in concert with other Republican-controlled executive and congressional offices prepared an information offensive replete with a series of institutional news flywheel mechanisms attached to its preferred version of events. Among the official actions that blocked a potential cascade of other sources and evidence in support of a challenging counterperspective were the following (with the dates they appeared in the *Washington Post*):

- On April 30, two days after the CBS photo story aired, an anonymous government official said the government "had taken several steps to stop the mistreatment of prisoners," while President Bush introduced the frame that he would consistently repeat: "The actions of a handful of soldiers . . . should not taint the tens of thousands who serve honorably in Iraq."
- The next day, on May 1, a televised statement by President Bush inserted in a Rose Garden photo-op with the Canadian prime minister referred to the "treatment" of prisoners but promised that "abuses" would be punished. (The *Post* echoed the term in its account, but also reported international shock, and introduced the term *torture*—from an article in *Tehran Times*.)
- On May 2, the Taguba report was released, which, although it used strong language to describe events at the prison, localized the "abuse" problem to, as the *Post* reported it, "the willful actions of a small group of soldiers" and "a failure of leadership" at the prison level.
- On May 5, Bush addressed the Arab world in two interviews on Arab television that characterized the "abuses" at Abu Ghraib as "abhorrent" acts that "represent the actions of a few people." (Secretary of State Powell attempted to smooth the way for the president that day by appearing at the United Nations to argue that Abu Ghraib had been the work of "a small number of troops who acted in an illegal, improper manner.")
- On May 7, Secretary Rumsfeld read a statement before a joint Senate-House Armed Services Committee hearing in which he took "full responsibility" for the events at Abu Ghraib and apologized "to those Iraqis who were mistreated by members of the U.S. armed forces." That same day, the House overwhelmingly passed a resolution that

deplored the "mistreatment" of Iraqi detainees and repeated the president's frame: "The alleged crimes of a handful of individuals should not detract from the commendable sacrifice" of U.S. soldiers in Iraq.

• On May 14, Rumsfeld made a surprise visit to Abu Ghraib and told reporters that the soldiers involved in the scandal would "be brought to justice." The next day, the Defense Department issued this punctuating statement: "No responsible official of the Department of Defense approved any program that could conceivably have been intended to result in such abuses."

This series of official activities with officials all repeating the same definition ensured that mainstream reporters would dutifully report the *mistreatment* and *abuse* labels, quickly establishing this as the predominant definition in news linked to Abu Ghraib. By May 19, while the Senate Armed Services Committee held hearings on the "abuses," the term *torture* had all but disappeared from the news. The official news narrative was all but complete within two weeks of the dramatic first airing of the photos.

The Bush administration's near monopoly of the story was due only in part to its news management campaign. We must also point to the lack of strong oppositional voices in the government, most logically but not necessarily those of Democrats. The absence of a strong challenge regarding how to define Abu Ghraib from either Congress or the Democratic presidential campaign made it harder for sources outside official circles to get into the news. The absence of official challenges also helped limit the exposure of the several high-quality investigative reports that emerged outside the daily news mainstream. Although some prominent Democrats used the congressional hearings to probe high-level culpability for the scandal, very few labeled events at Abu Ghraib as *torture*. In our *Washington Post* data, no prominent instances of the *torture* label were pegged to members of Congress, although a broader search found Senator Edward Kennedy cited deep in one story as saying, "Shamefully, we now learn that Saddam's torture chambers reopened under new management: U.S. management."[54] Though he would later call for Secretary Rumsfeld's resignation, Democratic presidential nominee John Kerry also repeated the president's framing virtually verbatim, saying, "We cannot let the actions of a few overshadow the tremendous good work that thousands of soldiers are doing every day in Iraq and all over the world."[55] When asked to react to Kennedy's statement, Kerry said, "He's my friend and I respect him, but I don't agree with the framing of that."[56] With President Bush affirming his faith in Rumsfeld early in the story, the avenues for sustaining a challenging story were closed, at least as played by the rules of the U.S. press system.

Alternative Explanations for Press Deference to Officials

There are, of course, alternative explanations for the media's reluctance to report prominent challenges to the Bush administration's definitions of Abu Ghraib. The relative absence of the word *torture* in the news about Abu Ghraib could stem, for example, from news organizations' caution about the possible legal implications of their language choices. As legal proceedings against individual soldiers loomed, these organizations would be careful, by this explanation, to use language that matched the legal charges that might be brought. This caution perhaps played some role in how the news presented stories about Abu Ghraib and the military trials that followed, and it may help to explain why, even in stories that mentioned *torture*, that term was often carefully segregated from direct descriptions of that detention facility. But as the documentary evidence mounted suggesting the administration's evolving policy on torture, legalistic caution seems an unsatisfying explanation for the press's reluctance to talk about torture even in broader thematic stories. As noted above, the *Post*'s editorial page on occasion carried unflinching torture allegations, as in one editorial that called for "the truth about how and why U.S. soldiers and interrogators committed scores of acts of torture and abuse in Iraq and Afghanistan."[57] Restraint in the news pages may have faded a bit, but only long after the heat of the initial Abu Ghraib story subsided. For example, one March 2006 *New York Times* piece reporting on the president's latest approval ratings opened with the bold sentence, "President Bush has survived rough scrapes before, bouncing back after the reports of torture by troops at Abu Ghraib."[58]

Another possibility is that the idea of U.S. forces engaging in torture represents a cultural incongruence that "short-circuits" open criticism because it is inconsistent with Americans' social identity.[59] Following this logic, the torture-policy frame would not be easy for Americans, including journalists, to entertain, because it does not fit our socially accepted image of ourselves as a nation. Nor would it fit easily within the "defensive" reporting style documented in studies of war coverage in which violence perpetrated by "our" troops is generally softened or obscured. "When one's own combatants are involved in killing civilians," one study finds, "journalists usually adopt techniques that lower the emotional impact of such stories."[60] This pattern extends to coverage of domestic policing as well, where the term *police brutality* is used only under particular and rather rare circumstances.[61]

But the cultural explanation is not fully satisfactory, because *torture* indeed *did* appear, if only briefly, as a candidate for a counterperspective at the outset of the story. The cultural filter, while no doubt at play here, was not so strong as to rule out any discussion of torture and torture policy altogether. Indeed, the term *torture* eventually became quite prominent in the news long after the height of the coverage of Abu Ghraib as Senator McCain and other leaders pressured the White House to support an amendment further limiting the cruel and inhuman treatment of war detainees. A search of the Nexis database shows that of 54 articles mentioning the McCain amendment in the *Washington Post* between October and December of 2005, *fully* 77% (42 articles) included the term *torture*—a dramatic contrast with the predominant pattern in coverage of Abu Ghraib.

These patterns suggest that, rather than meeting with a blanket cultural prohibition on discussing torture, the Abu Ghraib photos enabled an event-driven news pattern to briefly and tentatively challenge the news management capacities of officials, but the fragile event-driven news dynamic faded as the Bush administration aggressively took over the framing virtually unchallenged by other top-level officials. Within days of the release of the photos, the story began to fall into a familiar pattern of indexing as the counterframe of torture was pushed out of the news by a deluge of official events that promoted the terms *abuse* and *mistreatment* and discouraged the press from drawing connections between high-level policy makers and the events at Abu Ghraib.

Thus, we attribute the ultimate collapse of the torture policy frame in news about Abu Ghraib to the mainstream press's well-documented tendency to follow the lead of high institutional authorities and, correspondingly, to have trouble elevating available challenging perspectives when sources at institutional power points fail to corroborate them. The "torture policy" counterframe was pushed out of the news by a deluge of official events that promoted the "isolated abuse" frame, an effect reinforced by a lack of high-level public debate on torture such as occurred much later around Senator McCain's amendment. The curious result of these intertwined event-driven and official news management dynamics is a semi-independent press characterized by moments of relative independence within a more general pattern of compliance with government news management.[62]

The Semi-Independent Press Revisited

The conclusions drawn in this chapter about the limits of press independence should not be overstated. The nation's leading press *did* break the Abu Ghraib story, and CBS, the *Washington Post*, and the *New York Times*, among others, continued to probe the story of U.S. treatment of detainees long after public attention to Abu Ghraib had faded. As the data reported above show, Abu Ghraib became a significant news story to which considerable resources were devoted. The continued reporting by these leading news organizations over the next year and a half revealed links between the treatment of prisoners at Abu Ghraib and those at other U.S. military detention facilities in Afghanistan and Guantanamo Bay.[63] And several mainstream publications, such as *Newsweek* and the *New York Times Magazine*, published lengthy critical examinations of the larger practical and ethical questions involved in using torture in the War on Terror.[64] The shrewd reader will have noted that much of the information reported in this chapter was taken from mainstream media accounts.

What was lacking, we contend, was the kind of coherent and sustained challenge to the Bush administration's "isolated abuse" claim that would have created an information environment that might have enabled average citizens (who do not generally read newspaper accounts as closely as we have here) to assess alternative perspectives more clearly. Put simply, it mattered that the press converged on the "abuse" definition and used the term *torture* so gingerly, because those basic language choices structured public responses to the story. Even if public opinion still might have sided with the administration's accounts, and reached closure with the punishment of a few low-level offenders, simply holding up the possibility of torture and even torture policy to public view would have created a different climate of accountability in government. Indeed, this may be the most important reason for an independent press. Exposing the political elite operating in the comfortable isolation of Washington to the harsher images that typified how much of the rest of the world saw U.S. policies in Iraq might have emboldened critics in government to act sooner and differently than they did.

And so, for all the photos and the large body of available evidence suggesting a possible policy of torture laid bare, the appalling images from Abu Ghraib rather quickly became defined as a story of prisoner "abuse." To this ambiguous *abuse* label were attached lingering and ultimately unresolved questions, such as whether this abuse was set in motion by mixed signals from officials in the Pentagon—a news pattern discussed further in chapter 4.

The theoretical implication of the data presented here is that events like the release of the Abu Ghraib photos do offer opportunities for critical press coverage of stories that otherwise might never see the light of day, and create opportunities for the press to act independently of government to raise difficult issues. But the early, limited appearance of the torture frame followed by its quick demise suggests that event-driven news reporting, particularly in matters of high foreign policy consequence, is seriously constrained by mainstream news organizations' deference to political power. Lacking any consistent counterperspective from high-level officials, the national media declined to challenge fundamentally the Bush administration's claims. Indeed, Leonard Downie's dictum about lacking enough information to play up the torture angle in the *Post*'s coverage might be translated as the operating code of the mainstream institutional press: *who* (in the political hierarchy of sources) offered *what* (officially acknowledged) evidence of torture is the essential question. The photos may have driven the story, but the White House communication staff ultimately wrote the captions.

4

The News Reality Filter
Why It Matters When the Press Fails

> What can be heard around the world, in the wake of the invasion of Iraq, the prisoner abuse scandal at Abu Ghraib, and the controversy over the handling of detainees at Bagram [a U.S. airbase in Afghanistan] and Guantánamo Bay, is that America is less a beacon of hope than a dangerous force to be countered. This assertion, repeated in newspaper columns, on radio and television broadcasts, and via the Internet, diminishes our ability to champion freedom, democracy, and individual dignity— ideas that continue to fuel hope for oppressed peoples everywhere.
>
> U.S. DEPARTMENT OF STATE, SEPTEMBER 2005[1]

This lament appeared in a report titled "Cultural Diplomacy: The Linchpin of Public Diplomacy," written by the U.S. State Department's Advisory Committee on Public Diplomacy. Though the ACPD argued that world attitudes toward U.S. ideals and artistic culture were positive, its "discussions [with sources abroad] confirmed the message conveyed by recent polling—America's image and reputation abroad could hardly be worse. There is deep and abiding anger toward U.S. policies and actions."[1]

Consequently, many commentators and even some Bush Administration officials believed by mid-2004 that the United States might have "lost the moral high ground" abroad, endangering the nation's broader foreign policy goals. Speaking on CNN in May of 2004, Deputy Secretary of State Richard L. Armitage said that the Abu Ghraib backlash was even greater in Europe than among Arab nations. "For many of our European friends, what they saw on those horrible pictures is tantamount to torture, and there are very strong views about that. . . . In the Arab world, there is general dismay and disgust, but in some places we were not real popular to start with. So I think I'm actually seeing a European reaction quite strong—quite a bit stronger." In the Middle East, meanwhile, the images from Abu Ghraib were a boon for terrorists. According to Moises Naim, editor of the journal *Foreign Policy*, "If you want recruitment tools, these are the best anyone could imagine. They are a big blow and a stimulant to spur people to act against the United States. The real kicker for terrorism is indignity and humiliation, and that's what these pictures are about."[2]

Arguably, therefore, U.S. foreign and military policies and misdeeds in the aftermath of 9/11 have increased international tensions and even decreased national security. When high-level policies drive a wedge between the United States and other countries, can the press help the American public to understand what is at stake and hold leaders accountable? Our analysis in this chapter suggests that at precisely the time when the wedge was being driven, the public may not have gleaned from its press how other nations and cultures viewed our actions.

In chapter 3, we found that most discussion of torture in the U.S. news largely closed down within two weeks after the Abu Ghraib story broke. These news-framing choices were not random, but reflect implicit rules of the Washington press game. Absent a critical mass of high-level officials willing to sound the alarm about torture policy, the nation's elite press seemed unwilling or unable to sound the alarm itself—at least not clearly, consistently, or loudly. A crucial consequence of the narrowed range of debate about Abu Ghraib was, arguably, to shape the American public's moral judgment of that story in ways that inadvertently advanced the Bush administration's effort to mold public reaction. Segregating descriptions of Abu Ghraib from the word *torture* may have severed the public's moral disapproval of the abstract idea of sanctioning torture[3] from the chain of specific events at Abu Ghraib and elsewhere that raised reasonable questions about whether torture had already become U.S. policy. And while public support for the war declined after the Abu Ghraib story broke, it rallied again late in the summer, even as news of the Fay and Schlesinger reports might have offered an officially sanctioned jumping-off point for the press to follow an evidence trail toward high-level policy decisions.

This chapter explores other important political consequences of the prevailing news coverage patterns regarding Abu Ghraib and the Iraq war. One powerful result of the press's filtering of reality according to the Washington power balance was that the American public was less able to see U.S. foreign policy as others around the world saw it. Abu Ghraib was truly an international scandal in that its lurid images were publicized readily and widely in Europe and the Middle East, its symbolism seemingly self-evident in many foreign eyes. The American news media's reluctance to call Abu Ghraib torture or to prominently and persistently pursue the policy story behind it arguably deepened the cultural gap between foreign and American observers. That gap extended to coverage of the war in general, as we explore below. We also show how U.S. news coverage obscured the full story of how the detainees at Abu Ghraib and other U.S. military detention facilities came to be imprisoned. That gap in the story left the American public largely uninformed about policies that had created dismal conditions in those facilities and sanctioned the detention of large numbers of people with dubious links to terrorism or insurgency, factors that had caused considerable discontent among Iraqis and other foreign observers.

This filtering of facts in ways that walled off world reaction further supported a Washington power alignment that avoided serious official inquiries into higher-level culpability. With little high-level institutional response to the story, the news simply covered the legal proceedings for crimes that sent lower-level soldiers to jail.[4] Along these lines, we explore how the press handled questions about Secretary of Defense Donald Rumsfeld, who became a lightning rod for discontent about Abu Ghraib in particular and U.S. foreign policy in general. We find that despite significant evidence of his role, Rumsfeld's responsibility for policies that helped create the Abu Ghraib scandal remained obscured in the news, although the occasional pointed article seemed to beg for follow-up. Whether as cause or consequence of this limited analysis by the press, political momentum for holding him accountable dissipated until the voters spoke in 2006.

These various dimensions of the Abu Ghraib story are interconnected through the story-reporting choices made and shared widely among mainstream news organizations. On the question of responsibility, for example, framing the story in terms of "torture" might have more readily suggested intentionality, *and directed attention beyond the torturers to the policies of their superiors.* It was logically more difficult to move from the *abuse* label to the question of higher responsibility for those events. On the question of who the detainees were, the dominant news narrative took the meaning of *prisoner* for granted, obscuring how these people came to be imprisoned at Abu Ghraib or what the military hoped to gain from confining and interrogating them. On the question of world opinion about U.S. policies, foreign news sources did not uniformly label Abu

Ghraib as *torture*, but, as we show below, coverage in other countries was more likely to apply that label. Indeed, the press climate in most other nations, particularly those less politically and culturally aligned with U.S. policies in the War on Terror, reflected a widening gulf between U.S. and foreign opinion about the war and about the United States' role in the world. While the Realpolitik approach may be for powerful nations to ignore what others think of them, the eventual gap between foreign policies and their misperceived consequences is an oft-told story in the decline of empires. If the leaders won't tell the people of these dissonant realities, who will?

Ultimately, press coverage proved to be a weak mechanism for holding leaders accountable for policies that, in the view of many credible sources, circumvented U.S. and international law and sowed significant discord in Europe and in the Arab and Muslim worlds. On any of these levels, whether telling the story of the detainees, conveying world reaction to U.S. policies, or looking into the possibility of higher levels of culpability, the press demonstrated that it cannot play its watchdog role assertively without first being unleashed by debate or disarray among its most powerful sources.

The Victims of Abu Ghraib

While some detainees at Abu Ghraib were almost certainly members or supporters of the Iraqi insurgency, or people who had some knowledge about attacks against U.S. forces in Iraq, most were petty criminals and even innocent civilians with no connections to terrorism or the insurgency. According to the military's own reports, released during the heat of the scandal, most of these prisoners were subsequently released with no charges filed against them.[5] Most were taken prisoner in "cordon and capture" operations conducted by U.S. troops, who would have had little solid basis for determining individuals' connections to terrorist activities.[6] The Schlesinger report, one of the military's own investigations, concluded that

> as the pace of operations picked up in late November–early December 2003, it became a common practice for maneuver elements to round up large quantities of Iraqi personnel [i.e., civilians] in the general

vicinity of a specified target as a cordon and capture technique. Some
operations were conducted at night. . . .

Large quantities of detainees with little or no intelligence value
swelled Abu Ghraib's population and led to a variety of overcrowd-
ing difficulties. . . . Complicated and unresponsive release procedures
ensured that these detainees stayed at Abu Ghraib—even though most
had no [intelligence] value.

The report found that U.S. forces had often "reverted to rounding up
any and all suspicious-looking persons—all too often including women
and children. The flood of incoming detainees contrasted sharply with
the trickle of released individuals."[7] Quoting from a report written by
the U.S. Army's Inspector General, author Thomas Ricks describes army
operations in the late summer of 2003: "Senior U.S. commanders tried
to counter the insurgency with indiscriminate cordon-and-sweep operations that involved detaining thousands of Iraqis. This involved 'grabbing
whole villages, because combat soldiers (were) unable to figure out who
was of value and who was not.'"[8] Detention practices even went beyond
randomly sweeping up the innocent to more-targeted captures. According to one confidential military report leaked to the media later in 2004,
"It is a practice in some U.S. units to detain family members of anti-
coalition suspects in an effort to induce the suspects to turn themselves
in, in exchange for the release of their family members"—a practice that
according to the report's author "has a 'hostage' feel to it."[9]

The American public's support for using physical coercion against
foreign detainees is contingent on the circumstances. Support is greatest
when those detainees are portrayed as "ticking time bombs" hiding information that could save lives, but declines significantly when that contin-
gency is removed.[10] The news media's description of the detainees and the
circumstances of their incarceration could therefore have either aroused
or suppressed Americans' negative moral judgments concerning U.S. detention policies. Robert Entman provides a corollary example in U.S. news
coverage of the Soviet downing of Korean Air flight 007. The press framed
the 269 victims in an empathetic light and categorized the 1983 event as
intentional mass murder. This framing, he surmises, made "the [public's]
journey along the pathway to emotional, negative moral judgments . . .
instantaneous."[11] Similarly, if the news media described the Abu Ghraib

detainees as terrorists or terrorist-related suspects and/or as people who could yield vital information about the Iraqi insurgency, a negative moral judgment about Abu Ghraib would be less likely than if the detainees were described as people who had simply been caught up in U.S. military raids and whose connections to terrorism and intelligence value were, at best, unclear.

To assess how the public was cued to think about the detainees, we analyzed the full text of all *Washington Post* and *CBS Evening News* stories about Abu Ghraib that appeared between April and August of 2004—the same stories analyzed in chapter 3 (see appendix B.2 for methodological details). We wanted to know whether the news portrayed these people as linked to terrorism or, alternatively, simply as people, with families, jobs, and other humanizing characteristics. Accordingly, we examined each story for any specific words, other than *prisoners, detainees,* or cognate terms, that were used to describe them, such as *insurgents, terrorism suspects,* or terms that indicated their occupations, family relationships, or other identifying details.[12] We also looked for information about how the detainees ended up in Abu Ghraib prison (captured during attacks on U.S. forces; swept up in "cordon and capture" missions; already in prison under Saddam Hussein; etc.), and/or any claims about the detainees' intelligence value—they had no intelligence value, information extracted from them saved American lives, or any claim in between.

Our findings suggest that the news provided a highly obscured picture of the detainees and the circumstances of their imprisonment. Ironically, given the photographs, the victims remained in a sense invisible. The news rarely described the detainees as anything other than simply "prisoners," and provided little detail that would personalize them beyond a few isolated, horrific stories of what they underwent inside Abu Ghraib.

Interestingly, the detainees were rarely explicitly described as terrorists, insurgents, or somehow connected to the insurgency, although some stories, drawing from Bush administration and military officials, strongly implied that they were terror suspects and/or had high intelligence value.[13] The strongest example of this kind of framing came from Major General Geoffrey Miller (a key figure in bringing coercive interrogation tactics to Abu Ghraib, as we shall see below), who told reporters at a May 13 news conference with Donald Rumsfeld outside Abu Ghraib, "We want to keep the dangerous terrorists and murderers and things here."[14] Yet only 2% of

Washington Post articles described the detainees as insurgents or as security detainees, and 1% as terrorists; on CBS, less than 1% of stories used
these kinds of terms.

But if such negative labels were rare, humanizing information describing the detainees as mothers or fathers or sons, or mentions of female
or juvenile prisoners, was even more scant, appearing in just 1% of *Post*
articles and less than 1% of stories on CBS.[15] Only once on CBS (less
than 1%) and five times in the *Post* (1%) were the detainees described by
themselves or another source as "innocent," though explanations of how
innocent people had come to Abu Ghraib were even more rare.

Indeed, scant information was provided about how anyone, guilty or innocent, came to be held at Abu Ghraib. On CBS, only one story contained
such details: a brief mention that some detainees "were seized by soldiers
searching for Saddam loyalists." The general absence of this information
is remarkable given that reporters were not unaware of this dimension
of the Abu Ghraib story; of the twenty-one *Post* stories mentioning this
aspect, several included extensive descriptions of the circumstances of
detentions, including "aggressive roundups" and "indefinite captivity";
"delays in evaluating evidence" against those captured; and "arrests without clear evidence of wrongdoing." Several *Post* stories also mentioned
a report by the International Committee of the Red Cross claiming that
70% to 90% of the detainees had been arrested mistakenly (a figure the
Schlesinger report would soon confirm).[16]

But passages like these were lost in the sea of Abu Ghraib coverage, and
were offset by U.S. officials' claims that the detainees were far from innocent. Said one military official, "They are deemed to be a security threat by
a judge through multiple sources. It's that simple. If they were innocent,
they wouldn't be at Abu Ghraib." "You know, they're not there for traffic
violations," said another. In the cells where the harshest mistreatment
by U.S. forces took place, he said, "they're murderers, they're terrorists,
they're insurgents."[17] Most stories did not contain any information about
the detainees' value as sources of intelligence about Saddam Hussein or
the Iraqi insurgency. Of that fraction of news that did relate to this subject,
the reporting was slanted toward the suggestion by U.S. military sources
that these were terrorist-related detainees with high intelligence value;
such claims outweighed the contradictory ones that the detainees had little intelligence value by 3 to 1 in the *Post* and by more than 2 to 1 on CBS.

Thus, the overall picture of the Abu Ghraib detainees was murky, but weighted toward the negative depictions provided by U.S. officials. And though at least some reporters were aware of potential problems in the military's procedures for deciding whom to detain and for how long, this did not become a major theme of the reporting on Abu Ghraib. Though it may have been hard for Americans far from the scene to recognize, it seems that to many Iraqis, Abu Ghraib was not only a prison but also a crude intelligence-gathering site, with many hundreds of citizens being "processed"—that is, rounded up, questioned, held indefinitely, and for many if not all, ultimately released.[18] Even as these realities of the Abu Ghraib population became infamous rallying points in the Arab world, their obscurity to the American public only aided the Bush administration's efforts to contain an unpleasant political scandal.

It is interesting to consider the implications of this obscured picture of the detainees, for no matter how the question of their intelligence value was answered, it presented a serious potential challenge to the administration's framing of Abu Ghraib and the conduct of the war. If the prisoners abused at Abu Ghraib were not high-intelligence-value detainees, then not only the specific abuses captured in the widely publicized photographs but the overall operation might have seemed questionable: why were so many common citizens being held for months in captivity, with little legal recourse and little opportunity to prove their innocence? If the people mistreated at Abu Ghraib were high-value detainees, on the other hand, then it becomes easier to believe that the abuses photographed and broadcast around the world were part and parcel of the interrogation operation at the facility. That story line would directly imply that at least part of what had occurred there was indeed torture related to *interrogation*—a story line that the military and the administration adamantly denied. But the news gave the general public, who probably did not comb through it as closely as we have here, little opportunity to consider those questions.

The Gap between U.S. News and World Opinion

If mainstream news coverage left the American public less able to assess the policies and practices its government had authorized—including the "cordon and capture" of mostly innocent people and the use of physical coercion to extract information from detainees—that coverage also left Americans less able to assess the consequent impact on the United States' standing throughout the world. The press did not just shelter Americans from world opinion on Abu Ghraib. As shown below, from the beginning of the war, it filtered much of its stories' tone according to the political consensus in Washington, creating a considerable gap between U.S. news coverage and world news and opinion regarding the United States and the Iraq war. Abu Ghraib was thus easily assimilated into this established filtering process. Consider, by contrast, the findings from a study on the tone of coverage of the Bush administration across seven German television news programs. The tone dropped from somewhat positive before the war in late 2002, to very negative in May of 2004, right on the heels of the scandal.[19] One key to this difference is that, to many foreign eyes, Abu Ghraib looked more like torture and less like the isolated abuse the administration claimed it was. Our point, again, is not that this was necessarily the "correct" reading of the situation, but that such coverage brought questions to the forefront of foreign opinion that were more marginalized here at home. Americans were left less able to understand the intensity of foreign reaction to the scandal.

FOREIGN NEWS COVERAGE OF ABU GHRAIB.   Foreign news sources framed Abu Ghraib differently than the U.S. press did. A study by Timothy Jones compared U.S. coverage of the scandal with that of print media outlets from five different countries: the *Toronto Star* (Canada), the *Guardian* (England), *Der Spiegel* (Germany), *La Stampa* (Italy), and *El Pais* (Spain), from April 28, 2004, through April 28, 2005. Jones's data show that compared with the American press, all the news sources examined from other nations were more likely to use the term *torture*: "the Canadian press was 3 times more likely, the British press was 7 times more likely, the Italian press was 12 times more likely, the Spanish press was 14 times more likely, and the German press was nearly 15 times more likely." The study also found that in articles that used only one term for what happened at Abu Ghraib, "that term was 'torture' 21% of the time in the *Toronto Star*, 32% of the time in the *Guardian*, 64% of the time in *La Stampa*, 72% of the time in *Der Spiegel*, and 76% of the time in *El Pais*—compared to only 6% of the time in the *Washington Post*."[20]

Our own search of English-language foreign newspapers, including the *Toronto Star* and the *Toronto Sun* (Ontario); the *Times* and the *Guardian* of London as well as a collection of other broadsheets from the United

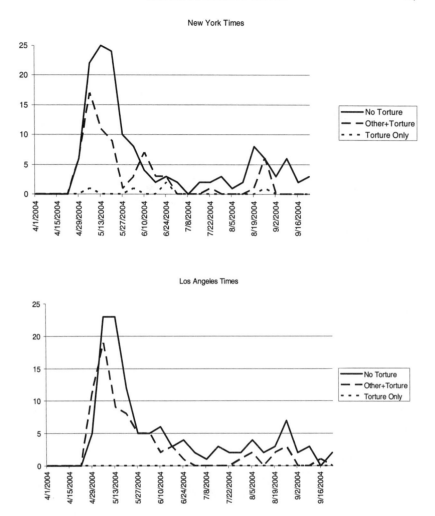

Figure 4.1: Mentions of *torture* and other labels in connection with Abu Ghraib in selected U.S. and international news outlets, news and editorial items, Apr. 1–Sept. 30, 2004.

Kingdom; and a collection of news story abstracts compiled by the BBC from news outlets throughout Europe, suggests a similar pattern.[21] Figure 4.1 offers a sense of the coverage we found in the United States versus other countries by focusing on four exemplary patterns.[22]

While the differences were not always stark, the percentage of stories that did not mention *torture* was on average higher in U.S. papers than in these foreign news sources. In eight out of ten U.S. papers, articles

UK Broadsheets

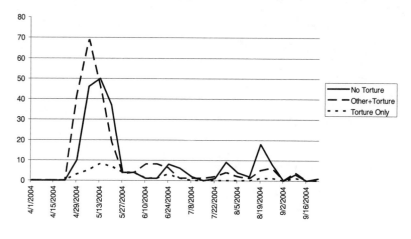

BBC International News Summaries

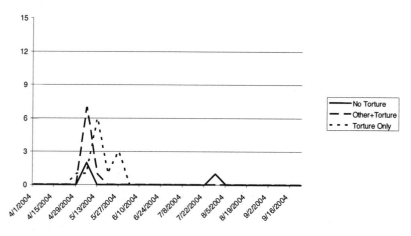

Figure 4.1: (*Continued*)

about Abu Ghraib that did not mention *torture* were more numerous than articles that used *torture* along with other labels, and much more numerous than articles that only mentioned *torture*. But in four out of six of the foreign news sources we analyzed, the reverse was true: more stories used *torture*, in combination with other labels—and even exclusively—to talk about Abu Ghraib.

Among the U.S. news organizations, the outlier was the *Los Angeles Times*; as shown in figure 4.1, the number of items at least mentioning *torture* was closer to the number that did not (though even in that news-paper, the number of items referring exclusively to *torture* was almost zero). The *New York Times*' coverage, in contrast, was close to average for our U.S. sources, with about twice as many items that did not make any mention of *torture* as those that did. The foreign news source closest to the typical U.S. pattern would be the conservative, Rupert Murdoch–owned *Times* of London (not shown in figure 4.1). But that paper was the outlier among the broad collection of foreign coverage represented in the UK broadsheets and the BBC International news review graphs. In fact, in the BBC stories, the "torture only" line actually dwarfs the "no torture" line (though the total number of stories overall is smaller than in most U.S. newspapers). In short, it appears that the foreign press generally used *torture* more freely than did its U.S. counterpart in talking about Abu Ghraib.

The discrepant realities presented in foreign and U.S. news existed from the beginning of the war, as illustrated in a study by Holli Semetko and Christian Kolmer. Their research measured the share of early war news devoted to positive statements about the U.S.-led "coalition of the willing." The study found that "during the first two weeks [of the war], the US maintained an average share of 25 percent of the news devoted to favourable statements about the Allies, which is three times more than appeared in Germany, five times more than in Britain, and over ten times more than appeared on Al-Jazeera."[23] U.S. news organizations were "more than ten times more likely than Al-Jazeera to evaluate the Allies positively, three times more likely than German television, and five times more likely than TV news in the UK."[24] Moreover, their data show that the reality gap between the U.S. and other national news media widened quickly between the first two weeks and the fourth week of the war. These data support independent journalist Michael Massing's assessment that "for the most part, US news organizations gave Americans the war they thought Americans wanted to see."[25]

THE AMERICAN PERCEPTION GAP.   As noted earlier, the reality gap in American coverage of Abu Ghraib was not an isolated incident, but re-flected the ongoing alignment of the U.S. press with the dominant Wash-ington line throughout the Iraq war. In light of the different tone of U.S. reporting, it is not surprising that many Americans not only perceived the war in favorable terms long after opinion in other nations had begun to turn, but also misperceived the state of world opinion. This palpable gap in perceptions was reflected in a study conducted by the Program on International Policy Attitudes at the University of Maryland, which, in a series of surveys, tracked American beliefs about U.S. foreign policy and the war in Iraq. In a report published in October of 2003 (well before the Abu Ghraib story broke), PIPA found that many Americans harbored several misperceptions about the war, including the notion that world opinion was supportive of the U.S.-led invasion of Iraq. (The other misperceptions measured in the survey were the beliefs that clear evidence had been found of a link between Saddam Hussein's Iraq and Al Qaeda, and that weapons of mass destruction had been found by U.S. forces in Iraq).

Because the survey linked the rate of misperceptions with the particular news outlets to which people were paying the most attention, it became widely known for showing how seemingly misinformed Fox TV viewers were, since 80% of those viewers held at least one misperception—the largest percentage across all media groups. But the more troubling finding of the survey was simply that so many Americans, almost regardless of which media they paid attention to, were misinformed. With the exception of regular viewers of Public Broadcasting and listeners of National Public Radio, majorities of *all* the other groups harbored at least one misperception about the war. Even between June and September of 2003, several months after the war began, 56% of the survey respondents believed either that a majority of people in the world favored the United States' having gone to war with Iraq, or that views around the world were "evenly balanced"; 47% shared those misperceptions about European opinion in particular. Moreover, the study observed, "Overall, those who paid higher levels of attention to the news were *not* more likely to know that world public opinion opposed the war against Iraq."[26]

This pattern of misperception was not the finding of a single survey, incidentally. As the 2003 PIPA report noted, "In polls conducted throughout the world before and during the war, a very clear majority of world opinion opposed the US going to war with Iraq without UN approval. However . . . polls conducted during and after the war [found] that only a minority of Americans were aware of this. A significant minority even believed that a majority of people in the world favored the US going to war with Iraq."[27]

What all this suggests is a media system in the United States that has increased, or at least failed to narrow, the perceptual and cultural gaps between Americans and citizens of other countries around the world. From Abu Ghraib to the Iraq war writ large, the American public sees a significantly different picture than citizens of other countries when it comes to how the United States flexes its muscle—in its wars and in its detention centers—around the world.

The Question of Higher Responsibility for Abu Ghraib

Perhaps different coverage of the significance of Abu Ghraib, or of the United States' being at odds with much of the rest of the world, would have set a better context for covering questions of responsibility for the torture of detainees. As it turned out, the press's framing of the responsibility factor was more complicated than perhaps any other element of the Abu Ghraib story. On the one hand, the nation's leading media paid more attention to questions of responsibility than to those about torture, the detainees, or world reaction to the story. On the other hand, the press predictably and continuously pegged its coverage to how the government itself engaged with the responsibility questions.

The U.S. press did raise serious questions about how high up on the chain of command responsibility for the scandal extended. Military investigations (at least obliquely) suggested command-level failures, and memos leaked from within the Bush administration showed that the White House had been briefed on strategies to create legal cover for the use of torture against U.S.-held detainees, and that the secretary of defense had approved coercive interrogation tactics. This body of evidence offered the media ongoing opportunities to press the question of high-level responsibility. Of course, as we argued earlier, these same documents also could have been used to raise the torture question more aggressively, but were not. The difference with regard to the responsibility question may be that "What did he know and when did he know it?" is a news script popular with Washington reporters ever since (if not before) the Watergate debacle. Unearthing a scandal that dislodges high officials has become, since the toppling of the Nixon administration, a highly valued, career-making prize.[28] If it was difficult for mainstream journalists to accuse U.S. forces of deliberately torturing innocent people, it was easier for those reporters to question whether people in high places had authorized or condoned the "abuse."

Yet although the responsibility question was raised fairly often in the news, it was not clearly answered, as our analysis below shows. The press raised the possibility that high-level military and civilian commanders might be at least indirectly responsible for Abu Ghraib, so that even while discussion of torture was fairly quickly contained, the question of responsibility for the "abuse scandal" was not. But the same political dynamics and news management strategies that shut down discussion of torture—such as Republican-dominated congressional hearings that gave top officials the opportunity to shape the story, and President Bush's repeated public statements of confidence in Defense Secretary Rumsfeld—also constrained discussion of responsibility. As with talk about torture, much of the examination of responsibility occurred on the editorial pages. When it became clear that neither the White House nor Congress was going to hold top leaders accountable for the scandal, there was little place—according to the rules of the Washington press game—for the accountability story to go. Meanwhile, low-level soldiers and officers were prosecuted and disciplined, and their claims about being ordered or encouraged by their superiors to "soften up" detainees for interrogation did not save them from punishment. Nor did those claims provide a lasting news hook for the story of higher-level responsibility.

THE UNANSWERED QUESTIONS.   In order to analyze how the press framed responsibility for Abu Ghraib, we looked closely at news stories and editorials in the *Washington Post* during the critical time period between the end of April 2004, when the Abu Ghraib story broke, through mid-September of that year. As the nation's preeminent "inside politics" newspaper, the *Post* provided perhaps the fullest picture of the dimensions of the responsibility story. We focused in particular on the question of Secretary Rumsfeld's responsibility. While many officials share authority over the actions of U.S. military forces, Rumsfeld's responsibility became a particular focal point, for several reasons. As the top civilian military authority, second only to the president, the secretary of defense is implicated (fairly or unfairly) in military scandals, particularly if those scandals appear to reflect official government policies. Indeed, immediately after the Abu Ghraib story first broke, Rumsfeld told the Senate Armed

Services Committee, "These events occurred on my watch as Secretary of Defense. I am accountable for them. I take full responsibility."[29]

Not only did Rumsfeld have general authority over detention and interrogation policies. As revealed in the early weeks after the Abu Ghraib story broke, he had authorized a list of interrogation techniques for use at Guantanamo Bay, including some that wound up in the Abu Ghraib photos. It also became known that he had authorized keeping some prisoners as "ghost detainees"—inmates whose identity and whereabouts would be obscured from outside observers such as the International Committee of the Red Cross. Thus, Rumsfeld's role in the treatment of U.S. prisoners was not insignificant. In fact, some close observers have recently suggested that President Bush was deliberately left out of the policy-making loop, to supply him with the all-important cover of "plausible deniability" in the event that the Bush administration's detention policies came under scrutiny.[30] If this is true, it increases the importance of Rumsfeld's role in developing and authorizing these policies.

Beyond the specifics of the connections between the high command and practices at military detention facilities, there is always the prospect that the secretary of defense can be held to account politically when a military scandal arises; that is, he can be fired or he can resign—as Rumsfeld eventually did after the 2006 midterm elections brought numerous Republican losses, with exit polls indicating the public's widespread dissatisfaction with the war. Throughout the early weeks of the Abu Ghraib story, speculation swirled about whether President Bush would ask Rumsfeld to pay the price of the scandal, giving us another reason to focus on Rumsfeld's responsibility as a proxy for the broader question of higher responsibility for Abu Ghraib.

We tracked claims about Rumsfeld's responsibility in several ways. For each story in the *Post* mentioning Donald Rumsfeld in conjunction with Abu Ghraib (a total of 189 news articles and editorials), we asked first whether it contained any claims about Rumsfeld's authorizing or being responsible for interrogation practices at U.S. military detention centers abroad. Because some controversial techniques were approved by Rumsfeld for use at Guantanamo but then "migrated" to detention centers in Iraq, we tracked claims related to any and all such U.S. facilities as well as claims that he was linked to practices at Abu Ghraib in particular. In addition, we tracked references to Rumsfeld's public apology for what

happened at Abu Ghraib, as well as his statements accepting responsibility for the scandal.[31] Finally, we looked for any claims in these articles that
he should resign or be forced out of his job.

We found that the question of Rumsfeld's responsibility was raised
fairly often, particularly in the initial weeks of the story and again in late
August when the Fay and Schlesinger reports were released. Overall, almost one-third (45 out of 150) of articles that mentioned both Abu Ghraib
and Rumsfeld included at least one type of claim regarding his authorizing
or being responsible for Abu Ghraib.[32] Moreover, 28% of articles contained
calls for or discussion of his possible resignation.[33] But the precise nature
and extent of his responsibility, as presented by the *Post,* remained murky.

Initially, to the degree that his responsibility was discussed at all, various sources in the *Post* mainly blamed Rumsfeld for failing to deal with
the scandal effectively after the photos came to light. For example, *Post*
columnist David Broder criticized his after-the-fact response: "When he
appeared before the Senate Armed Services Committee on Friday, Rumsfeld candidly admitted that he did not recognize the explosive potential
of the scandal and did not alert either the president or Congress to its
calamitous worldwide effects."[34] By late August, Rumsfeld's personal responsibility for shaping the practices at Abu Ghraib—not just his handling of the public scandal—was being raised more often.

Yet even though the question came up fairly regularly, the *Post's* discussion of Rumsfeld's responsibility remained muddled. One manifesta-
tion of this lack of clarity echoed a pattern we found with regard to the
labeling of Abu Ghraib: a significant gap between the news and the editorial pages. This gap became particularly noticeable at the key moment
after the release of the Schlesinger report—the one government investigation that portrayed Rumsfeld's office as in some way responsible for Abu
Ghraib. In comparison to its editorials, the *Post's* news coverage of the
report was tame, carefully limiting the scope of Rumsfeld's responsibility
to what was explicitly outlined in the reports. As a page-one article put it,
the Schlesinger report "found that actions by Defense Secretary Donald
H. Rumsfeld contributed to confusion over what techniques were per-
missible for interrogating prisoners in Iraq."[35] But the *Post* reacted much
more strongly on its editorial page. There the editors noted that the report
"demolished the fiction, clung to until now by President Bush, Mr. Rumsfeld and the Pentagon's whitewashers, that prisoner abuse in Iraq was an

aberration for which no senior officials were responsible." According to these editors, the report revealed "the truth most fiercely resisted by the administration and its allies: that the crimes at Abu Ghraib were, in part, the result of the 2002 decision by the president and his top aides to set aside the Geneva Conventions as well as standard U.S. doctrines for the treatment of prisoners."[36]

Of course, journalists are granted a greater degree of freedom to express their views in editorial pieces—that is the very purpose of the "opinion" section of the newspaper. Our point here is that the *Post's* editors did something more significant than simply expressing an opinion: They framed the story fundamentally differently on the editorial page, focusing on aspects of responsibility for the scandal that were not emphasized in their paper's *news* coverage. Fact claims in editorials decrying decisions made at the highest levels of government regarding treatment of detainees barely surfaced in the *Post's* news-page coverage of the Schlesinger report. Those pages narrowly documented the latest officially provided dots of evidence, while the editorial page was left to connect the dots to sketch the larger picture of high-level culpability.

Overall, our data show that claims about Rumsfeld's responsibility for Abu Ghraib were more likely to come from editorial pieces than from the news pages. Out of 103 news stories mentioning Rumsfeld and Abu Ghraib, 23% contained some claim about his direct responsibility; out of 47 editorial items, 45% contained such claims. If the news pages, because of the assumption of objectivity, convey greater credibility to the ideas expressed there, then the notion of Rumsfeld's responsibility for Abu Ghraib was comparatively marginalized. Which raises an intriguing puzzle: why was it not acceptable to talk as freely about Rumsfeld's possible role in the *news* pages?

WHO WAS RESPONSIBLE? THE STORY WITH NOWHERE TO GO.   One explanation for these journalistic decisions might simply be the alleged "liberal bias" of the *Washington Post,* for one might suppose that the editors consequently used the editorial page to "bash" Rumsfeld. But we propose a different explanation—one that can also diagram similarly muddled patterns of reporting even in cases where the ideological stripes of the players are reversed: the same dynamics we have pointed to thus far in our study of news coverage related to the Iraq war. As with the main Abu

Ghraib story, reporters had documentary evidence and plenty of suggestions that Rumsfeld might be held accountable for the crisis his policies
had helped to create. What they lacked were the institutional cues that
would sharpen and sustain the story.

Perhaps most important among the constraints on how the press filtered the responsibility story was the fact that President Bush quickly and
unequivocally defended Rumsfeld from his critics and made clear he would
not allow him to leave office. On May 5, a week after the Abu Ghraib story
broke, the White House leaked to reporters that the president had "chastised" Rumsfeld in a meeting for his handling of the scandal (the president,
reporters were told, learned about it only after it was aired on CBS).[37] But
the next day—one day before Rumsfeld testified before committees in both
the Senate and the House—Bush said in televised remarks from the White
House Rose Garden that he was "sorry for the humiliation suffered by Iraqi
prisoners and the humiliation suffered by their families," but insisted that
Rumsfeld would remain in office. On May 7, Rumsfeld performed the
requisite ritual of political absolution—the public apology, stating at the
hearings that he was personally responsible and "accountable" for the Abu
Ghraib abuses. Asked whether it would be better for America's standing in
the world if he were to resign, Rumsfeld responded, "That's possible." But
he would not resign, he insisted, simply because "people try to make a political issue out of it."[38] The president reportedly twice rejected Rumsfeld's
offers to resign immediately after the Abu Ghraib story broke, and continued to defend him long into his second term. As Bush famously declared in
April of 2006, "I'm the decider and I decide what's best. And what's best is
for Don Rumsfeld to remain as the secretary of defense."

Without an official acknowledgment of high-level responsibility, as
one journalist observed, "the Abu Ghraib scandal eventually ebbed, in
part because of the lack of proof that the president had ordered the mistreatment of prisoners."[39] Even so, the causal chain connecting the president and Rumsfeld to Abu Ghraib was rather long, with several key but
somewhat hazy links. Rumsfeld authorized his most controversial interrogation practices for detainees held at Guantanamo, not in Iraq. Those
practices then allegedly "migrated" (a term often used in news stories) to
Iraq via Major General Geoffrey Miller, who told investigators he had been
dispatched to Baghdad by Undersecretary of Defense Stephen Cambone
after Cambone had a "conversation" with Rumsfeld.[40] This complicated

and sometimes speculative trail of evidence made the story of responsibility a more difficult one for reporters to tell on the news pages.

One institutional arena in which that story might have been reconstructed, thus giving mainstream journalists license to explore it fully on the news pages, were the numerous official investigations that followed Abu Ghraib. But, as discussed above, even the most damning governmental fact-finding effort, the Schlesinger report, did not draw clear, bright lines connecting Rumsfeld's policy decisions with the treatment of prisoners photographed at Abu Ghraib. Instead, it pointed rather vaguely to the Pentagon's role in allowing the prison "conditions" that led to abuses.[41] Indeed, the various investigations into the Abu Ghraib debacle left significant gaps in the larger picture, perhaps deliberately. As one former government official observed at the time, the investigations in fact may have been a "carefully designed strategy to have lots of activity going on around the center of this thing without probing the center itself."[42] Thus, the institutional cues that might have sustained the responsibility story in the mainstream press were muted.

The other institutional arena in which the question of responsibility was raised was the military trials of soldiers involved in the scandal. But despite these soldiers' claims that they had been following orders, or at least that their actions had not been frowned upon by their superiors, these proceedings did not produce clear links to higher authorities. In part this was due to unique features of military trials. As one expert put it, "there is no central prosecution office run by commanders" in the military justice system, "so you don't have a D.A. thinking, I'm going to follow this wherever it leads."[43] In part it was because the army judge in charge of the trials of Charles Graner, Lynndie England, and other Abu Ghraib defendants denied the defense attorneys' requests for testimony from Secretary Rumsfeld and other high-level commanders, ruling that the commanders' actions did not bear on the conduct of these low-level soldiers. Moreover, Major General Miller, with whom the Guantanamo interrogation methods presumably migrated to Iraq, invoked his right against self-incrimination to avoid testifying in the trials of two military dog handlers charged with abusing Abu Ghraib prisoners.[44]

According to one independent journalist who attended those trials and wrote about them in *Harper's* magazine, the by-then extensive record on U.S. torture policy was "both critical background and inadmissible

evidence." In addition, the U.S. Army's internal review process had ensured that "only the lowest-ranked soldiers would be court-martialed, and
only photographs they took that supported the government's limited narrative [of low-level abuse] would be introduced. Anything that threatened
to open more disturbing doors . . . was eliminated."[45]

In the absence of presidential, congressional, military, or judicial censure, the Washington press corps had nowhere to take the story of high-
level responsibility as long as they adhered to the common rule of limiting their coverage according to the power index operating in government
decision-making processes. And, put bluntly, when it became clear that
no high-level heads were going to roll, news outlets playing by the rules
of the Washington press game no longer had a "big story" on their hands.
To their credit, reporters at the *Post* as well as the *Times* and some other
elite news organizations continued to probe the question, and every newly
leaked memo and new government investigation allowed the lingering
question of responsibility to be raised again. But lacking any institutional
mechanism to enforce it, the press could not of its own power make accountability happen.

Instead, the news followed the well-established "game frame" script in
which the political fortunes of the powerful rather than the substance of
their policies become the main story.[46] Many articles focused on the *political* ramifications of Abu Ghraib for Rumsfeld and the Bush administration.
As one front-page *Washington Post* story on the Schlesinger report duly
noted, even that relatively hard-hitting report "does not appear to threaten
Rumsfeld's position as defense secretary, especially because all four panel
members emphatically rejected the idea of calling for his resignation yesterday at a Pentagon news conference to release their conclusions."[47]

In short, lacking institutional initiatives—investigations, court proceedings, firings—that would provide the press with a politically safe way
to tell stronger stories about who was responsible for the international dis-
grace of Abu Ghraib, mainstream news coverage about culpability often
seemed muted and confused, and the country was caught in what independent journalist Mark Danner described as "frozen scandal"—"the icebergs are floating by," but nothing really happens. As Danner observed,

A process of scandal we've come to know, with an expected series of
steps, has come to an end. Before, you had, as Step 1, revelation of

wrongdoing by the press, usually with the help of leaks from within an administration. Step 2 would be an investigation which the courts, often allied with Congress, would conduct, usually in public, that would give you an official version of events. We saw this with Watergate, Iran-Contra and others. And finally, Step 3 would be expiation—the courts, Congress, impose punishment which allows society to return to some kind of state of grace in which the notion is, Look, we've corrected the wrongdoing, we can now go on. With this administration, we've got revelation of torture, of illegal eavesdropping, of domestic spying, of all kinds of abuses when it comes to arrest of domestic aliens, of inflated and false weapons of mass destruction claims before the war; of cronyism and corruption in Iraq on a vast scale. You could go on. But no official investigation follows.[48]

As the icebergs floated by, the mainstream media's inability to name those responsible independently and push for accountability was revealed.

Where Is the Watchdog Press?

During the spring and summer of 2004, when the Abu Ghraib scandal was ripe and the public's attention was focused, the news framing of responsibility for the detainees' mistreatment was confused, contradictory, and unresolved. Though there was no evidence that Secretary Rumsfeld or anyone else high in the chain of command had authorized the more perverse and egregious sexual humiliation of prisoners at Abu Ghraib, survey data suggested that even at the height of the story, the majority of the public did not understand that the secretary of defense had indeed authorized some of the interrogation practices pictured in the photos—unclothing and hooding prisoners, forcing them into prolonged stress positions, and threatening them with unmuzzled dogs.[49] Beyond that type of specific knowledge, the public lacked a clear picture of the linkages between high-level decision makers and the debacle of Abu Ghraib. As the other data presented here show, they also lacked a clear sense of who was being detained and by what means they were chosen for detention, or how other nations viewed the scandal and the larger war that framed it.

Democratic theory often supposes that the press is a "watchdog," and even a "fourth branch" of government that counterbalances the power of the other three. Through the news media's independent scrutiny, in theory, the public can understand what its leaders are doing and call them to account for their policy decisions. But the confused story about responsibility for Abu Ghraib provided little traction for the public to hold its leaders accountable. Those difficulties were magnified by the *abuse* label so prevalent in the story, which made the question of higher responsibility less urgent and compelling; by the obscured picture of the detainees themselves, who were rarely portrayed as merely petty criminals and average citizens who probably should not have been in a prison for insurgents and terror suspects at all; and by the considerable gap between U.S. and foreign coverage, which arguably left Americans less aware of how the story had impacted U.S. prestige around the world.

Elections, of course, are the primary mechanism of accountability in a democracy. But elections are supplemented by other mechanisms, chiefly news coverage and public opinion polls, that, in theory at least, keep citizens informed of ongoing policy developments and keep leaders apprised of the public's will. It is a prized ideal in the American political culture that the news media serve as the eyes and ears of a public that cannot see for itself inside the highest offices of its government.[50] The implicit promise of this watchdog ideal is democratic accountability: the public can only hold its leaders accountable if it knows what those leaders have been doing. This is a lofty standard, to be sure, the achievement of which any news media system might be bound to disappoint. But the particular media system described here is virtually guaranteed to fail at those moments when it is needed most. The press cannot itself bring about democratic accountability—particularly when it plays by the deeply entrenched rules of the Washington press game. When the government will not hold itself responsible for scandals, errors, and failures, a media system tied so tightly to those very same government institutions will have little basis for independently raising and sustaining critical questions on the public's behalf.

5

Managing the News

Spin, Status, and Intimidation in the
Washington Political Culture

We're an empire now, and when we act, we create our own reality. And while you're studying that reality—judiciously, as you will—we'll act again, creating other new realities, which you can study too, and that's how things will sort out. We're history's actors . . . and you, all of you, will be left to just study what we do.

A BUSH ADMINISTRATION OFFICIAL, AS REPORTED
BY RON SUSKIND, OCTOBER 2004

People who really knew Washington knew that if you went after the Bush administration on something that mattered to them, they would be the targets of Karl Rove's revenge. That pattern was pretty well established. So I think people were afraid.

RICHARD CLARKE

In June 2005, Senator Richard J. Durbin, a soft-spoken moderate Democrat from Illinois, compared the behavior of U.S. troops at Abu Ghraib to the torture techniques used by the Nazis, the Soviets, and the Cambodian Khmer Rouge. Deeply troubled by American interrogation techniques at Abu Ghraib, Durbin expressed strong emotions about what he regarded as a blot on U.S. prestige. What happened next illustrates the less visible Washington political dynamics that go into the finer-grained management or regulation of news stories while their broad narratives are tied to more formal power relationships. In a behind-the-scenes glimpse into how Washington political debate is regulated, Shailagh Murray of the *Washington Post* described an orchestrated campaign to discredit Senator Durbin. "Quick to pounce were conservative Web commentators and radio talk-show hosts, followed by other media outlets with a strong conservative following, including Fox News and the *Washington Times*." After a week of intense pressure, a shaken Durbin apologized for making the comparisons. Referring to the conservative movement, he remarked: "They are extremely well organized, and inevitably, they drag the mainstream media behind them."[1]

In this chapter, we highlight the factors that help explain Senator Durbin's experience and the similar experiences of others who took their policy criticisms of the Bush administration public. We argue that the administration operated from the premise that because perceptions of reality are malleable, so too is reality itself. Just as light bends as it passes through a prism, perceptions of reality bend to power. The press facilitates this "reality management" by habitually turning to a narrow range of sources it considers legitimate and credible. Indeed, the more important a story—the higher the political stakes—the more likely the press is to turn to powerful spin machines to take control of its telling. In the ideologically driven media environment of all-news-all-the-time cable television and sharp-elbowed bloggers, the safest place for the elite press to be is in the "nonideological" space found in an implicit understanding of news as whatever the most powerful officials say it is. The press docs this as if official sources were somehow free of unbiased intent. The ironic consequence of the explosion in alternative news outlets is that the establishment press is driven deeper into the political consensus of the moment.

Journalists, Sources, and Forging the Washington Consensus

According to the indexing model developed in this book, sustained debate in the news is usually produced by disagreement among political elites who are perceived by the press to wield enough power to affect the course of policy. The volume, clarity, and shape of messages from those powerful sources, in turn, depends on the quality of their communication resources, which, in turn, is often related to who wields the most effective communications strategies. Because policy powers are particularly circumscribed in the area of foreign affairs (compared to broader, multileveled, and often more complex processes in such areas as education, environmental regulation, or crime), this news formula means that a fairly limited range of officials, most often from the executive branch and Congress, set the parameters of national debate.

This model of news making has been well established in research. What has been less examined is the *culture of consensus in Washington politics* that reinforces these kinds of news decisions day in and day out.

Consensus around what a story is about does not simply emerge fully formed. The constant underlying process of sources jockeying for news position gives the Washington consensus a dynamic quality, including its potential for sometimes dramatic and rapid change following crisis, scandal, election-related shifts, or reversal of policies. The promotion of strategic images and perspectives on events through the complex political and social networks of Washington is often referred to in such loose terms as *spin, buzz, PR,* or *conventional wisdom.* This chapter takes a closer look at how this daily negotiation and management of major stories operate through a variety of mechanisms, some subtle and others not. We want to know more about the journey from the many private debates concerning policy to the few public ones that surface in the press. What factors encourage the continued privatization of potentially important public debates about policy?[2] What factors beyond just their positions of institutional power influence the timing and availability—the supply—of news sources and their story lines? Our look behind the news is aided by the firsthand accounts of various players, including journalists, public relations consultants, and news sources, who have shared their experiences with us in interviews. (The protocol for these interviews is available in appendix D.)

In order to understand how a Washington consensus may emerge around a particular story, and how various conformity-enforcing dynamics work, it helps to remember that many Washington reporters, particularly those working for the most powerful and elite news organizations, are part of, not separate from, the political environment they cover. As one longtime observer of the scene has put it, most Washington reporters "can't operate without being part of the system. . . . Everybody wants to be at Versailles. Washington is Versailles. They want to be close to *le roi soleil* [the sun king], they want to be part of the power structure."[3]

Journalists as Active Agents in Building the Washington Consensus

Robert Callahan served in a number of high-profile public affairs positions in the State Department, including embassy spokesperson in Honduras during the Contra wars in the 1980s. More recently, he served as spokesperson and press attaché at the American diplomatic mission in Baghdad, and then as the director of public affairs for the newly created Office of the Director of National Intelligence. According to Callahan, journalists "seem to write their articles to a formula. Sure they'll say Secretary of

Defense Rumsfeld said this, but they will then run to some critic of the war. Rumsfeld says something about the war in Iraq, and then they'll run to (Representative John) Murtha or (Representative Nancy) Pelosi and ask for a contrary opinion, and then they alternate paragraphs."[4] In Callahan's view, the range of debate is constrained even at its most expansive moments. "We have to recognize that the press is a part of this establishment, a prominent part of this establishment. They [reporters and policymakers] all see each other and deal with each other. And the whole political spectrum, when we are talking about Washington . . . is very narrow." Even at its healthiest, press coverage of high-stakes political issues is too often conformist in nature. When oppositional debate fails, as it did, for instance, prior to the 2003 Iraq war, the press tends to fall almost completely in line with existing policy frames. As Robert Entman notes, "Journalists canvass their networks of legitimate and customary sources (for example, the White House and Pentagon press secretaries, key members of Congress) to learn how they are connecting ideas and feelings: are sources saying the same thing in unison, are they arguing with each other, are they quiet on particular matters?"[5] Clearly, news is constructed according to the contours of official dialogue and debate—or at least that part of official debate made in public.

As a result, much of the dialogue in the news seems disjointed and often obscure in its significance. In part this is because journalists are attempting to fashion something from what may well (and often does) turn out to be nothing much at all. In part, however, the journalistic search for responsiveness from often very narrow ranges of officialdom is useful for both officials and journalists as daily measures of stories' positioning and stability. But this still begs the question of why news sources argue with one another in a way that only occasionally allows the press and the public to access the disagreement. Why, in other words, do critical ideas gain a public hearing in the news only at certain moments?

These questions seem particularly interesting given the increasing role in news making played by think tanks, conservative media outlets, various media watchdog groups, and bloggers. Each tries to shape public debate on a wide variety of political issues. Media watchdog groups, for example, apply pressure to news organizations in an effort to promote "balance," that is, encourage favored political views in the news and discourage opposition views. Likewise, the creation of think tanks such as the Heritage Foundation and cable news channels such as Fox News Channel, along with the rise of conservative talk radio, has created new venues for conservative ideas.[6] Less successfully, liberal views have looked for a home on syndicated radio, such as the talk network Air America Radio. These developments provide a rich array of *potential* voices and views to the mainstream press, which only raises the question: given the richness of the political environment, why does such a narrow range of voices typically make its way into the mainstream press?

Debates, disagreements, and strongly felt policy differences exist in Washington much more frequently than one would surmise from reading the newspapers. But the disagreements are muted, the arguments private, and the public left unaware. Indexing and other models of press-state relations are about the *public* component of a larger corpus of *private* disagreements among officials, former officials, and others in a position to speak authoritatively to the pressing issues of the day. And so, unless the press senses that shifts in power balances are occurring, the daily news often turns repeatedly on the same grand narratives, filled in daily and sometimes hourly with updated and often disjointed exchanges among officials.

However, the consensus that keeps this news control game going is often threatened by far more serious disagreements and discussions going on behind the scenes. Sometimes those critical policy conversations surface in the press in the form of former generals, executive branch officials, or legal advisers who speak out on issues that have the potential to change the story itself. In these cases, dominant news sources often seek to suppress that conversation, via discrediting or outright intimidating other sources. Thus, officials are agents in constructing the Washington consensus, not only in trying to dominate the news and spinning their positions through influence networks, but in the stealthy warfare they wage against competing sources.

Consensus Regulation through News Source Management

It is well known that policy debates sometimes rage behind the scenes, with fuller public knowledge of those debates coming only much later from memoirs or policy histories, long after the relevance of the debate has passed. We fully recognize the importance—indeed, the necessity—of conducting some policy deliberation away from the public's gaze. That said, we are less accepting of extreme secrecy or the silencing of policy critics that serves to protect dubious reputations, shore up shaky power positions, or prevent opponents from publicizing more creative solutions for failing policies. Unfortunately, a Washington consensus built on power and its behind-the-scenes management, and sustained in part by the lack of clear press accountability standards, makes it hard for many players to distinguish among different grounds for suppressing competing perspectives in public debate.

One way that high-level sources attempt to regulate the Washington consensus is through what we call the *tactical management of competing news sources*—the means and methods used in Washington politics to silence dissent and discourage potential news sources from participating in political debate. The reasons why sources step forward may range from principled and sometimes heroic disagreement with prevailing policies to self-aggrandizement. Less scrutiny has been given to the reasons why sources may decide to remain silent, even when their professional judgment and conscience tell them otherwise. There is similarly less attention paid to the costs borne by those who do decide to become public critics. Those costs become all the higher when, as often happens, the Washington consensus remains unable to embrace publicly what lower-level or ex-officio critics have to say, and the press consequently proves unable to give their stories much play.

In this chapter we focus on *disincentives* rather than incentives for sources to step forward and offer their views to the press. Involved here are often hard-nosed political tactics designed to silence or short-circuit oppositional participation as a news source, from whatever quarter it may come. As played in the big-league politics of Washington, DC, particularly by the Bush administration, this game operates more by the rules of Tony Soprano than *Robert's Rules of Order*. Potential sources are discouraged from dissenting from the Washington consensus by intimidation and threats to personal reputation, among other means. The tactical management of news sources influences which (and how many) critics will dare step forward to try to shape and change the policy debates to which the news is generally indexed. While the threat of retaliation has been a long-standing news management technique, the administration relied heavily upon it, sometimes with considerable success.

Machiavelli Discovers the Media: Bush Rules of Government

Given journalists' lack of clear political accountability standards beyond those chosen by government itself, and the jockeying of sources seeking to create realities that suit their political purposes, it is no wonder that we have witnessed the ascendance of a particular approach to governing practiced during the Bush years. That approach is rooted in assumptions concerning the malleable and subordinate nature of reality, the elastic human capacity to perceive it, and the mechanisms used to shape it. The core premise, whether witnessed in the masterful selling of the Iraq war or the inept, emperor-has-no-clothes response to Hurricane Katrina, is that narratives matter more than material reality. Indeed, narratives create perceptions of reality itself, opening the way to the use of power to create those realities.

Resting behind the tactical management of the daily news is a deeper epistemological premise concerning the nature of knowledge, truth, and the construction of meaning. That premise asserts that power bends reality into conformance with political goals. This governing style is often attributed to Deputy Chief of Staff and senior adviser Karl Rove, who was surely the chief architect of the Bush communication strategy. But this narrow attribution does not give nearly enough credit to the cadre of neoconservatives who captured top policy positions in the administration, particularly late-in-life converts to the neoconservative school such as Richard Cheney and Donald Rumsfeld. The degree to which their original promises and continuing accounts of the war clashed with available evidence on the ground was matched perhaps only by the venom they injected into attacks upon those (both news makers and journalists) who would disagree with them in public.

Put simply, the administration assumed it could bend mass perceptions of reality even against massive evidence to the contrary, with only occasional challenges from the press and dissident sources. And indeed, the ultimate surprise is not the hubris or the monumental presumption on which this governing style was based, but that it worked as well as it did for so long. From the early days leading up to war in Iraq through the Abu Ghraib prison scandal, the press rarely questioned the administration's justification for war and largely bought the idea (at least in reported news, although we suspect private conversations among journalists sounded different) that Abu Ghraib was the consequence of "a few bad apples."

Which brings us full circle, back to the daily context within which the news game is played out, the ecosystem that keeps it functioning: the Washington political culture that encourages conformity to conventional wisdom. In the tight circle of friends, sources, colleagues, and former colleagues that describes so much of Washington politics, one always runs the risk of social and professional ostracism if one ventures too far from the fold. What makes the published conventional wisdom of this era one for the history books are three hallmark factors: (1) governing based on reality narratives forged from an alchemy of convenience and grand illusion, (2) relying heavily on back-channel public relations and spinning conventional wisdom to prime the Washington culture of compliance to support the narrative, and (3) using personal intimidation to silence those who were sufficiently shocked and dismayed to express their public dissent at the near delusional results. We describe each of these three factors in more detail below.

The Malleability of Reality: Truth and Politics
in the Bush Administration

Independent journalist Ron Suskind captured well the Bush administration's stance concerning the relationship between power and perceived reality when he described his exchange with a senior administration official. The official took exception with one of Suskind's earlier criticisms of the administration. Suskind's account of the exchange puts the epigraph at the opening of this chapter in context:

> The aide said that guys like me were "in what we call the reality-based community," which he defined as people who "believe that solutions emerge from your judicious study of discernible reality." I nodded and murmured something about enlightenment principles and empiricism. He cut me off. "That's not the way the world really works anymore," he continued. "We're an empire now, and when we act, we create our own reality. And while you're studying that reality—judiciously, as you will—we'll act again, creating other new realities, which you can study too, and that's how things will sort out. We're history's actors . . . and you, all of you, will be left to just study what we do."[7]

In all its hubris and conceit, we believe these remarks illustrate the administration's organizing principle when dealing with the press and politics. Power bends reality to its will. Power is a prism through which facts are filtered and distorted to fit preferred versions of reality. For a nominally conservative administration, the Bush White House embraced a keenly postmodern epistemology. Like so many social constructionists or linguistic relativists, it seemed to believe that human engagement with material reality is mediated by social constructs. It is almost as if Karl Rove and George Bush were reading French theorist Jean Baudrillard.[8] What *is* isn't nearly as important as what is thought to be. Reality is first constructed to fit policy preferences and then reinforced through continuous news management, including pressure and intimidation. Several examples illustrate these points.

One area where this operating philosophy has been most evident is in science policy, and in the stories of scientists finding themselves at odds with the administration's preferred interpretation of reality. James E. Hansen, director of NASA's Goddard Institute for Space Studies, accused the Bush administration of keeping scientific information from reaching the public. Political appointees at NASA demanded to see his and other scientists' lectures and publications in advance.[9] Remarkably, a twenty-four-year-old political appointee to the NASA press office named George C. Deutsch prevented reporters from interviewing Hansen, telling colleagues he did so because his job was to "make the president look good."[10] "It seems more like Nazi Germany or the Soviet Union than the United States," Hansen told a gathering of scientists at The New School in New York.[11] Administration watchdogs also muzzled scientists at the National Oceanic and Atmospheric Administration.[12] Moreover, the federal Environmental Protection Agency issued "talking points" to local environmental agencies to help their spokespeople play down an Associated Press article exposing the disproportionate impact of pollution on impoverished neighborhoods.[13] In still another case of alleged political pressure on scientists, Susan F. Wood, the director of the Office of Women's Health at the Food and Drug Administration, resigned in protest of the administration's efforts to twist science and delay FDA approval of over-the-counter emergency contraception.[14]

The debate about global warming and the role of fossil fuels offers another instance of politics shaping science. Despite his lack of scientific qualifications, Philip Cooney, a White House official who once led the American Petroleum Institute's efforts to deemphasize the connection between global warming and the burning of fossil fuels, altered several government reports concerning global warming.[15] Controversy generated by a whistleblower from within the bureaucracy eventually forced Cooney to resign his White House post. But a Bush administration spokesperson claimed that the timing of Cooney's departure was entirely coincidental, having nothing to do with the altered reports; he simply wanted to spend more time with his family. What the White House didn't say was that the day after he resigned, Cooney was hired by ExxonMobil to fill an undefined job.[16] From the American Petroleum Institute, to the White House, and back to the oil industry, Cooney completed the circuit. Kert Davies, U.S. research director for Greenpeace, put it best in an interview with the British newspaper the *Guardian*: "The cynical way to look at this is that ExxonMobil has removed its sleeper cell from the White House and extracted him back to the mother ship."[17]

David Baltimore, president of the California Institute of Technology and winner of a Nobel Prize, said that he had grown accustomed to the administration's habit of "misrepresenting scientific findings to support its policy aims." It is no accident, he said, "that we are seeing such an extensive suppression of scientific freedom. It's part of the theory of government now, and it's a theory we need to vociferously oppose."[18]

Creating reality also had its place in the administration's foreign policy process. Between 2000 and 2005, Paul R. Pillar served as the National Intelligence Officer for Near East and South Asia in the Central Intelligence Agency. In a 2006 article in *Foreign Affairs*, he presented a scathing criticism of the administration's use of intelligence before the start of the Iraq war. "In the upside-down relationship between intelligence and policy that prevailed in the case of Iraq, the administration selected pieces of raw intelligence to use in its public case for war, leaving the intelligence community to register varying degrees of private protest when such use started to go beyond what analysts deemed credible or reasonable."[19]

Perhaps second only to its desire to believe that Iraq possessed weapons of mass destruction (WMDs), the administration was eager to demonstrate a link between Saddam and Al Qaeda.[20] Its desire to find such a link led to the creation of a special intelligence analysis unit inside the Pentagon called Policy Counterterrorism Evaluation Group. Headed by Douglas

Feith, a leading neoconservative, this alternative intelligence shop "was dedicated to finding every possible link between Saddam and al Qaeda, and its briefings accused the intelligence community of faulty analysis for failing to see the supposed alliance."[21] The U.S. intelligence community was mobilized around the effort to create the facts around political objectives.

Centralization of policy making to a few key players, combined with a distrust of the bureaucracy and the perceived necessity of fitting facts to desired policy, meant that compliance enforcement was paramount. Describing the policy process, Tori Clarke, former assistant secretary of defense for public affairs, told us,

> When it comes to Afghanistan, when it comes to Iraq, the overwhelming majority of the analysis of what was going on and what the approaches ought to be . . . were done by a very small handful of people: Bush, Cheney, Rumsfeld, Powell, Rice. Unlike decades and decades of foreign policy and national security and foreign policy development and execution in which it tends to work its way up from the bottom . . . this was top-down. You can argue back and forth whether or not this is right, but it was a very small handful of people who had any influence and made any decisions.[22]

Lawrence Wilkerson, Colin Powell's Chief of Staff at the State Department and an aide when Powell was chairman of the Joint Chiefs of Staff, put it in harsher terms. In a widely noted speech in Washington, DC, he referred to a "Cheney-Rumsfeld cabal that flummoxed the process." He continued,

> So you've got this collegiality there between the secretary of defense and the vice president, and you've got a president who is not versed in international relations and not too much interested in them either. And so . . . decisions often that are the opposite of what you'd thought were made in the formal process.[23]

Concentration of policy and decision making in the hands of a small coterie of officials, coupled with an administration having a penchant for spin, encouraged a system of news management by intimidation. The political hymnal was handed down from on high, and everyone was expected to sing along—and in the right key.

For example, in November 2002, CIA station chiefs from around the Middle East were called to London for a meeting seemingly as much about attitude as it was about intelligence gathering. Said one attendee, "This was to be a come-to-Jesus meeting, one in which officials from headquarters would make clear that it was time for the skeptics among them to drop their reluctance to engage on Iraq."[24] But in fact, many CIA officials—from rank-and-file analysts to senior managers—knew before the invasion that they lacked sufficient evidence to prove the existence of Iraq's weapons programs or the Al Qaeda connection. According to *New York Times* reporter James Risen, "Those doubts were stifled because of the enormous pressure that officials at the CIA and other agencies felt to support the administration."[25] Tyler Drumheller, a CIA analyst involved in assessing the alleged WMD program, told Risen, "Why didn't anybody say anything before the war [about how weak the intelligence was]? I did. And I can tell you it was hard, because nobody wanted to hear it, and they made it very clear that they didn't want to hear it."[26] Whether it was the CIA, National Oceanic and Atmospheric Association, or NASA, a political cadre pressured professional scientists and analysts to come up with politically supportive answers and scientific findings. When they failed to stick to the script, pressure was put on them to be silent and get in line.

These examples illustrate the Bush administration's epistemological stance toward facts and truth. Other examples reveal that, at times, the administration's management of news and perception had a surprising lack of sophistication. The more ham-fisted methods of perception management included simply buying the news outright. Armstrong Williams, a prominent media pundit, was paid $240,000 to promote the No Child Left Behind Act of 2002 on his syndicated television program and in his newspaper columns. Williams didn't disclose the funding until after *USA Today* learned of it through a Freedom of Information Act request.[27]

While the American public got Armstrong Williams's payroll punditry, the Iraqi people read manufactured news courtesy of the Lincoln Group, a shadowy PR firm hired by the Pentagon to create pro-U.S. news in the Iraqi press. The Lincoln Group did this by bribing editors and journalists in Iraq to use stories written by American ghostwriters. The Pentagon's outsourcing propaganda to the Lincoln Group appeared to stem from the collapse of what was intended to be an in-house operation. In 2002, news accounts revealed that the Pentagon was planning the creation of something called the Office of Strategic Influence. Among other things, OSI was expected to plant false stories in the foreign press.[28] When a public outcry led to the abandonment of the program, the Lincoln Group took its place.

In November 2005, the *Los Angeles Times* reported that the Lincoln Group was at work, helping the Pentagon covertly place articles favorable to the United States in the Iraqi press. In that year, dozens of pieces written by psychological-operations specialists in the U.S. military were published, a practice that continued into 2006. "The operation," noted the *LA Times*, "is designed to mask any connection with the U.S. military."[29] Stating that the program violated no law or Pentagon rules, George W. Casey, the commanding general of U.S. forces in Iraq, said in March 2006 that the military would continue paying Iraqi newspapers to publish pro-U.S. articles, as he saw no reason to discontinue the program.[30]

Casey's conclusion that the Lincoln Group broke no laws in its PSYOP campaign was at odds with findings in a report produced by the Pentagon in 2003. The "Information Operations Roadmap" noted that "information intended for foreign audiences, including public diplomacy and PSYOP increasingly is consumed by our domestic audience, and vice-versa." The report, released in a Freedom of Information Act request made by the National Security Archives at The George Washington University in Washington, DC, was classified secret and dated October 30, 2003.[31] It concluded that PSYOP messages disseminated to any audience except individual decision makers—and perhaps even then—will often be "replayed by the news media for much larger audiences, including the American public."[32] Significantly, it stated that it is illegal for the U.S. government to disseminate domestically information intended for a foreign audience.[33] Did this occur? It is difficult to say. But in today's global media environment, "news" from one part of the world is available around the globe in a matter of seconds. What is also clear is that more direct examples of what the General Accountability Office called government propaganda are available.

"I'm Karen Ryan, reporting from Washington." Was this the sign-off of a journalist wrapping up the latest news from the nation's capitol? Not exactly. Karen Ryan was a government employee pretending to be a reporter. The Bush administration was passing off video news releases extolling the virtues of its policies as real news—and succeeding. VNRs look and sound like real newscasts or "packages." In one feature, President Bush receives a standing ovation as he signs controversial Medicaid legislation.[34] The administration even offered news anchors (the real ones) a suggested script to introduce the VNR: "In December, President Bush signed into law the first-ever prescription drug benefit for people with Medicare. Since then, there have been a lot of questions about how the law will help older Americans and people with disabilities. Reporter Karen Ryan helps sort through the details." Ryan's VNRs ran as news segments on about fifty local television stations around the country, in many cases without noting its origins.

Similarly, news stations nationwide aired a story by a Mike Morris describing plans for a new White House campaign to discourage teenage drug use. As with the earlier "news" about the No Child Left Behind Act and the Medicare VNRs, the government produced Morris's piece—something the GAO had already concluded constituted illegal "covert propaganda." "You think you are getting a news story," remarked Susan A. Poling, managing associate general counsel at the GAO, "but what you are getting is a paid announcement."[35]

VNRs were also produced concerning pressing issues of foreign policy. In 2002, State Department public affairs contractors produced a segment on how America was helping liberate Afghani women. Intended to build support for administration policies in its global War on Terror, the fake news segment ran almost in its entirety on a Fox affiliate station in Memphis.[36]

Another example of the federal government supplying news is the Pentagon's Hometown News Service. With a staff of forty U.S. Army and U.S. Air Force military and civilian personnel, the service produces both print and broadcast "news" that is used by local newspapers and television channels. According to its Web site, in one year it produced and distributed 750,000 individual news releases to the "14,000 newspapers, television and radio stations subscribing to Hometown's free service."[37] According to the New York Times, the service's "good news" segments have reached 41 million Americans via local newscasts, in most cases without the station acknowledging their source. Meanwhile, the Pentagon Channel became available to Americans via their satellite and cable-company service providers. As the conservative Washington Times put it, "The Pentagon has created its own 24-hour television channel to cut out the middle man—the national media—in covering news events at the headquarters of the world's most powerful military."[38]

As alarming as each of these examples of news fabrication and perception management might be to some, it is the cumulative nature of the
Bush administration's efforts that is most striking. According to a GAO
report released in 2005, the administration spent more than $1.6 billion
in public relations and media contracts in a two-and-a-half-year span.[39]
Another $197 million was spent on public relations firms, and $15 million more was spent on individuals such as Armstrong Williams and news
organizations. The Department of Defense alone spent some $1.1 billion
of the $1.6 billion total. Getting out the preferred version of reality was an
expensive undertaking.

If the administration couldn't buy or go around the national press corps,
they simply infiltrated it. This seems to be the logic of the strange story
of Jeff Gannon, whose real name is James Dale Guckert (a.k.a. "the Bull-
dog"). He worked as the White House correspondent and bureau chief for
a conservative Web site called Talon News, a virtual news service without
an actual newsroom or office. Gannon drew unwanted attention to himself after asking President Bush whether he could deal with Senate Democrats "who seem to have divorced themselves from reality."[40] Besides
softball—and ironic—questions such as this, critics noticed that for Gannon, reporting from the White House sometimes involved cutting and past-
ing White House press releases directly into his "news" stories. Following a
flurry of liberal blogger digging, he left Talon News in February 2005.

The controversy sparked questions about why the White House had
cleared Gannon for briefings in the first place, especially in light of the
fact that he had been denied a press pass on Capitol Hill, where already
credentialed reporters control the credentialing process. Critics wondered
how someone with no journalistic experience, working for a Web-site
news service with no substantive presence in Washington, gained daily access to the White House (including presidential news conferences) using a
fake name. As any unofficial visitor to the West Wing of the White House
understands, the Secret Service requires a real name and social security
number—or an equivalent government identity number—so that it may
perform a background check. Without this, one is not permitted on the
grounds, much less given access to the president of the United States. The
conclusion reached by many critics was that Gannon was a foil, someone
the White House used to divert attention when questions grew too testy.
In this view, Gannon was a safety valve.

Like the accretion of damning facts that drifted by during the flaps over so many Iraq-related events, much of the reality fabrication of the Bush administration simply continued to move along, greeted with occasional howls of outrage and shrugs of helplessness. What to do when the government does not play by the conventional rules of decency, civility, or transparency on which democracy, to a considerable extent, depends? Protest and public challenges are among the conventional reactions, but they generally become effective only if they are publicized and given daily credence in the press. Relying on the press to remain active members in constructing the Washington consensus was thus an important element of the administration's governing strategy.

Relying on the Culture of Consensus to Support the Narrative of Power

Political pressure, video news releases, Pentagon-sponsored news programs, and White House correspondents with dubious qualifications do not, by themselves, account for the larger pattern of successful news control by the Bush administration, or for the mainstream press's reluctance to take on the administration. After all, these fabricated realities were not so convincing that they somehow replaced reality in the minds of most journalists, and they surely did not lull policy opponents to sleep. Indeed, all the incidents reported in the last section were eventually exposed by the press itself. The question becomes, what happened next? Why did these streams of relentless propaganda fail to trigger a swift, credible public response—if not by the Democrats, then by the press? Why was there no cumulative effect that somehow produced a front-page scandal or a press feeding frenzy that set the administration back on its heels?

By contrast, the hapless Clinton administration suffered serial scandals and feeding frenzies at the hands of the press over seemingly lesser offenses. The difference, it would seem, is that the Republicans during those years found various institutional platforms from which to stir up those press responses (impeachment being the grandest of them all), while the Democrats during the Bush years lacked the power, and perhaps the imagination or the will, to follow suit. Either way, the press responded within the bounds of the government power dynamic, as calibrated daily through the networks that establish the Washington consensus.

Journalists working for mainstream news organizations, by definition, work within the limits set by the daily sense of who is in and who is out, and what is important and what is not, based on sampling and participating in the social and political circles that constitute the Washington consensus. As a result, things that may seem to be big news to many on the outside don't look the same on the inside. Consider, for example, the reaction of Keith Richburg, the foreign desk editor at the *Washington Post*, to the Downing Street Memo. As explained in chapter 1, this term came to refer to an intelligence brief given to Tony Blair, the British prime minister, before the war in Iraq began. It described the British intelligence community's concern that U.S. intelligence findings had been shaped by the Bush administration's desire to invade Iraq. The clear implication of the document, leaked to the British press in 2005, was that the White House knew the claims concerning WMDs and links between Iraq and Al Qaeda were inaccurate at best. At worst, it suggested the administration deliberately misled the American public and the world about Iraq. But to Richburg, the Downing Street Memo was old news. Indeed, the *Post* eventually covered the story only in response to Internet critics. "We had made a decision that there was no new news it," Richburg said. "We didn't cover it. But the blogs beat up on us so we had a big page-one spread about it just to shut them up."[41]

Something similar occurred in 2006, and again it involved a leaked British document. On March 27 of that year, a *New York Times* article confirmed that contrary to Bush's repeated claim that he was reluctant to go to war with Iraq, privately the President had expressed a preference for war, regardless of the facts concerning WMDs or Al Qaeda connections.[42] The *Times'* basis for this assertion was a memo written by a Blair aide and first revealed on February 3 by the British newspaper the *Guardian*, and in a book written by Philippe Sands, a law professor at the University of London.[43] The leaked document summarized a January 31, 2003, Oval Office meeting between Bush and Blair. In it, Bush appears dead set against any outcome but war. Indeed, the president "was determined to invade Iraq without the [United Nations'] second resolution, or even if international arms inspectors failed to find unconventional weapons."[44] He even suggested painting an American aircraft to look like a UN plane with the intent that it would be shot down and thereby create a pretext for war. As presented in this memo, the president was gunning for war. Yet his continued public statements at the time painted a very different picture.[45]

On February 10, less than two weeks after his meeting with Blair, Bush said, "If war is forced upon us—and I say 'forced upon us,' because use of the military is not my first choice. . . . But should we need to use troops, for the sake of future generations of Americans, American troops will act in the honorable traditions of our military and in the highest moral traditions of our country."[46] On March 6, just two weeks before the invasion of Iraq, Bush said, "I've not made up our mind [sic] about military action. Hopefully, this can be done peacefully."[47] Nonetheless, the memo summarizing the January Oval Office meeting calls into question these and several other similar assertions the president made before launching the war.

Surprisingly, despite the weight of the matter—confirmed evidence clearly indicating that Bush had misled the American people and launched a war on what he himself knew to be false pretenses—the story was underplayed or overlooked altogether. While it may not be surprising to learn that Fox News ignored the story, so did CBS and ABC, as well as the *Washington Post*, the *Los Angeles Times*, the *Wall Street Journal*, and *USA Today*. All failed to run follow-up stories on the memo.[48]

Why would the *Post* draw such a narrow view of news regarding the Downing Street Memo, and other news organizations do the same with the Oval Office meeting memo? Previous research findings are reinforced by our own investigation that suggests that the bigger the story and the greater its political significance, the more cautious the establishment press becomes. The irony here is that such caution is just as likely to lead to erroneous and misleading reports as it is to factual accuracy. Dependence on official sourcing makes the establishment press vulnerable to skewed intelligence offered up as news and the occasional prevarication presented as a major scoop—exemplified by Judith Miller's single-source reporting in the *New York Times* concerning Iraq's WMD program.

Leonard Downie Jr., the *Post's* executive editor, underscored this attitude when he told us that in order for the *Post* to call the events at Abu Ghraib torture, it would need additional outside sources. Similarly, as noted in chapter 3, editors at the *New York Times* claimed not to realize that people were "reading things into our not using 'torture' in headlines" when covering Abu Ghraib. These self-imposed limitations of imagination, necessary in order to operate in the big leagues of Washington media and politics, are another important feature of the Washington-based news media environment. Journalists operate in a media mind-set established by a dominant political culture in the nation's capital, one that is ironically limited by concerns of violating the unspoken code that will determine future access to the inner circles of power, as well as future professional and social acceptance. Echoing what Robert Callahan noted above, another veteran journalist suggested that strongly challenging the political consensus of the moment, rather than working within it, "puts you out of step with 95 percent of your colleagues and. . . . you feel left out . . . you stop getting invited to parties, and people say you're a crank and a weirdo. You're not part of the team anymore."[49] In Washington, journalists and officials operate in the same narrow circle; and it is by the rules of that circle that they play.[50]

This is the more difficult and perhaps more controversial aspect of our analysis, because it is about a Zeitgeist that offers few clear methods of measurement. One cannot conduct an experiment to gauge the variation in a Zeitgeist. Instead, understanding comes from years of experience and observation of a media-political system where the same people—journalists and politicians—attend the same social functions, send their children to the same private schools (St. Alban's[51] and Sidwell Friends are two of the preferred options), and attend the same parties. They also tend to live in the same communities—Bethesda, Chevy Chase, and Potomac in Maryland, old-town Alexandria in Virginia, or a Washington address followed by NW.[52] The Zeitgeist is measured in the microdemographics of a Washington dinner party celebrating the launching of a book written by a journalist who married into a powerful Washington political family. Among its members, the family counts two former members of Congress, a national television and radio pundit, and one of the most powerful lobbyists in the land. Those attending the party were some of the same journalists, politicians, and lobbyists who earlier that day engaged in the battles, debates, and press conferences that went little further than the same ritualistic press conferences from the day before.[53] Expectations are high, but the price for breaking the rules is even higher.

As a consequence, news is often trivialized—and the press exercises the full measure of its independence—by the pursuit of surrogate issues. When for example Vice President Cheney shot a seventy-eight-year-old man in a hunting accident, the story received saturation coverage for days. On the one hand, it seems reasonable that the news media would regard the shooting of a man by the vice president as newsworthy. But in the view of former White House press secretary Mike McCurry, something else explained the saturation coverage. He told us that it was also a reaction to the limitations the press feels in reporting about the Bush administration. "They can't go after the big issues so they go after what they can, such as Cheney accidentally shooting a fellow hunter."[54]

And so the dominant public image of Iraq and other presidential policies reflected the Bush doctrine of government by narrative, with its trappings of message discipline, loyalty among administration officials, and a relentless drive to exploit every opportunity to set the agenda and framework of debate. But the administration could not have accomplished this without the support of a press corps fearful of being out of sync with the Washington Zeitgeist (even when they were well aware how far out of step that Zeitgeist was with world opinion about Abu Ghraib or the war in Iraq).

Suddenly, Hurricane Katrina struck. For a time, the specter of cronyism, incompetence, and callousness caromed off the mounting casualties and signs of policy failure in Iraq. The White House seemed temporarily overwhelmed, and the news touched on realities that had been awkwardly kept in the background or out of the picture entirely. Until this collision of catastrophic events produced a crack in the consensus, the administration was remarkably adept at controlling the press and the sources that inform it. And even afterward, when the administration rededicated itself to commanding the news, the words of its officials returned to positions of prominence in the headlines.

With a cowed and ineffective Democratic Party, the only source of alternative perspectives to those spun by the White House media machine were occasional voices speaking out from the ranks of policy professionals. Some, such as Richard Clarke, the former counterterrorism chief, were relatively successful in making themselves heard. Others, such as Treasury Secretary Paul O'Neill, were less so. Understanding how the White House dealt with dissent is the final part of our analysis of consensus maintenance in Washington, DC.

Silencing Dissent

The narrowness of the "legitimate" debate that forms the basis of most news is reinforced by the use of subtle and sometimes not-so-subtle forms of political pressure, including threats and intimidation. As more than one critic of the Bush administration learned, when an authoritative source stepped forward to criticize policy, his or her reputation would be attacked and credibility undermined. The very basis of their authoritativeness—their status as an inside player and knowledgeable and legitimate source—became embattled.

Lawrence Wilkerson, the former Colin Powell aide who spoke out about the "Cheney-Rumsfeld cabal," told us that he had been warned about the "Corleone effect," a metaphorical reference to a mob hit by a member of the fictional organized-crime family in *The Godfather*. As Wilkerson put it, "You may not get it on Monday but you'll get it a year down the road."[55]

Perhaps the most famous example of the administration's determination to silence critics involved Joseph Wilson, a former ambassador to Gabon and the husband of a now famous CIA operative. In February 2002, Ambassador Wilson was asked to investigate whether Iraq had purchased or attempted to purchase "yellowcake" uranium from Niger in the late 1990s. The implication was that Iraq was trying to build WMDs, as the administration so adamantly claimed. After interviewing sources in Niger, Wilson concluded that Iraq had not sought uranium, and reported his findings to administration officials. With that he thought the issue had been put to rest.

But Wilson was stunned to hear President Bush reassert the claim in his now infamous sixteen words uttered during the 2003 State of the Union address: "The British government has learned that Saddam Hussein recently sought significant quantities of uranium from Africa." In a column published in the *New York Times* four months after the war began, Wilson accused the Bush administration of "exaggerating the Iraqi threat" in order to justify war. "Based on my experience with the administration in the months leading up to the war, I have little choice but to conclude that some of the intelligence related to Iraq's nuclear weapons program was twisted to exaggerate the Iraqi threat."[56]

Shortly thereafter, while musing on the choice of Wilson for the Niger mission, columnist Robert Novak noted that Wilson's wife was an operative for the CIA. Novak wrote, "Wilson never worked for the CIA, but his wife, Valerie Plame, is an Agency operative on weapons of mass destruction. Two senior administration officials told me Wilson's wife suggested sending him to Niger to investigate the Italian report."[57] Revealing the identity of intelligence operatives is a federal offense, and the Justice Department assigned a special prosecutor to conduct an investigation. Who provided Novak with Plame's identity? The subsequent investigation led to a dramatic confrontation between various news organizations and the special prosecutor, Patrick J. Fitzgerald. The details of much of this case beyond the indictment of Cheney aide Lewis (Scooter) Libby, and a near brush with indicting Karl Rove, may take historians years to sort out.

Wilson told us that his involvement in the debate about Iraq came in two parts.[58] The first came before the start of the war and dealt with U.S. policy options concerning Iraq. Generally, his position paralleled the realist position articulated by former national security adviser Brent Scowcroft and other GOP leaders distressed by the neoconservative rush to war (discussed further below).[59] Wilson supported the use of limited military action to eliminate any suspected sites that might contain WMDs. "The position I staked out was not that far apart from what others from the first Bush administration had taken."

Looking back on the prewar debate, Wilson acknowledged the futility of a lone individual standing up against the media machine turning out the White House line. "In that debate, we were outgunned and outmanned. The other side was able to put many more voices onto the airwaves much more frequently." Despite the futility of the enterprise, Wilson, Scowcroft, and retired Marine general Anthony Zinni kept up the effort. At one point in December 2002 Wilson received an e-mail from Zinni saying that the debate on whether to go to war in Iraq was over and that the president had made his decision. Wilson phoned Scowcroft and asked his opinion. Scowcroft, according to Wilson, said it was not over and that he should "continue doing what he was doing."

However, at the end of the day, the debate about whether to invade Iraq was a foregone conclusion, Wilson said, and "those of us arguing for a different approach were merely gadflies to this administration. And the fact that not a lot was done about us or to us was an indication that we weren't worth their time or effort." He observed too that the nature of the attacks from the White House during this early, prewar phase of the debate was different from what came later. "At the time of the debate during the runup to the war there wasn't the same sort of smearing of us as occurred later. There wasn't the character assassination that you saw with O'Neill,

Clarke, myself, and others afterward when people started questioning the underlying justification for the war." It was the collapse of the WMD rationale that put the attack machine into gear.

The second part of the debate involved challenges to the Bush administration concerning the integrity of the intelligence process and the administration's claims that Iraq was pursuing WMDs. The column Wilson had published in the *New York Times* on July 6, 2003, asserted that the administration was manufacturing information to fit its intent to invade Iraq. As he wrote in his book, *The Politics of Truth*, "The decision of the president's people to come after me and make me an example arose from no concern over the emergence of secrets related to my mission—there weren't any—but rather from the worry that the pressure they had placed upon intelligence analysts, in order to manipulate data to conform to their already determined political ends, would be exposed."[60] This is the pressure that former CIA analyst Pillar described in his article for *Foreign Affairs* in 2006.

Wilson told us that it was clear from testimony that "Libby and Rove and perhaps others were pushing the story out to the press in this time frame and maybe even before my article appeared." As early as March 2003, he claimed, well before the appearance of the column in the *New York Times*, but after the criticisms Wilson raised prior to the war, the vice president's office had done a "workup" on him. "It is very clear that they had all of the information they needed and decided what their line of attack was going to be." The July 6 column questioning the president's sixteen words in the State of the Union address was only the trigger to an already loaded gun.

In his book, Wilson said, "I realized that my credibility would be called into question, and I was steeled for that."[61] He told us, "I had every expectation that they were going to come after me. I had taken out my pictures of me with the first President Bush and my handwritten notes and I had dusted them all off. It was very clear to me that they were going to come after me." In his estimation, the administration felt compelled to do so for three reasons.

First, the administration wanted "to change the subject from the sixteen words to Wilson and his wife." Second, "I think it was a clear attempt to send a message to the foreign policy community and the intelligence community that if you do to us what Wilson just did to us, we will do to you what we just did to his family." He concluded this observation with a reference to *The Godfather,* the same movie that Lawrence Wilkerson had invoked in an earlier conversation: "Be afraid; be very afraid."

Third, the attack was motivated by a desire for revenge.[62] "That is what appeals to Rove. Get rid of the cockroaches; get rid of the Democrats. What they activated in all of this was the RNC [Republican National Committee] and the right-wing echo chamber. The whole political apparatus from the Right was activated in order to do this."[63] Senator Durbin's observations quoted at the beginning of this chapter are echoed in Wilson's description of his own encounter with the GOP attack machine.

As of 2006, the investigation into the leaking of Plame's CIA affiliation had resulted in the indictment of Lewis Libby. He "testified to a federal grand jury that he had been 'authorized' by Cheney and other White House 'superiors' in the summer of 2003 to disclose classified information to journalists to defend the Bush administration's use of prewar intelligence in making the case to go to war with Iraq, according to attorneys familiar with the matter, and to court records."[64] Wilson was made to pay for speaking out against the administration. (As of this writing, Wilson and Plame had filed a civil lawsuit against Lewis Libby, Dick Cheney, and Karl Rove, alleging violations of their civil rights in an effort to "discredit, punish, and seek revenge against" Mr. Wilson).

Another oft-cited example of the administration's retribution for speaking out involves General Erik Shinseki, a former U.S. Army Chief of Staff. When testifying before the Senate Arms Services Committee before the start of the Iraq war, General Shinseki was asked to provide his professional judgment concerning the appropriate size of the postinvasion stabilization force. He said that several hundred thousand troops would be needed for that operation. Almost immediately, Deputy Defense Secretary Paul D. Wolfowitz declared that the general's estimation was "wildly off the mark." Although it would be inaccurate to say that Shinseki was dismissed for his remarks—a point Toni Clarke made emphatically to us—it can be said that he suffered public rebuke from the Pentagon civilian leadership. Defense Secretary Donald Rumsfeld said Shinseki had a right to his opinion, but that this one would be proved wrong.[65] As the *New York Times* noted, Rumsfeld's and Wolfowitz's "public comments were unusual and were widely interpreted in Washington as a rebuke to General Shinseki, who is scheduled to retire in mid-June." When Shinseki left office, neither Rumsfeld nor Wolfowitz attended his retirement ceremony—"a breach of protocol that raised eyebrows across the service."[66]

There is no shortage of examples of pressure being applied or retribution sought from authoritative sources of news and interpretation—counterframes—at odds with the Bush administration. That said, it is also important to remember that the effectiveness of the administration's efforts had its limits. Not everyone could be cowed and intimidated.

The Limitations of Intimidation

Vulnerability to intimidation and fear is distributed unevenly among the administration's critics. Not everyone can be bullied into silence, and elite journalists will pay closer attention to the claims of certain kinds of critics than to others. In these exceptions one sees an important difference between the indexing system we have described throughout this book and some alternative models of press-government relations, particularly models that understand the news media to be little more than a closed-loop system for advancing government propaganda.[67]

Teflon Sources

We believe that part of what enables some dissenters to speak up and be heard—and avoid or at least weather political attacks in the process—stems from their ability to convey high political status while presenting a nonideological veneer. Career military officers and others who have worked for both political parties are examples of this sort of news source. They are attractive (even if short-lived) news sources because they implicitly define the boundaries between the mainstream press vis-à-vis alternative media. The mainstream press responds to the alternative-media environment of ideological bloggers and cable television pundits by positioning itself as a "nonideological" keeper of journalistic standards. Critics who offer policy criticism from the ranks of career specialists without evident political affiliations are an asset to both news gathering and the political positioning of the mainstream press. This is particularly true when sustained challenges from an oppositional party are missing. Nonideological technocrats are sometimes the only sources available to the mainstream press when it seeks to offer "the other side of the story" in terms the Washington consensus will allow. General John M. Shalikashvili, former Chairman of the Joint Chiefs of Staff,[68] White House counterterrorism czar Richard Clarke, and CIA analyst Paul R. Pillar are all examples of critical sources that emerged from nonpartisan technocratic backgrounds.

Consider, in this light, what happened when Clarke stepped forward to take on the Bush administration. That episode constituted a near perfect storm—and the first sustained postwar, pre-Katrina storm—of criticism for the administration. Within the same week in March of 2004, Clarke appeared on the 60 Minutes news program; his book, Against All Enemies, arrived at bookstores; and he testified before the 9/11 Commission hearings. These high-profile venues, plus an uncharacteristically sluggish response from the White House, created the first dimming of the administration's post-9/11 aura of invincibility. Looking back on the more critical assessments of the administration that began to emerge following Hurricane Katrina and the mounting casualties in Iraq, Clarke's criticisms in 2004 might seem tame and conventional. But at the time they constituted one of the first cracks in Bush's post-9/11 armor. The episode also illustrates both the nature of the administration's tactical measures to silence critics and how, on occasion, those efforts failed.

Clarke began his public attack by telling 60 Minutes correspondent Leslie Stahl that the president had been fixated on deposing Saddam Hussein, and that he had pressed Clarke into drawing connections between Iraq and the 9/11 attacks. "The president dragged me into a room with a couple of other people, shut the door, and said, 'I want you to find whether Iraq did this.' Now he never said, 'Make it up.' But the entire conversation left me in absolutely no doubt that George Bush wanted me to come back with a report that said Iraq did this." Clarke continued: "I said, 'Mr. President, we've done this before. We have been looking at this. We looked at it with an open mind. There is no connection.' He came back at me and said, 'Iraq! Saddam! Find out if there is a connection.' And in a very intimidating way. I mean that we should come back with that answer."[69] In response to Bush's directive, Clarke initiated another review of possible connections. After FBI, CIA, and other experts looked at the evidence, their report was sent to the White House. According to Clarke, "It got bounced and sent back saying, 'Wrong answer. Do it again.'" Reality needed to be fixed around policy objectives.

Clarke's book was available in stores immediately after his 60 Minutes interview was aired. He told us that he began writing Against All Enemies out of a desire to tell the story of what happened inside the White House on September 11, 2001. But what began as an account of events that day soon became a critique of the path that led the country into a costly war in Iraq. "As I was engaged in the writing process, it became clear to me that they really were going to do the war in Iraq come hell or high water," Clarke said.[70] "I found myself getting more and more angry about what they were going to do." In his view, the war was a strategic blunder in the war against the real terrorists in Afghanistan and elsewhere.

Clarke was certainly cognizant of the consequences of criticizing the Bush administration publicly. As he told us,

> I was aware that writing this book would make me a pariah with the Bush administration and, therefore, [with] a lot of their friends. So I was going to pay a big price for writing the book. We were starting this consulting firm [Good Harbor], and a lot of the consulting work that we were doing—or hoping to do—might disappear, because this White House is very vindictive. But I also thought it was worth paying those prices because people were being so quiet, noncritical.[71]

When asked why other potential critics remained silent, Clarke said that fear was a central factor. "People who really knew Washington knew that if you went after the Bush administration on something that mattered to them, they would be the targets of Karl Rove's revenge. That pattern was pretty well established. So I think people were afraid." What qualities or countertactics allowed Clarke to dodge "Rove's revenge"? What made him the perfect storm of public criticism for the administration?

Richard Clarke offered a rare storytelling opportunity for the news media. As the former counterterrorism policy czar in the White House and the man who essentially ran the immediate response operations on 9/11, he was a well-established nonpartisan official who was also highly critical of not only the Bush administration but the president himself. When asked why efforts to marginalize him failed after he went public with his scathing criticisms, Clarke said the answer was twofold. "One, I had been in Washington for thirty years and an awful lot of the news media people knew me and knew that I was not a partisan guy and knew that if I was saying these things I was saying them because I believed them."

His background and the Washington press corps' familiarity with him served as a defense against the administration's first response to Clarke's

60 Minutes interview and his book, which was to claim that Clarke was partisan and really hoping to benefit Senator John Kerry's candidacy for the presidency in 2004.[72] In other words, the first response was to try to categorize Clarke as just another political hack rather than a career technocrat. The White House wanted to strip him of the very quality that made him so dangerous.[73] But Clarke had served in a number of senior positions, stretching back two decades and across both Democratic and Republican administrations. He was "nonpolitical," a technocrat respected for his expertise in assessing terrorists' threats and devising counterterrorism measures. The charge of partisanship simply did not stick. Consequently, Clarke presented the mainstream news media with an opportunity to address the frustrations and professional embarrassment felt over its uncritical coverage of the lead-up to the war. As he put it,

> I think there was beginning to be an awful lot of bottled-up, pent-up frustration in the media. [There was] beginning to be a realization that they had been giving the Bush administration a free pass on a lot of things, and that it had resulted in some unfortunate results, like Iraq. And they also saw in my allegation that the Bush administration had done nothing for 9/11—a pretty good story that they had missed, or at least not published. So I think a lot of the reaction was, "I think this guy is probably right."[74]

Besides being no match for his technocratic credibility, the administration simply misjudged the impact of Clarke's appearance on national television. "It was interesting to watch as a participant," Clarke said, "because I think this White House, despite all of its political antennae and sophistication, really was surprised by the *60 Minutes* interview."[75]

CBS had approached the White House for a spokesperson to rebut Clarke's statements before the story aired on March 21, 2004, but it was slow to respond. As his nationally televised assertions "reverberated like thunder,"[76] the White House scrambled to regain its footing. "I don't think they really understood until the day of the *60 Minutes* interview the extent of the damage that could have been done, was being done by what I was saying. They didn't have a game plan."[77]

In the week after Clarke's appearance on *60 Minutes*, the Bush administration launched a full-scale attack against him. A video montage used by NBC News's *Meet the Press* as a lead-in to his appearance on its March 28 program captured and amplified the White House response. Tim Russert introduced the tape by noting that "the administration unleashed a ferocious counterattack" against Clarke. White House Chief of Staff Andrew Card is seen first, saying "The reflections in his book and what we hear in the media today are not the reality." Then White House spokesperson Scott McClellan charged that Clarke was "deeply irresponsible. It's offensive and it's flat-out false." Next came Deputy Defense Secretary Paul Wolfowitz, who tried to undermine Clarke by questioning his cognitive abilities: "It just seems to be another instance where Mr. Clarke's memory is playing tricks." Finally, Condoleezza Rice declaimed, "I just don't think that the record bears out Dick Clarke's assertion." Beyond these charges, Vice President Cheney told Rush Limbaugh's radio audience that Clarke "wasn't in the loop, frankly, on a lot of this stuff" and added that "he may have a grudge to bear there, since he probably wanted a more prominent position" in the Bush administration.[78]

The White House was joined in its attacks on Clarke by its congressional allies. Senator Bill Frist (R-TN), the Senate majority leader, claimed on *Meet the Press* that Clarke "has told two entirely different stories under oath." He maintained that Clarke's testimony given in July 2002 conflicted with that given during his appearance before the 9/11 Commission. "It is one thing," Frist said, "for Mr. Clarke to dissemble in front of the media, in front of the press, but if he lied under oath to the United States Congress, it's a far, far more serious matter."[79]

Clarke responded by asking that all six hours of his July 2002 testimony be declassified, as well as many of his White House memos and e-mails. "Let's take all of my e-mails and all of the memos that I've sent to the national security adviser and her deputy from January 20 to September 11 and let's declassify all of it."[80] His challenge went unmet.

Moreover, he was practiced at keeping the focus on the issues he wanted to discuss. When Tim Russert echoed one of the administration's attack themes—that Clarke was a disgruntled job seeker out to get the administration because he had been passed over for a high post—Clarke replied,

> Now, here we go again, you know, with it's about Dick Clarke and it's about his motivation, when really this is what the White House is trying to get you and others to do is to focus on me. I'll answer the

question, Tim, but I want to point out again that this is about the president's job in the war on terrorism. This is about how going into Iraq hurt the war on terrorism. This is not about Dick Clarke.[81]

Just as the White House and the GOP attack machine wanted to draw attention toward Joseph Wilson and Valerie Plame and away from the questions Wilson raised about the misuse and abuse of intelligence, it wanted to make Richard Clarke—and not the substance of his charges—the object of scrutiny.

The Bush administration knew that the 9/11 Commission hearings would present Clarke with still another opportunity to level his criticisms against it. Its counterattack against Clarke's *60 Minutes* appearance and his book apparently was timed in anticipation of this testimony. And once again, the strategy rested on an effort to discredit Clarke, thereby sending the media after him, not the substance of his charges. For example, two hours before Clarke's 9/11 Commission testimony, the White House leaked to Fox News information intended to damage his credibility: at one time he had provided a background briefing to reporters in which he extolled the Bush White House counterterrorism policies.[82]

But the attacks on Clarke were beginning to backfire on the administration, serving only to generate more attention for his book and to keep the story alive.

> Within about a week you could almost feel the shift in the force field in Washington, you could almost feel that they had shut off a switch, because about a week into it, they stopped. What I heard at the time through the grapevine was that they stopped because they realized, (a), they were selling my book. You couldn't find the book in bookstores anywhere in the country, and Simon and Shuster couldn't print them fast enough. And (b), they were getting extremely bad press for attacking me.[83]

Clarke's professional and reputational status, along with his well-timed, prominent public appearances, helped inoculate him against the White House attacks. Other technocratic and nonpartisan news sources dot the press landscape as well, offering their own critical takes on the war in Iraq and the conflict with Al Qaeda. But despite their successes in overcoming the Bush administration's attempts to silence its critics, Clarke and the other dissenters that were heard occasionally, such as Paul Pillar, were unable to compensate for the absence of an effective oppositional party capable of sustaining an effective counterframe. The closest thing to that came instead from opposing wings of the Republican Party itself.

A Family Feud: GOP Rifts on Iraq

Though it has been studied most closely in terms of conflict between the two major political parties, the indexing norm also works when power splits occurring within a party have the potential to alter policies, as happened among the Democrats during the Vietnam War. Moreover, full-throated public criticism emanating from within the White House or the ranks of a party and directed at another faction of that party add to the news value of the story for mainstream journalists by feeding their standard preoccupation with political conflict. Further, internal divisions in ruling parties may play out in institutional flywheels, such as hearings or legislative processes, that keep stories going even beyond the capacities of publicity-savvy individual sources such as Richard Clarke.

Even before the war in Iraq, the Republican Party had begun fracturing along ideological lines. The neoconservatives in the Bush administration had introduced a new brand of Republican foreign policy, one sometimes referred to as neo-Wilsonianism or Wilsonianism with teeth. As foreign policy scholar Francis Fukuyama notes in his book *America at the Crossroads*, strong public support for the war before 2006 stemmed from a surprising compatibility of political sentiments between neoconservatives and more traditional conservatives, who tend toward nativism and isolationism and are typically not inclined to pursue overseas interventions in the name of abstract ideals. As Fukuyama notes, "The Iraq war was promoted by an alliance of neoconservatives and Jacksonian nationals, who for different reasons accepted the logic of regime change in Baghdad." At the same time, he notes, the neoconservatives "sidelined the realists in the Republican Party like Brent Scowcroft and James Baker, who had served in the senior Bush's administration and were skeptical about the rationale for the war."[84] Perhaps the culmination of the realist-neoconservative split occurred between the forty-first and forty-third presidents of the United States. James Risen describes a telephone conversation between George W. Bush and his father that degenerated into a shouting match. The senior Bush "was disturbed that his son was allowing Secretary of Defense Donald Rumsfeld and a cadre of neoconservative ideologues to exert broad influence over foreign policy, particularly concerning Iraq, and that he seemed to be tuning out the advice of moderates, including Secretary of State Colin Powell."[85]

But the realists were never completely sidelined, as Fukuyama argues. Indeed, what little official opposition there was prior to the start-up of the war often came in the form of factional fighting between the realists and the neoconservatives. Then in September 2002, six months before the U.S. invasion of Iraq, Brent Scowcroft, a long-standing Republican foreign policy insider, former national security adviser, and perhaps George Herbert Walker Bush's closest friend, joined former secretaries of state Lawrence Eagleburger and James Baker in mounting a campaign against pursuing the war.[86] In the view of one media scholar, "All in all, for a couple months during the summer of 2002, Republicans behaved like Democrats."[87]

Some critics of the war combined a technocratic veneer with their GOP credentials. Blending elements of a career national security technocrat and a GOP insider, Lawrence Wilkerson felt compelled to come out strongly against the administration for which he had once worked. While investigating the Abu Ghraib scandal at the direction of Secretary Powell, Wilkerson came to the conclusion that, as he put it, "this is a radical government. It is radical in ways that makes it very dangerous. If someone wasn't taking it on frontally, it was needed."[88] Despite his strong criticisms, the White House didn't attack him after his "cabal" speech because, he surmised, "Powell gave me cover. Perhaps they were afraid I was speaking for Powell." Secretary Powell's stature and popularity made him a threat to the administration and the most untouchable of potential White House policy critics. Wilkerson's remark underscores the sensitivity with which the White House treated Powell. In Wilkerson's case, intraparty loyalties combined with a technocratic character gave him room to criticize without retaliation.

While some might admire the strength of Wilkerson's convictions, others might find his timing problematic. He gave his speech in 2005, not 2003, when it might have made a greater difference. Internal splits within the dominant political party are often muted and sometimes come too late to affect the course of events. But the rules of the Washington press game guarantee that such splits are one of the few ways that debate can make the front pages and critical ideas gain a wider hearing. As noted earlier, the legislative effort of Senator John McCain to reaffirm American commitment to its laws and treaties concerning enemy detainees not only brought the issue of torture more squarely into the news—it forced Mr. Bush to squirm within the fractured reality of simultaneously denying that his administration had approved torture while opposing the legislation, and finally being forced politically to accept it and shake hands (healing the power rift) with McCain. What is consistent through all of these episodes is that the news was driven by the dictates of power and the daily adjustments and perturbations within the Washington consensus.

The Washington Power Game: From Corleone to Consensus Politics

In this chapter we have tried to illustrate how the tactical elements of news source management combined with the long-existing culture of consensus in Washington journalism to support the questionable governing methods of the Bush administration. The result was years of news about one of America's most historic and dubious political adventures that avoided political accountability issues not formally addressed by the government itself. To the administration, reality could be bent to the will of power, and power was exercised by active news management—even news *production*—and intimidation. The intent was to create a reality that supported the administration's desires and dreams, no matter how far-flung from material reality they were. Greenhouse gases don't cause global warming; death and carnage in Iraq are signs of progress; and the physical abuse of prisoners at Abu Ghraib and elsewhere—right up to the threshold of organ failure—wasn't torture. And too often, the Washington press went along with the story.

But the failure of accountability is not borne by the press alone. In a robust democracy, opposition parties offer alternative policy positions while critiquing the party in government. For most or all of the twenty-first century, the Democratic Party has failed to meet its responsibilities as the opposition party. Even in the aftermath of the Bush administration's inept handling of Hurricane Katrina, and the mounting casualties and growing chaos in Iraq, Democrats seemed incapable of identifying a coherent political strategy or unifying message.[89] Into this vacuum stepped forward, on occasion, a handful of dissenters with the courage of conviction to speak out, but not the institutional legs to create a sustainable alternative narrative of national politics. An occasional speech by a Lawrence Wilkerson or a column by a Brent Scowcroft or a John Shalikashvili cannot by themselves sustain a counterframe. As significant as Richard Clarke's trifecta—60 *Minutes,* a bestseller, and the 9/11 Commission— was, it could not take the place of a political party.

Of course, there is probably only so much that can be expected from the minority political party when it so seriously lacks institutional power. Outnumbered and continually outmaneuvered in Congress, and hamstrung by the post-9/11 culture of patriotism and fear, the Democrats offered little sign of the power momentum to which the press typically hitches its news coverage—reminding us that the weaknesses and failures of the press are often part and parcel of the weaknesses and failures of the larger political system. We take up the enduring problems of the press, the political system, and government accountability next.

6

Toward an Independent Press

A Standard for Public Accountability

Dear Mr. President:

We heard you loud and clear Friday when you visited our devastated city and the Gulf Coast and said, "What is not working, we're going to make it right." Please forgive us if we wait to see proof of your promise before believing you. But we have good reason for our skepticism. . . . Every official at the Federal Emergency Management Agency should be fired, Director Michael Brown especially. In a nationally televised interview Thursday night, he said his agency hadn't known until that day that thousands of storm victims were stranded at the Ernest N. Morial Convention Center. He gave another nationally televised interview the next morning and said, "We've provided food to the people at the Convention Center so that they've gotten at least one, if not two meals, every single day." . . . Lies don't get more bald-faced than that, Mr. President. Yet, when you met with Mr. Brown Friday morning, you told him, "You're doing a heck of a job." . . . That's unbelievable.

OPEN LETTER TO PRESIDENT BUSH PUBLISHED BY THE
EDITORS OF THE *New Orleans Times-Picayune*,
SEPTEMBER 4, 2005

It was a tough week in America, but an inspired one for the press. Reporters from many news organizations made it to New Orleans as a level 5 hurricane closed in on the city in late August 2005. Intrepid journalists broadcast live reports of the storm, the flood, the human suffering, and the failure of government officials to comprehend and respond to the disaster. NBC anchor Brian Williams won a Peabody Award along with NBC News for coverage that began on August 28. On that day their crew arrived at the Superdome, where thousands of storm evacuees were gathering for shelter. Williams noted in his blog that he had received en route to New Orleans a National Weather Service report on his Blackberry that seemed so dire that he urged his colleagues to verify its authenticity:

166

```
URGENT-WEATHER MESSAGE
-----------------------------------------------------------------------------------------
NATIONAL WEATHER SERVICE NEW ORLEANS LA
1011 AM CDT SUN AUG 28 2005
    . . . DEVASTATING DAMAGE EXPECTED . . .
HURRICANE KATRINA . . . A MOST POWERFUL HURRICANE WITH
UNPRECEDENTED STRENGTH . . . RIVALING THE INTENSITY OF
HURRICANE CAMILLE OF 1969.
MOST OF THE AREA WILL BE UNINHABITABLE FOR WEEKS . . .
PERHAPS LONGER.
AT LEAST HALF OF WELL CONSTRUCTED HOMES WILL HAVE ROOF
AND WALL FAILURE. ALL GABLED ROOFS WILL FAIL . . . ALL
WOOD FRAMED LOW RISING APARTMENT BUILDINGS WILL BE DE-
STROYED . . . ALL WINDOWS WILL BE BLOWN OUT.
THE VAST MAJORITY . . . OF TREES WILL BE SNAPPED OR UP-
ROOTED. ONLY THE HEARTIEST WILL REMAIN STANDING . . .
BUT BE TOTALLY DEFOLIATED.
POWER OUTAGES WILL LAST FOR WEEKS . . . AS MOST POWER
POLES WILL BE DOWN AND TRANSFORMERS DESTROYED. WATER
SHORTAGES WILL MAKE HUMAN SUFFERING INCREDIBLE BY MOD-
ERN STANDARDS.
```

New Orleans mayor Ray Nagin was one official who heeded the warning. Calling Katrina the storm that everyone had long feared, he ordered the city to be evacuated and opened large public facilities such as the Superdome and the Morial Convention Center to house those who could not leave. By the next day, August 29, the storm surge breached the city levees and New Orleans began flooding. Eighty percent of the city was underwater by August 31.

When NPR's Robert Siegel interviewed Homeland Security Secretary Michael Chertoff on September 1, he asked how long before aid would reach the thousands stranded in the convention center. Chertoff referred to heroic efforts to reach evacuees in the Superdome, and continued to refer to the dome and not the convention center throughout the interview. Siegel inquired whether Chertoff even knew of the plight of the center's stranded thousands. Chertoff admonished Siegel and his listeners not to listen to rumors. Siegel bristled, saying that his reporter was a veteran of wars and disasters and was not reporting rumors. By the end of the interview, it was clear that Chertoff was not aware of much that was going on in New Orleans, yet continued assuring Siegel that aid was being delivered.[1]

That night, Michael Brown, director of the Federal Emergency Management Agency, was interviewed by Ted Koppel on ABC's *Nightline*, and seemed equally unaware of what was happening in the city. Brown admitted that he had just learned earlier that day about evacuees stranded in the convention center. Koppel noted that the news media had been giving live reports on the deteriorating situation for two days, and asked incredulously, "Don't you guys watch television? Don't you guys listen to the radio?" He then berated the official for waiting five days to get to the point of talking about help that might be delivered in the next couple of days.[2]

When Brian Williams interviewed Brown earlier on September 1, he opened his report with an awkward signal to the audience that he felt compelled to move beyond his customary role as a journalist who would normally defer to officials. He opened with the odd disclaimer, "Well, however fair this is," and noted that he had known Michael Brown for some time. He then introduced his new function by saying, "But tonight, really, my role is viewers' advocate and for the folks here." He then asked Brown why the helicopters flying overhead all day couldn't be used to drop water, food, and medical supplies to the stranded survivors in the convention center. Brown admitted that he had just learned about the crisis there and promised to get relief to those people soon. Williams closed with the admonition, "Sir: The folks here and watching are going to hold you accountable to those words."[3]

Whether on radio, TV, or in the papers, journalists were suddenly and surprisingly taking adversarial positions with officials, and even informing those officials about the realities of the situation at hand. This was indeed a rare reversal of the more familiar pattern of reporting official accounts of situations that journalists often know are being spun to gain political advantage. It was a heady moment. Everywhere one tuned, there seemed to be an impassioned journalist expressing public outrage and seeking to hold officials accountable. One news account of this rare moment noted, "There were so many angry, even incredulous, questions put to Bush administration officials about the response to Katrina that the Salon Web site compiled a 'Reporters Gone Wild' video clip. Tim Russert, Anderson Cooper, Ted Koppel and Shepard Smith were among the stars."[4] Brian

Williams even told his audience that Katrina might change the nature of journalism, which had been marked by too much dependence on those in power to define the news.[5]

As it happened, the news system was not so easy to turn around, even with the best intentions of individual journalists. Slowly but surely, familiar patterns settled back in. The daily routines of press politics were reestablished. Michael Brown resigned, hearings were held, mistakes were acknowledged, and Congress poured money into damaged areas along the Gulf Coast. Yet Katrina does tell us something about what it takes to create a moment of truly independent press coverage: White House communication and spin operations were shut down (the entire top tier of the administration had been literally on vacation when the hurricane struck); officials were not even aware of a critical situation; journalists were on the scene to see the devastation for themselves, and had the technical capacity to show that reality directly to viewers (Brian Williams even dispatched a photo of the damaged Superdome taken on his cell phone); and reporters had just enough access to critical officials to keep the news accounts from appearing overly partisan or crusading. In short, journalists had entered the eye of a no-spin zone. But it was just a matter of time before the official mechanisms that routinely generate and spin the news were again fully geared up to reestablish the normal dependence that characterizes the press-government relationship.

Yet even in the early stages of this exceptional case, the Katrina story took on familiar patterns. While some news organizations such as the *Times-Picayune* at the epicenter of the disaster felt emboldened to challenge the president independently,[6] most began searching for official sources that would express critical positions—and there were plenty willing to do so. We gathered a sample of *New York Times* news articles about Hurricane Katrina that also mentioned Michael Brown, FEMA, or President Bush and were published between August 29 and September 7. The impressive yield of 133 articles included 46 that contained specific mentions of government failure or incompetence. However, only 8 of those instances in which the government's response to the disaster was criticized lacked a corroborating statement from a state, local, or national official.[7]

Toward the end of that first week after Katrina struck, the *Times* devoted a lengthy analysis piece to the revival of the Democratic Party as an organization capable of challenging the administration, stating that the "Democrats offered what was shaping up as the most concerted attack that they had mounted on the White House in the five years of the Bush presidency."[8] The article contained quotations from the House minority leader, the party's 2004 presidential and vice presidential candidates, the party national chair, and various senators, along with rebukes from Republican leaders. The power analysis that guided the narrative asserted that the Democrats felt emboldened to criticize the Mr. Bush's competence because many Republicans had broken ranks and joined the chorus of critics, and because the minority party felt comfortable with an issue that would not draw fire about their patriotism, as would the war in Iraq or the War on Terror. Thus, the *Times* revealed implicit assessments of Washington power balances and political gamesmanship as the key underlying factors that drove the story. In our view, it was that same assessment that controlled the news gates as the story developed. Within a week of the disaster, however, the news had begun to reestablish familiar journalistic patterns of assessing balances of power and bending the definition of issues according to the institutional forces that manage them.

Why Can't the Press Be Independent All the Time?

If Katrina is the exception to press dependence that proves the rule, we need to examine why the U.S. press system reverts so readily to its deference toward the most powerful actors in government to craft their definitions of reality. Nearly all the indicators tell us that the press guides its coverage along the lines of power in government at key institutional decision-making points that set the course of policy. The steering mechanism that keeps coverage on course in between those decisive moments when policies are challenged or reaffirmed is the inside-the-Beltway consensus discussed in chapter 5. Insider conventional wisdom about the realities of power is heavily shaped by government communications officers and their public relations agents, whose primary targets are other officials and journalists.

The sheer weight of this preoccupation with power acts as a daily minder for reigning in any challenges from the press. For example, *Times* reporter Elizabeth Bumiller was asked at a public forum on the first anniversary of the war why journalists were so docile at President Bush's press conference on the eve of the U.S. invasion of Iraq, given the weakness (and, ultimately, the systematic wrongness) of the administration's rationale for the war. She cited the inhibiting weight of challenging power in the context of the perceived inevitability of history:

> I think we were very deferential, because in the East Room press conference, it's live. It's very intense. It's frightening to stand up there. I mean, think about it. You are standing up on prime time live television, asking the president of the United States a question when the country is about to go to war. There was a very serious, somber tone that evening, and I think it made—and you know, nobody wanted to get into an argument with the president at this very serious time. It had a very heavy feeling of history to it, that press conference.[9]

Challenging the president on the eve of war may have been an imposing prospect, but there were many missed opportunities before that point that were avoided on other grounds of deference to power. As reality bends through the prism of power, those in authority become emboldened to believe their own fantasies, misperceptions, and follies. This is the timeless lesson of history.

The core preoccupation with power and partisan gamesmanship is largely what turns citizens off about their own government and the news messengers who seem implicated in the game. In this view of politics, citizens are reduced to being spectators in often unpleasant contests of political advantage that seldom involve perspectives beyond those introduced strategically and methodically by powerful players trying to use their institutional positions to gain advantage. The skeptical reader may say that since this is what politics is all about, why should the press hide it from view? To this, the reader concerned about democracy might counter with: why, in the face of ill-considered policies (of the sort that continued to play out in Iraq and the War on Terror), and a cowed opposition, should the press become a conduit for government propaganda? This not-uncommon result fuels critics such as Edward Herman and Noam Chomsky, who proclaim that the corporate-minded press is nothing more than a propaganda outlet for the state.[10] Our view is that it is a bit more complicated than this. Indeed, on those occasions when democracy is working relatively well, with diverse factions publicly debating policies with different considerations about the public interest, the news gates open to more diverse viewpoints. Yet in those moments when power exercises its corrupting effects and government officials choose not to correct the problem, the press indeed functions as though it were an information ministry. As media scholar Robert McChesney puts it,

> Journalists who question agreed-upon assumptions by the political elite stigmatize themselves as unprofessional and political. Most major U.S. wars over the past century have been sold to the public on dubious claims if not outright lies, yet professional journalism has generally failed to warn the public. Compare the press coverage leading up to the Spanish-American War, which is a notorious example of yellow journalism—before the advent of professional journalism—to the coverage leading up to the 2003 Iraq war and it is difficult to avoid the conclusion that the quality of reporting has not changed much.[11]

This strangely encumbered system of press politics that characterizes American democracy today depends so much on insider perceptions of power to define the news reality that it is hard for the press to activate what Entman refers to as a "cascade" of challenging views from lesser sources.[12] This difficulty with inserting other credible evidence into news coverage applies most of the time, so that government, for whatever reason, has proved incapable of policing itself. In keeping with this overarching rule, even the critical journalism that characterized the latter stages of the Vietnam War was driven by continuing challenges issued by mid-level administration officials, active-duty military officers, and important factions in the Democratic Party breaking with the Johnson administration's war policy and planning. Only when the inside-the-Beltway consensus shifted and the "sphere of legitimate controversy" expanded did media coverage more strongly reflect the war's critics.[13] Numerous examples since Vietnam illustrate the same pattern, from coverage of the first Gulf War and other U.S. military forays to the savings and loan debacle of the 1990s.[14]

The Consequences: One-Sided Realities and Credibility Gaps

The prospect of the disintegration of Iraq into the mother of all failed states was, of course, what deterred George W. Bush's father (and his

advisers, who included Colin Powell) from taking Baghdad during the
Gulf War of 1991. Unfortunately, the junior Bush's efforts to somehow
complete his father's mission went awry. But few in government and thus
few among its press monitors challenged what, at its inception, seemed
to be a dubious rationale that linked the Iraq foray to the War on Terror.
Despite their availability, similarly few credible sources were offered sustained news space to challenge the perverse post-Vietnam plot twist of a
reverse domino theory in which democracy would spring forth throughout a region with precious little experience or even desire for it.

Sources challenging the Bush administration's reality gap existed,
but many would-be critics (for example, most Democrats) had so compromised themselves with their silence at the outset of the war that they
risked denunciation as weak fair-weather patriots and liberal wafflers.
The reason that these otherwise banal denunciations prove so withering
for the Democrats is due, in part, to the fact that the press brings them
centrally into the story, and thus subtly shifts the entire terms of debate.
And so the hapless Democrats seemed even less newsworthy in moments
such as when Wisconsin senator Russ Feingold introduced a resolution to
censure the president for violating the law and citizens' rights by tapping
the personal phone calls of Americans.[15] The only movement in the party
was a mad rush away from being associated with the initiative. The result
was that Feingold was branded a "maverick" by the *Washington Post* headline accompanying the story. A *New York Times* account, placed on page 11,
gave the Senate's one-day censure hearing little play and, while highlighting the political plusses and minuses for Republicans and Democrats of a
possible censure vote, duly noted in the lead paragraph that the hearings
would go nowhere. Yet a poll conducted at the same time showed that
52% of the public felt that Congress should initiate an impeachment inquiry if it turned out that the president had wiretapped American citizens
without approval of a judge.[16]

Meanwhile, after being granted a year to prepare its public defense of
its eavesdropping program by the *New York Times'* decision to not publish
its story on the matter, the Bush administration characteristically went on
the offense. The news media dutifully reported the administration's view
that it did not need judicial authorization in light of constitutional powers allegedly reserved for presidents in wartime—an opinion provided by
Alberto Gonzales, who had been promoted to attorney general following

his creative legal work as White House counsel during the Abu Ghraib scandal, helping to redefine the torture of foreign prisoners. Throughout this and other challenging moments of the administration, the press seemed consistently unable to do much more than record these novel legal rationales for the record.

And so, as the domestic spying story unfolded, official voices rapidly took over the narration of events, and the news lost its critical edge. With Republicans fully in power and Democrats in retreat, there seemed to be little interest within government or among news organizations in pursuing charges of high crimes against the Bush administration. Thus, the story took twisted paths through government institutions bent more on making problems disappear from the news than addressing them on their merits. As a result, the nation saw a few Democrats calling weakly for hearings, again reflecting the party's lack of news-making prowess and its uncanny inability to send a message to challenge an increasingly vulnerable president. Meanwhile, the Republicans awkwardly discussed retroactive legislation to enable whatever the president had done, while admitting that even this solution would prove difficult since they were in the dark about what his deeds actually were. In the end, the domestic spying story, like Abu Ghraib before it, veered away from underlying issues of lawbreaking by the government and possible damage to core values of American democracy, disappearing into the news thicket of power and politics.

During the long arc of the Iraq story, many other voices, of course, were heard for a typically brief time in the news. Some dissenters were less, and others more successful at surviving the withering fire of the administration, as epitomized by challengers like Joseph Wilson and Richard Clarke. Overall, however, remarkably few newsworthy critics who stepped forward could trigger sustained independent news challenges to the growing number of weak links in core administration stories. Journalism's commitment to its prime operating rule of driving stories through the sources and institutional processes of government power is particularly interesting, given the steady erosion of public support for the war throughout 2005 and 2006.

It is clear that the almost daily episodic news reports describing the mayhem and lack of progress on basic reconstruction plans in Iraq, along with the rising price of gasoline and soaring budget deficits at home, all took their toll on support for the president's handling of the situation in

Iraq. For example, *Newsweek* polls conducted by Princeton Research Associates showed that approval had dipped below 40% after the spring of 2005 and had fallen toward 30% by early 2006. An ABC News–*Washington Post* poll showed that by the summer of 2006, a solid 64% felt that the Bush administration had no clear plan for handling the situation in Iraq. (A like number in that poll also felt the same way about the Democrats, but the *Newsweek* poll showed that a significant plurality would still prefer the Democrats to have a chance to handle it.) Perhaps the most damning opinion trend was the 53% majority registered by the summer of 2006 in a CBS–*New York Times* poll saying that Iraq would never become a democracy. Consistent with this judgment, over 60% of respondents in *Newsweek* polls taken in mid-2006 said that the war in Iraq had not made the world safer from terrorism, and the bottom-line conclusion was that the war was not worth fighting.[17]

Washington news that is indexed to power is troubling, whether it shapes or defies public opinion trends. While it seems likely that the administration's bold news management helped bolster public support for entering into a war on questionable pretenses, that support later fell away, even as the news continued to take its cues from the highest levels of government. Our overall point here is not that the dominant narrative in the news always shapes opinion, particularly over long periods of time when that narrative is at odds with available evidence. It is well established that people have many points of reference for their opinions as situations develop over time and begin to hit home in direct ways.[18] Rather, our main point is that the press remained so slavishly committed to reporting an increasingly unbelievable story. As explained below, this association with often implausible government narratives may contribute to the loss of public confidence in the press—a trend that has become entwined with the spiraling decline of confidence in Congress and the executive branch of government in recent years (with an understandable but brief rebound following 9/11).

Adhering to such a limiting standard of accountability does not mean that reporting is easy. Indeed, journalists are often uncomfortably constrained by their own process, and express many signs of longing for more substance in the stories they cover. In their best moments, leading news organizations offered up possible openings for cascades of political challenges to break out, as happened in the first two weeks of the Abu

Ghraib case (as well as in the continued probing by the *Times*, for example, regarding U.S. detention policies) and the occasional investigative reports about the Bush administration's lack of planning for the war. At each of those junctures, however, the press generally "balanced" the voices of critics with the (dominant) voices of top officials; pegged its reporting to government processes (often dominated by a unified Republican leadership)—and then characteristically stepped back and allowed these same political forces to take over narrating the story.

Ironically, the main source of eventual change in the story about the war came, though grudgingly, from inside the Bush administration itself. By 2006, the daily reports of bombings, beheadings, and rising violence in Iraq—coupled with the prospect that an unpopular war had become an election issue—all finally seemed to put too much strain on the long-running administration story that things were going better in Iraq than they seemed. An administration not known for its learning curve seemed to be taking a modest reality check. Among the early signs of gradual story change was Defense Secretary Rumsfeld's acceptance of the reality of an Iraqi "insurgency," a term that suggests something more than his and Vice President Cheney's earlier references to a few dead-enders and foreign terrorists causing the unrest, done to dismiss the nightly scenes of televised violence. The idea of an insurgency suggested an organized resistance against the U.S. military occupation and the Iraqi government, which might imply the need to consider a different military strategy. But the insurgency story line, too, lagged well behind the reality curve. Ongoing episodic news reports surrounding the administration's efforts to impose meaning on the violence described large numbers of sectarian killings, along with suggestions that the violence stemmed from militias and death squads associated with Iraqi government and military officials and police. And so, in testimony before Congress in August 2006, Generals Pace and Abizaid—flanked by a nearly silent Rumsfeld—finally acknowledged that civil war in Iraq was all but at hand.[19]

Once this even newer version of the story was given such high-level official sanction, the news gates could again open a bit wider. As before, however, the story change came well after it had been available for independent reporting that might challenge the administration to address important aspects of the situation it was clearly ignoring.[20] In these and other ways, the grand irony of the U.S. press system is that what may be the world's freest press suffers the (largely accurate) popular perception that press and government are tethered together in ways that may undermine public confidence in both. This may be the greatest cost to democracy in the entire journalistic process.

Press Dependence and the Loss of Public Confidence

The press-politics system that produces this kind of news is so inward-looking that it threatens to sever the government from the people. Indeed, because the focus among Washington players is on partisan positioning and political advantage, the Democrats gained relatively little public esteem from the Bush administration's failings. And, as long as the press reports mainly on the political game, the citizenry is marginalized, and the players remain bound by a strange code of public relations–driven politics that permits little movement beyond the bounds of the Washington consensus of the moment.

Meanwhile, citizens' groups must fight to get into this picture. They have a far greater chance of getting their views into the news when the institutions are divided on issues, as has been the case on abortion policy for the past several decades. On other issues, as we described in the last chapter, newsmakers with a power advantage are often able to suppress opposition by challenging the patriotism, fiscal responsibility, or toughness of potential challengers: conditions under which fruitful public deliberation in the news generally disappears. This closed news scenario means that citizens' organizations or policy experts outside government seldom lead public debates on the issues.[21] The result for many consequential issues is that most individual citizens seldom receive independent perspectives that are framed clearly enough so that they might assess leading policy initiatives independent of journalistic prejudgment about where the political momentum is heading. This scenario often produces hasty and ill-considered policy. The quagmire in Iraq and the deterioration of the War on Terror into potentially counterproductive activities such as torture, illegal detention, and domestic spying stand as painful evidence of this.

These judgments are not ours alone. At the time of this writing, majorities of Americans had turned against the president, his war, and his general handling of international affairs, as had world opinion.[22] But the bitter experience of once again being fed a diet of propaganda—passed from calculating (and ultimately inept) politicians through the compliant press to the public—only adds to the public's acquired distaste for politics and the press. The puzzle, of course, is why a free press has no publicly articulated accountability standard of its own to guide it in such politically charged situations.

The adage that history repeats itself is based in part on predictable institutional patterns and behaviors. The press system in the United States is so uniformly organized across mainstream news organizations that it qualifies as an institution: the media, when it comes to news, is singular.[23] Though journalists would point to their vigorous competition to get the news first as evidence to the contrary, they also often freely admit that the competition is generally limited to tidbits such as exclusive interviews with inside sources or a scrap of inside information that nobody else got. In matters of press-government relations, then, history becomes strikingly patterned. At some point, the press pack will turn against the hand that feeds it, but only when all the conditions are in place to question whether those in power still hold a grip on their own policies.

Thus, one can safely predict that the occurrence of some catastrophic failure or alarming signals of electoral outrage would eventually trigger a cascade of political challenges and a press feeding frenzy that might change the course of government policy. During the Vietnam War, for example, the challenges came swiftly and furiously following the Tet offensive and alarming signs that U.S. troops no longer could distinguish friend from foe and had begun to fire upon civilians. Parallels in Iraq built up for years behind the leaky dam of government spin and press compliance. For example, the U.S. killing of civilians in Haditha, Iraq, might have become the My Lai of the Iraq War, if the will to pursue it had emerged on the part of either the Bush administration or the press. But again, the lack of an independent press standard of public accountability means that the dam might burst too late to avert disaster or give the public confidence in their governing institutions.

The crucial consequence of reporting important issues refracted along the lines of power politics is that it becomes difficult to have a focused national conversation about whether the assertions of those sources deemed most newsworthy by the press are true, realistic, or in the public interest. It also becomes difficult to know collectively—although one might suspect that many citizens consider this privately—whether the ideals of democracy are endangered, or what to do about it if they are. Is the law whatever the president says it is, as long as there is no opposition to challenge him? How would the people know otherwise?

The reigning system of press deference to political power is deeply ingrained. But perhaps the press could operate one degree of separation farther from their reference point of simply letting the current balance of power in Washington effectively settle our public understandings of important issues. How might this occur?

What Standard of Accountability Might the Press Adopt?

Why should the press stake its precious position in the public sphere so close to the sphere of government power? After all, the "watchdog" role of holding the government and other social institutions accountable to independent public-interest standards is a widely accepted ideal for the U.S. press (even though, as we discuss below, it has proved difficult for the press as presently organized to attain). Even the simple ideal of objectivity might enable the press to stand further apart from the government it monitors. However, the routines of news production often bear little resemblance to the watchdog ideal, while the hallowed journalistic tradition of "objectivity" often becomes confused with deference to authority and power.

The confusion about standards of political accountability starts with the implicit journalistic shortcut that assumes that reporting to the citizenry what those at the center of power are doing is the most reasonable and unassailable thing to do. After all, the people elected the government, and if they don't like what it is doing, let the people fix it. As we know, however, this is a dim hope in an age of distracted citizens who feel manipulated and cut off from the government by the very news that is offered as their primary civic tool for understanding it. However, setting the news agenda independently, while producing a refreshing diversity of information, would also bring noisy criticisms of bias and crusading—from the very same powerful officials who have come to depend on the current news system as a tool of public relations and governance. This curious confusion of objectivity with power is so profound that journalists who depart from narratives reported by the rest of the press pack are typically challenged by their editors for not getting the story right. The power angle in mainstream news reporting means that policies lacking opposition from opponents deemed capable of actually influencing or defeating them are seldom given sustained public attention by the press.

Press deference to power is deeply engrained and continually reinforced in the culture and routines of mainstream journalism. Indeed, the institutional approach to the news media that we take in this book emphasizes the organizational and political forces that produce and maintain the particular style of journalism practiced in the United States. The lesson of that analysis is that there are no easy fixes for recurring institutionalized patterns of behavior.

Nevertheless, we are also struck by a peculiarity of this system of press politics: journalistic deference to power is almost entirely voluntary. While there are identifiable empirical reasons why the press often bends to power, it is also clear that when they choose to, journalists are willing and able to stand up to authority. What is needed, we contend, is a news standard that can better guide journalists and the public, particularly in those moments when political power is lopsided and government is bent on constructing a reality narrative seemingly at odds with the facts and even with the democratic system itself. When other institutions fail to set the factual record straight, vet major policies, or observe the rule of law, shouldn't the news media more readily or reliably step in to hold their feet to the fire? According to the reigning professional code of mainstream journalism, the answer is no—or more precisely, only if and when those in government take up that challenge first. As is, journalists seem to see their duty as "raising questions"—usually the questions that those in power are already raising—and then stepping back to allow the officials in charge to sink or spin. Too often, government gets by with spin rather than with genuine responses, thus undermining political accountability in between elections, and reducing the chances of accountability at election time.

In approaching an improved accountability standard for the press, it is possible—and crucial—to identify goals that are consistent with existing journalistic ideals and press performance principles that resonate with national tradition and values. Perhaps the greatest irony—and tragedy— of the press patterns we have analyzed here is that they violate many journalists' own beliefs about the purposes of their profession. In their interviews with hundreds of American journalists, media critics and former journalists Bill Kovach and Tom Rosenstiel found strong agreement that journalism must (among other things) serve as an independent monitor of power and provide a forum for public scrutiny of officials.[24]

At least three coherent ideals already exist from which to build an improved accountability standard: the traditional model of the press as an institutional watchdog; the long-standing notion of the press as a marketplace of ideas; and the newer (and ironically controversial) model of civic or public journalism. As noted in the next section, each of these is resonant with American traditions, and though each faces serious challenges, each model offers principles and standards worth reinvigorating in contemporary journalism.

To suggest this reevaluation of journalistic ideals reminds us that even the best efforts to address press standards creatively have been fraught with difficulty in the past—not least because journalism remains more art than science, making a clear standard difficult to construct. Moreover, since journalism is not (for good First Amendment reasons) a licensed profession, a new standard of accountability would, of course, prove difficult to enforce. Yet journalism arrived at its current set of standards through a fairly focused self-examination process early in the last century. It is time for another self-examination that looks squarely at the issues of political accountability and dependence on those in power. Without a serious reexamination of its current practices in light of American journalism's higher ideals, the press will find itself caught again and again in the same dilemmas, while the public—and perhaps American democracy itself—loses out.

The last grand effort to address the role of the press in democracy was the Hutchins Commission, which met in the 1940s at a time of considerable change in both the news media and the American state. Termed a "magnificent failure" by media scholar Stephen Bates, the commission had its origins at a board meeting of the *Encyclopaedia Britannica,* where *Time* publisher Henry Luce and his old friend, University of Chicago president Robert Hutchins, had the following exchange of notes:

> *Luce:* How do I find out about the freedom of the press and what my obligations are?
> *Hutchins:* I don't know.

Luce: Well, why don't we set up a commission on freedom of the press and find out what it is?

Hutchins: If you'll put up the money, I'll organize the committee.[25]

Blue ribbon in its makeup and lofty in its ambitions, the commission produced a report that was at once eerily prescient in its strong concerns about media consolidation and the diminishing sense of social responsibility, and curiously weak in its recommendations for a watchdog journalism that was somehow to be established through market-based solutions and self-regulating citizen press councils.[26] Media historian Victor Pickard describes the commission and its legacy as follows:

> By the mid 1940s a media crisis was unfolding not unlike the one we're experiencing today. Concerns over propaganda, overt commercialism and concentrated ownership led to questions about the democratic role of the press. . . . The members of the commission concluded early on that media were simultaneously becoming more powerful and more commercialized. Focusing on ways to make the press more democratic and responsible, their initial critique and recommendations were fairly radical. For example, Archibald MacLeish argued that public access to media was paramount and thus the press should be treated as a common carrier. William Hocking compared the news to the public education system, arguing that neither should be left to the profit-driven whims of the marketplace . . . Harold Lasswell suggested that one-newspaper towns should be protected by content regulation based on a public utility model. They also considered increasing competition by aiding start-up newspapers through government subsidies.
>
> These more radical proposals gradually faded from the discussion once the commissioners faced the question of enforcement. By the time the final report came out in early 1947, much of the original fiery language and radical proposals had been removed. The report did identify three core tasks for the press: provide information; enlighten the public; and serve as a government watchdog. But the fear of state involvement in the media led the commission to trust the news industry's good will in self-regulating, though failure to self-correct, they suggested, would merit state intervention. As a halfway measure,

they recommended an autonomous citizens council to issue annual reports on press performance.

Despite its arguably toothless prescriptions, industry response to the Hutchins Report was fierce and quick. . . . Under the headline "A Free Press (Hitler Style) Sought for U.S.," the Chicago Tribune condemned the report as a "major effort in the campaign of a determined group of totalitarian thinkers . . . to discredit the free press of America . . . who are composed entirely of men who have left-wing, Socialist convictions ranging from New Deal pink to Communist red."

So, though the Report was dismissed by industry and to some extent forgotten, it did articulate what was later dubbed "the social responsibility theory of the press." Many of its tenets were seamlessly incorporated into Journalism-school textbooks, codifying for the first time a direct link between freedom of the press and social responsibility.[27]

The time seems ripe for another national conversation about these issues of press independence and standards of accountability.[28] News audiences are dwindling, a reflection of the public's lost confidence in the press as an institution, and journalists as a profession.[29] While some journalists may argue that it is impossible to satisfy fickle and increasingly polarized audiences, this argument misses the point that the press may be actively contributing to own its death spiral by failing to embrace a clear standard of public responsibility or accountability. Media scholar Thomas Patterson has found that the predominant style of news today, which is quick to pounce on politicians' minor gaffes and wrongdoings but light on substance, is driving away news audiences. The sensationalized soft news that "passes for watchdog journalism," he contends, "needs to give way to a more credible form of journalism," a type of journalism that neither ignores official wrongdoing nor "turn[s] the media agenda over to the newsmakers."[30]

Indeed, the loss of public confidence may be caused in part by the press's inconsistency in challenging those in power on important issues, its inability to keep many investigative reports in the news long enough to engage public attention, and its inability to prevent bending those reports through the prism of power when they do continue to make the news. And while fear of public reproach may sap the will for change among the press, there is little evidence to suggest that change could do more harm than maintaining the status quo. Media scholars Timothy Cook and Paul Gronke offer a hopeful point of departure by noting that while Americans disdain the insider posturing and the ritualistic adversarialism that mark the current media culture on display in the news, most genuinely endorse an independent press that raises real questions about the substance of public policy.[31]

Another indicator that the time is ripe for open deliberation about the role of the press in democracy is the unprecedented public reaction to proposed rule changes by the Federal Communications Commission in 2003 that would have allowed greater consolidation of media ownership in even fewer hands. Despite very little news coverage, and spurred in part by activist organizations devoted to rolling back increasing economic concentration in the media industry, citizens of many political stripes helped pressure Congress to block the proposal.[32] As heartening as this level of public participation may be, what is needed now is not just a hard look at the economic regulations (or lack thereof) that shape the news media's underlying corporate structure, but also a serious discussion of the norms and routines that tethered the news to political power long before today's era of hyperconcentrated media. While increasing bottom-line pressures certainly have done little to improve the quality of the news, they are not the only reason the news falls short.

An ironic challenge to press reform is that the American news media's relative freedom and autonomy create an ongoing dilemma of decision making. Media "freedom" seems to require that no strings be attached to First Amendment protections. Yet without some shared standard of accountability to guide them through the government's ongoing attempts to manage the news, the media's power to decide what's news risks deterioration into merely echoing the safe contours of the Washington consensus.[33] Sociologist Michael Schudson has suggested that the lack of a clear accountability standard may be one of the curiously defining qualities of the American press.[34] A survey of press standards in the world's democracies indicates so many alternative models with competing virtues and shortcomings that it is hard to know how to proceed in the abstract.[35] This is why we recommend starting with a consideration of ideas and values that are already consistent with the American tradition, and that have been partially incorporated (albeit with limited success) in previous eras of journalistic crisis and self-examination.

Since American political culture has displayed such abiding faith in the hidden hand of providence as guided by the Constitution, we begin by noting that any attempt to challenge the marketplace basis of the American media and their First Amendment protections seems a nonstarter. We note, however, that earlier historic moments have flirted with such variations on the free-marketplace model as government protection of the public interest, press commitments to play the watchdog in public life, and press efforts to report news guided by greater public input into the news agenda.

Models of Press Performance: The Watchdog, Civic Journalism, and the Marketplace of Ideas

One of the best-known and most often invoked ideals of press performance in the United States is the notion of the press acting as a "watchdog" or even as a "fourth branch" of government that checks and balances the other three. This ideal envisions the press keeping a skeptical eye trained on the government, guarding the public's interest and protecting it from misinformation, incompetence, and corruption. According to this ideal, the press holds the government to account on the public's behalf—a key rationale for the freedom the press has been granted under the Constitution. Supreme Court justice Potter Stewart stated this expectation in formal terms when he argued that the First Amendment's free-press clause was intended to enhance the "organized, expert scrutiny of government" by the press, and "to create a fourth institution outside the Government as an additional check on the three official branches." [36]

This view of the media's responsibilities to the public is not necessarily supported by many corporate owners, who see profits to shareholders as their primary responsibility. As window dressing for the more pressing incentives of making profits and maintaining minimal government regulation, one routinely hears impassioned defenses of the "marketplace of ideas." Despite its more cynical uses by corporate media lobbyists, the marketplace ideal has deep roots in American political thought and First Amendment jurisprudence: the ideal that the media should provide robust public debate among a diversity of views so that the "best" or "truest" ideas can rise to the top and societal consensus on public issues can emerge. [37] The allusion to free-market economic theory is deliberate, since this model envisions the free exchange of ideas among privately owned media as the best regulator of truth and effective public deliberation.[38] As with the watchdog ideal, the marketplace ideal is frequently invoked as a rationale for press freedom: The press must be free from government control so that the public has access to wide-ranging debate that will allow it to choose among competing political leaders and policy options.

While both the watchdog and marketplace models resonate strongly with American ideals, both have proved difficult for the news media to live up to. There have been times in history when the market conditions seemed better suited to more diverse and lively public debates than today. Indeed, earlier eras have witnessed a comparatively vibrant marketplace of ideas in which no single block of mainstream media operated in unison to restrict public debate. For example, the turn of the twentieth century saw a large-circulation, critical and investigative press that was supported by social movements pressing for reforms of labor practices, product standards, women's rights, and government corruption. However, this moment died fairly quickly through a combination of political attacks, such as Theodore Roosevelt's charge that journalistic "muckrakers" were undermining public confidence in institutions, and social changes, such as the rise of a professional press increasingly in thrall to objectivity, along with an economic recession that killed many investigative publications.[39]

If the turn of the last century witnessed better market conditions for the survival of an independent press, the turn of this century may represent the worst: extreme concentration of media ownership, a generally withdrawn public, and an avowedly timid professional press that generally shuns anything approximating crusading journalism. According to media law scholar Edwin Baker, such market conditions make an unregulated media system anathema to the health of democracy.[40] Just as governments require careful design and occasional reform, the design of media markets must proceed with careful consideration of what democratic results are realistic and desirable. The nominally free economic marketplace, in other words, does not automatically produce a vibrant marketplace of ideas, even given the First Amendment protections enjoyed by the press.[41]

Likewise, the watchdog ideal has proved to be a difficult standard for the news media to meet, especially in an era of increasingly controlled information by the government, tightening market imperatives, and shrinking news audiences. Media scholar Bartholomew Sparrow has concluded that despite the centrality of the watchdog role to American political thought, today's institutionalized news media do not in fact serve as a countervailing power to the government. Rather than a fourth branch, Sparrow suggests, the media usually serve as the "fourth corner" in the so-called iron triangles that characterize much of government policy making.[42]

In the face of the media's continuous inability to live up to the watchdog ideal, political scientist John Zaller has proposed a more forgiving standard of press performance: it should operate as a burglar alarm for a busy and often distracted citizenry. This standard admonishes the press to sound warnings and "rouse ordinary people to action" only when truly vital public problems arise, since "journalists cannot talk about every potential problem because their audience would ignore them."[43] Unlike the traditional watchdog ideal and the "full-news" standard of news quality that many academics favor, the burglar alarm standard emphasizes feasibility, attempting to reconcile high cultural expectations of the importance of news in a democracy with the realities of a commercialized news system constrained by diminished audience attention and tastes. On the face of it, this proposal seems in keeping with the spirit of these conservative and market-obsessed times—something of a "watchdog-lite." The problem is that without concerted discussion about how to implement this standard, the press may continue on its present course of sensationalism and responsiveness to official pronouncements of crises. The result would be the sounding of repeated false alarms that numb the attentiveness of the citizenry, along with the failure to sound alarms about high-level policy problems when not prompted by the government.[44] Moreover, as Zaller himself notes, it is still important that *some* news organizations—the elite press we have focused on this book—fulfill the full-news standard so that other news organizations around the country know what alarms to sound.

In response to these recurring dilemmas and discouraging patterns of press performance, some news organizations have experimented with a third model, called public or civic journalism. Its advocates argue that conventional news sours the public on civic life by highlighting conflict, scandal, and sensation. According to journalism professor Jay Rosen, one of the intellectual leaders of this movement, the goal of public journalism is to reenvision journalism as "democracy's cultivator, as well as its chronicler," to "restyle the work of the press so that it support[s] a healthier public climate."[45]

Practitioners of public journalism advocate shifting away from the conventional journalistic habit of simply depicting both sides of any given political controversy. Instead, they want the press to proceed toward "explanatory" news stories that move beyond the usual narrow array of official sources to provide greater context and a wider range of viewpoints. They also advocate allowing the public to set the news agenda actively through opinion polls, focus groups, and town hall meetings. Like the watchdog and marketplace models, public journalism purports to derive from the Constitution itself: The press, Rosen claims, "is singled out for special protection because its independent status is what keeps a free people free. . . . [T]he deepest purpose of journalism . . . is to amplify and improve" public deliberation.[46]

Yet many mainstream journalists object to the notion of surrendering journalistic control of the news agenda to the public, which, they believe, threatens the prized ideal of objectivity. In fact, its critics argue, public journalism replaces the ideal of objective news with news in which journalists become advocates for various community causes and thus venture into crusading.[47] And despite the seemingly sensible idea of bringing the public into the conversation about what the news should be, many elite journalists have vigorously opposed the idea, either because it can be deployed as a marketing program in disguise, or because it may pander to public sentiments rather than encouraging independent journalistic judgments about what matters in public life.[48] If only more news organizations proved capable of consistently making such judgments in terms of some identifiable public standard, this criticism might seem more credible.

Meanwhile, both the watchdog and the marketplace ideals are often invoked by media elites as a defense of press freedom—but without much evidence that those ideals are productively in play. That most news organizations, most of the time, report much the same stories from much the same perspectives suggests that the market in ideas is not working as it should. And many observers within and outside journalism agree that the enterprise reporting that is the hallmark of watchdog journalism is on the decline[49]—notwithstanding some significant exceptions, such as the *Washington Post*'s revelations of secret U.S. "black sites" for holding and interrogating suspected terrorists indefinitely; the *New York Times*' reporting on the National Security Agency's domestic surveillance program; and, later, the uncovering by the *Times* and other papers of government surveillance of private international financial transactions to root out monetary support for terrorism. The watchdog ideal was articulated nicely by Bill Keller, the *Times'* executive editor, in a response to the angry denunciations of the latter story from the Bush administration and its supporters:

> It's an unusual and powerful thing, this freedom that our founders gave to the press. Who are the editors of *The New York Times* (or the *Wall Street Journal, Los Angeles Times, Washington Post* and other publications that also ran the banking story) to disregard the wishes of the President and his appointees? And yet the people who invented this country saw an aggressive, independent press as a protective measure against the abuse of power in a democracy, and an essential ingredient for self-government. They rejected the idea that it is wise, or patriotic, to always take the President at his word, or to surrender to the government important decisions about what to publish.[50]

Yet as Keller noted in the same letter, the *Times* and other news organizations had been criticized "for not being skeptical enough of the Administration's claims about the Iraqi threat" prior to the war. In other words, to defend the recent, more independent news decision, Keller harked back to an earlier, far less independent decision. As these shifting news decisions illustrate, mainstream journalism lacks a publicly articulated standard for putting the watchdog ideal into consistent practice—a standard that does not simply serve as a rationale for reproducing the very patterns of power-based news analyzed in this book. Moreover, as we have tried to document, even when the press raises questions about a government policy, it then often steps back and allows government officials to take over the narrative, or allows the narrative to get lost in the thicket of insider politics. And fundamentally, the appearance of watchdog news seems to depend far too often on political context. When the president's political power is at its peak, a news media that plays by the rules of the Washington game is the least willing and able to challenge that power.

In sum, as a result of failing to engage creatively with public standards for press accountability, mainstream journalism has come, however unwittingly, to let the government (and those players perceived to have the power to influence it) define the range of public debate. Decades of scholarly research have shown that the mainstream news media often do not demonstrate the kind of independence from government implied in any of these yet-to-be-realized models. Instead of careful and continuous scrutiny, the press shows moments of critical independence within an overall pattern of dependence on government for the raw materials of news and the legitimization of "acceptable" viewpoints. And instead of being open to continuous and wide-ranging debate, the news gates are generally closed to societal voices that don't wield political power. The degree of critique (the watchdog ideal) and the breadth of debate (the marketplace ideal) that can be found in the news are spurred less by the press's deliberate, consistent "scrutiny of government" than by the occasional disruption of the power balance or the eruption of unexpected news events, which offer some of the few regular paths through which the contemporary media fulfill either journalistic standard.[51] Indeed, the U.S. press often seems hard pressed to live up to even the limited expectations of the burglar alarm model. Rather than exhibiting consistent independence from government so that it might be reliable in sounding alarms about failures in democratic politics, the press can best be characterized—as we have argued throughout this book—as *semi*-independent.[52]

Are Our Expectations Too High?

Before we go on to highlight what these three ideals might still contribute to a new standard of press performance, it is important to take up the counterargument: the problem is not really with the news delivery, but with prevailing news quality standards. One might argue (as John Zaller and some other scholars have)[53] that the problem is not so much in the media coverage as in scholars' impossibly high expectations of it. Indeed, the great-grandfather of the study of American political communication, Walter Lippman, observed many years ago that it was misguided to expect the press to supply truth and enable popular sovereignty.[54]

Aside from the objection that the press does not—and perhaps cannot—live up to its own ideals, we would note that in fact, a semi-independent press is not necessarily an unreasonable model of the role of news in a well-functioning democracy. It certainly appears that journalists adhere to the rules of the Washington power game, at least in part, out of a sense of their democratic obligation to leave the agenda setting to the public's elected representatives. After all, journalists are not elected, yet they wield tremendous potential power to define and alter the civic political agenda. If the news media today seem unconcerned with that power when it comes to promoting all forms of crass commercialism and sensationalism, it still appears that the nation's top reporters and editors believe that they should wield their influence to set the *policy* agenda with great caution.

In a well-functioning representative democracy, it might make sense for the news media simply to follow the lead of elected officials in defining key issues for debate. If elected officials adequately represent the public's views, have adequate incentive to engage in substantive policy debates, and are held adequately accountable through the electoral system by publics not highly dependent on the media for their political information, there might be little need for the press to be more than semi-independent. However, a cautious media reluctant to set the agenda proactively on important political issues does not serve democracy well if these sanguine assumptions about the wider political system do not hold. Instead, the semi-independent press arguably fails democracy when democracy most needs it: when officials and their policies do not reflect stable public opinion and deeply held public values, or when the government's own "organized, expert scrutiny" of policy options and governmental performance breaks down.

Mainstream journalism—Washington journalism in particular—perches on a precarious and circular paradox: while journalists may know that their sources in government are self-interested, corrupt, even lying, they *need* those same sources to continue producing what their bosses and peers will recognize as legitimate "news." For this reason, more than one close observer has characterized Washington journalism as deeply cynical.[55] Moreover, as sociologist Gaye Tuchman recognized in her pioneering study of media decision making, journalism as presently practiced seeks the legitimacy provided by the government's voices and views; if those were openly acknowledged to be corrupt, the very foundations of mainstream news would be disrupted.[56]

Publicly calling government misinformation by its proper name would leave journalists uncertain of *what* to report, as the *Washington Post's*

Ben Bradlee observed: "There's no question, in my mind, that a vigorous uncovering of lies in government is essential, it must continue and must be a major element of what the press does. But I do think we have to go a step farther, which is to replace the lies that we uncover with some form of truth, and therein lies the difficult part."[57]

This paradox, with its working premise (or fig leaf) of a well-functioning democracy, helps explain why even premier journalists, when pressed, are often unable to offer an independent standard to defend their news judgments regarding, for example, the Bush administration's rationale for going to war in Iraq. In a series of interviews with well-placed reporters and editors, journalist Kristina Borjesson repeatedly explored this puzzle. The response from former *Nightline* anchor Ted Koppel—certainly one of the most respected journalists of his era—illustrates mainstream journalism's dilemma:

> *Borjesson:* You don't just take their word for it, do you?
> *Koppel:* No, I don't just take their word for it. But when they tell me why they're going to war, I certainly have to give proper defer-ence to . . . [sic] if the president says I'm going to war for reasons A, B and C, I can't very well stand there and say, "The president is not telling you the truth, the actual reason that he's going to war is some reason he hasn't even mentioned." I as a reporter have to say, "Here is what the president is saying. Here's what the secre-tary of defense is saying. Here's what the director of the CIA is saying. Here's what the members of Congress are saying." And indeed, when everyone at that point who has access to the clas-sified information is with more or less one voice agreeing that, yes, there appears to be evidence that Saddam Hussein still has weapons of mass destruction—maybe not nuclear, but certainly chemical and probably biological—are you suggesting that the entire American press corps then say, "Well, horse manure"?[58]

Koppel's candid response underscores well the limitations of Washing-ton journalism—note the highly placed sources on his list of those views to which he must defer—and its deepest dilemma: if all those high of-ficials are saying the same thing and yet not necessarily telling the truth, what is the respectable professional journalist to do?

In answering Borjesson's questions, independent journalist Ron Suskind—one of the most probing and savvy reporters to have covered the Bush administration—inadvertently captured the deeper dilemma:

> *Borjesson*: They said it [their reason for going to war] was weapons of mass destruction and connections to Al Qaeda.
>
> *Suskind*: Right.
>
> *Borjesson*: Wasn't that clear?
>
> *Suskind*: There were no connections to Al Qaeda.
>
> *Borjesson*: Whether it's true or not is a separate issue from what they said.
>
> *Suskind*: They offered all manner of justifications. The fact is that the administration in large measure within itself knew that many of them were hollow.
>
> *Borjesson*: But what about the press?
>
> *Suskind*: What about the press? Why didn't we get it? We still haven't gotten it.
>
> *Borjesson*: Why?
>
> *Suskind*: Why haven't we . . . 'cause it . . .
>
> *Borjesson*: I have to make a note here that there's a long pause, a long silence on your end.
>
> *Suskind*: I think the answer is the one I offer. Look, it is a sacred, solemn duty of the leaders of a nation to explain to the true sovereigns—the voters, the citizens—why we should go to war against another nation. There is a long history of this being a solemn and sober obligation. It can't just be a good reason. It has to be a reason that Americans, on balance, think is worthy of the ultimate sacrifice.
>
> *Borjesson*: Well, we've been lied to before on this same issue. . . . What is the press's role in this exchange?
>
> *Suskind*: The press's role was to try to figure this out, but the press was up against a strategic model to keep not just them but the American public and their representatives in Congress from seeing clearly the true reasons and motivations that ultimately drove us to war.[59]

Suskind's difficulty in answering the question "What about the press?" leads him to the deeper problem: if officials do not communicate in good faith, there is little that professional journalism—as conventionally imagined—can do to set the record straight. Suskind further observed that the "solemn obligation" of officials to explain themselves to the public "is increasingly viewed as quaint and part of the arcana of our past because it runs right into the current news management ethos based on message discipline and message control. The pertinent idea is that saying something over and over again—through as many different venues and portals as possible—and just sticking to the script, is a strategy that ultimately wins out."[60]

It seems to be a safe assumption that this approach to governing will not disappear when the White House changes occupants. Mainstream journalism will confront this dilemma again. Which again raises the question: is there a news standard that can better guide journalists—and the public—in the brave new world of twenty-first-century politics?

Toward a New News Standard

Each of the three models reviewed above—watchdog (or its more passive variant, burglar alarm) journalism, civic journalism, and the marketplace of ideas—offers antidotes to the pitfalls of a semi-independent press. While it would be unrealistic to expect any of these models to be fully realized in the American news media system, the principles they articulate can serve as the starting point for a new public conversation about the role of the press in democracy:

- *The press enjoys its constitutional protections from overt government censorship in order to serve democracy and the public interest.* Press freedom is not granted merely to enhance its ability to do whatever it wishes, but to enable it to be the eyes and ears of the public—*particularly* when the regular democratic mechanisms of accountability may not be functioning properly.
- *Political conflict among the powerful is not the only—or even the best— framework for exploring the merits of government policies.* While high-level conflict is certainly an appropriate cue for critical coverage, the press is well within its democratic charter to subject major government policies and proposals to sustained attention and critique, *whether or not* the government itself is doing so.

- *The press's legitimate role includes bringing a variety of viewpoints to bear in scrutinizing public policy—and not simply to tally the "wins" and "losses" of power politics.* The best ideas only have hope of rising to the top when an array of substantive alternatives is brought into public deliberation. Like it or not, the mainstream news media are still the only place where large-scale deliberation can realistically occur. The press's job is to host that discussion, and to broaden it, rather than preemptively narrowing the options according to journalists' calculations of which ones already have political momentum.

- *Ultimately, the press's job is to offer more than scattershot scrutiny of the issues as dictated by its calculus of power.* When an administration is working hard to sell its policies to the public—even in the name of national security—the press can and should provide the public with coherent counterperspectives. When major policies are being considered and a counterperspective is not being offered by those in the top circles of power, the press can and should move beyond that circle—not just reporting objections for the record, to be buried deep on the inside pages of the newspaper, but sustaining a coherent critique, in the interests of full public deliberation and democratic accountability.

While these standards might be difficult to incorporate into every single news article produced, they could certainly be used to guide editorial decisions about the overall content of a news organization's coverage. More independence by individual news organizations—more willingness to break free of the "pack"—would in turn lead us closer to the marketplace-of-ideas model of press performance. While it may be unreasonable to expect every news organization to provide within its own coverage an all-inclusive selection of information and ideas, each one acting more independently could better approximate that ideal than the current system of news, which is dominated by conformity to the lead of top officials and top news organizations.

Finally, in thinking about news that better serves the citizen, Entman offers a useful standard for measuring how independently the news media define issues and events:

The media should provide enough information independent of the executive branch that citizens can construct their own counterframes of issues and events. It is not enough for the media to present information in ill-digested and scattered morsels. Rather, what citizens need is a counterframe constructed of culturally resonant words and images, one that attains sufficient magnitude to gain wide understanding as a sensible alternative to the White House's interpretation.[61]

When does the news fulfill its democratic responsibility? The answer is surprisingly simple: News meets this important responsibility when information obtained from the administration is challenged by information obtained independently from other sources and presented to the public in coherent and culturally resonant ways. On occasion one sees what we are proposing in, for example, lively deliberations on important issues, such as the ongoing debates on abortion.[62] But if we are serious about cultivating informed public opinion regarding war and peace and supporting the tenets of democratic accountability, we must guard against media that are too beholden to a single perspective manufactured by White House spin machines.

Final Thoughts

The rich array of episodes during the Bush years, from the lead-up to the war in Iraq, to Abu Ghraib, to Hurricane Katrina, to the domestic eavesdropping scandal, all tell us something important about the conditions under which the press is more and less dependent on the government's information management in reporting events. In the process of understanding the press as something of a dim national conscience, we also hope to learn something about this moment in time—this time of 9/11, terrorism, and the Iraq war that will surely go down in history as marking one of America's most controversial and consequential forays into the world. A war at odds with world opinion and increasingly with its own stated policy goals, compounded by grisly images of what much of the world saw and defined as torture, has challenged the American promise of freedom, democracy, and civility. (The ongoing detention of hundreds of foreign prisoners who have never been formally charged, some of them not even formally acknowledged by our government, has extended and sharpened that challenge.) Yet the absence of vigorous mainstream media debate about these matters left most Americans confused about what happened, why it happened, and what to do about the increasingly unhappy aftermath of these poorly examined policies. We write this book in the spirit that these issues are too important to leave to historians alone. Our evidence suggests that the recurring pattern of the government leading the press should prompt news organizations and citizens to take a close look at a press system that often fails when democracy needs it most.

The main problem with journalism that filters facts through its practitioners' perceptions of power is that it often bypasses the public. Of course, coaxing inattentive citizens to form informed opinions and find ways to express them in national policy debates is not the role of the press as envisioned by most Americans. Few citizens are informed about issues that fall outside the daily experiences of job, family, health, safety, or personal morality. Indeed, for the news to inform or even get the attention of most of the people most of the time seems impossible. But there is a vicious circle here: if the news preempts public consideration of important policies just because power formations in Washington have hardened quickly on an issue, then publics are peremptorily excluded and consigned to ignorance.

Ultimately, the public conversation we propose is unlikely to materialize without a concerted effort among leading news organizations to reexamine and develop a different conception of the journalistic profession. Until some more independent standard is discussed and adopted by the press, we will continue to see failures of the American press system in those very moments when its independence is most needed: when critical debate within government is limited and government is therefore prone to ill-considered, poorly planned, corrupt, or disastrous actions. Of course, when those poorly examined policies go badly, as they often do, journalists later show up to deliver the bad news in the form of scandals and finger-pointing that turn the public against both the press and politics. Yet journalists themselves often point to this cycle as an implicit defense of the current news system. Seeing "crusading" as inappropriate, the only path left open to them, they believe, is to wait for democratic processes to finally, if imperfectly, begin to realign the balance of political power in Washington.

By late summer 2006, when American combat casualties in Iraq were approaching three thousand and tens of thousands of Iraqi civilians were dead, the Washington political consensus seemed to have shifted enough to enable the establishment press to embrace a more critical stance toward the Bush administration's policies in the Middle East. Yet the conditions for that shift were consistent with the rule of power. As the press reported that declining public support for the war might become an election issue in 2006 and beyond, this and other factors seemingly began to reshape the conventional wisdom of the Washington consensus: beyond the poll numbers on the war, Bush was also receiving low marks from the public on the domestic economy; chaos in Iraq continued to mount along with worldwide criticism of the treatment of U.S. prisoners at Guantanamo; more Republican politicians broke ranks with the president on various issues; and the embattled press had surely grown weary of the administration's relentless spin. While later studies will ascertain whether the news indeed became more critical of the president in 2006 and beyond, a key test of our theory will be whether a changed constellation of political factors can be linked to a shift in the news climate.

But the charge of too little, too late must be applied to any such shift in the press's tone at the end of the Bush years. By then an emboldened Iran had exercised its influence across the region, Israel's northern territories were under attack by Hezbollah, much of Lebanon was in ruins, and chaotic violence in Iraq continued to make a mockery of the administration's "Plan for Victory" PR campaign. In August 2006, in an article assessing the deteriorating conditions in Iraq, the New York Times entertained the possibility that the country had slipped into civil war; of course, it did so only after General John P. Abizaid, the American commander of all U.S. forces in the Middle East, used the phrase in testimony before the Senate Armed Services Committee earlier in the week. Yet again, the Times waited for official cuing before it too ventured into the chilly waters of reality: "For some who have watched the public relations campaign closely," the Times reporter observed, "General Abizaid's statement . . . represented a tacit acknowledgement that there was no use spinning this conflict."[63] Not anymore, anyway.

Better late than never? Perhaps not. Perhaps it is time to fix a news system that has demonstrated a crucial failing. The reporting of reality after it is filtered through the news management of high officials and journalistic perceptions of power—at the expense of credible and timely competing perspectives that might promote greater public accountability—explains a good deal about the quality of public information in the United

States. When government is vigorously considering and contesting alternative policy perspectives, the news becomes filled with lively exchanges and contrasting perspectives. Yet when government most needs public scrutiny—that is, when government fails to openly debate policy options—the American press often fails to provide it. Need we remind the members of the press that filtering public information through the dictates of power is a measure commonly used by democracies to define less desirable forms of government?

APPENDIX A

Evidence suggesting a connection between Abu Ghraib and U.S. torture policy as reported by the *Washington Post*, Mar. 1–Aug. 30, 2004

Source of evidence	Description	Date produced/ released	Date first reported in the *Post*
Human Rights Watch report: *"Enduring Freedom": Abuses by U.S. Forces in Afghanistan*	Reported interviews with Afghans detained by U.S. forces at Bagram airbase in 2002. These individuals described prolonged confinement and mistreatment, including being "continuously shackled, intentionally kept awake for extended periods of time, and forced to kneel or stand in painful positions for extended periods," and doused with freezing water.	Mar. 8, 2004	Mar. 9, 2004
Taguba report: *Article 15-6 Investigation of the 800ᵗʰ Military Police Brigade*	Administrative review of allegations of prisoner abuse in Iraq, specifically at Abu Ghraib prison, conducted by U.S. Army Major General Antonio M. Taguba. Findings included a lack of communication, fragmentation of authority, lack of training and supervision of prison guards, and morale problems at Abu Ghraib; that the prison had effectively been put under the control of military intelligence, in violation of U.S. Army regulations; that a pattern of "sadistic, blatant, and wanton criminal abuses" at the prison was "substantiated by detailed witness statements and the discovery of extremely graphic photographic evidence"; and that some guards claimed that military intelligence personnel commended abusive soldiers for making detainees compliant. Criticized the practice of keeping "ghost detainees"—CIA prisoners who were kept off official rolls and hidden from International Committee of the Red Cross investigators. Recommended that Brigadier General Janis Karpinski be relieved of her command and reprimanded for command failures.	Mar. 9, 2004; leaked to press late Apr. 30, 2004; made public early May 2004	Apr. 30, 2004

Appendix A (continued)

Source of evidence	Description	Date produced/ released	Date first reported in the Post
Ryder report: *Assessment of Detention and Corrections Operations in Iraq*	Confidential survey by U.S. Army Major General Donald J. Ryder, later appended to the Taguba report. The report did not find widespread abuse in detention centers, or that military intelligence had ordered military police to pressure detainees before interrogation, but only what it called "flawed or insufficiently detailed use of force and other standing operating procedures or policies (e.g., weapons in the facility, improper restraint techniques, detainee management, etc)." In the *Post's* words, the report "highlighted numerous prison short-comings that had stoked friction between the detainees and their U.S. guards . . . which led in turn to riots and other protests that prison guards put down with the abuses documented in photographs" and in the Taguba report.	Nov. 5, 2003; released March 2004	May 2, 2004
International Committee of the Red Cross: *Report on the Treatment by the Coalition Forces of Prisoners of War and Other Protected Persons by the Geneva Conventions in Iraq during Arrest, Internment, and Interrogation*	Confidential summary report on the ICRC's investigations of fourteen detention centers in Iraq conducted between March and November 2003; sent to the Provisional Coalition Authority and its administrator, Paul Bremer, in February 2004. The report found a "consistent pattern" of "brutal behavior during arrest." It included graphic descriptions of evidence of physical abuse, humiliation, and excessive force; reported that some detainees exhibited "physical marks and psychological symptoms" that "appeared to be caused by the methods and duration of interrogation"; charged that military police had repeatedly engaged in "excessive and disproportionate use of force . . . resulting in death or injury"; and also reported estimates by military intelligence officers that 70% to 90% of "the persons deprived of their liberty in Iraq had been arrested by mistake." In a May 7, 2004, press conference, the ICRC reported it had made "repeated requests" to the Provisional Coalition Authority to correct the treatment of prisoners.	Jan. 2004; leaked by State Department officials in Feb./Mar. 2004; made public by the ICRC May 7, 2004	May 8, 2004

Appendix A (*continued*)

Source of evidence	Description	Date produced/ released	Date first reported in the *Post*
Senate Armed Services Committee Hearings	U.S. Army Major General Taguba testified that the the military guards at Abu Ghraib had been made "subject to the tactical control of interrogators" but attributed the incidents at the facility to "willful" conduct of individual soldiers. Defense Secretary Rumsfeld apologized for the treatment of Iraqis by U.S. forces, promised additional investigation, and proclaimed, "These events occurred on my watch. As Secretary of Defense, I am accountable for them and I take full responsibility." The committee also released the "Interrogation Rules of Engagement" reportedly posted on the walls of Abu Ghraib prison which included—subject to approval by Lieutenant General Ricardo S. Sanchez, commander of U.S. forces in Iraq—nine high-pressure interrogation techniques, such as the use of prolonged sleep deprivation and muzzled dogs.	May 5–7, 2004	May 6, 2004
Amnesty International: *Iraq: Amnesty International Digest*	AI released a press statement on April 25, 2003, condemning U.S. soldiers in Iraq for stripping detainees naked and humiliating them, citing a Norwegian newspaper story as its source. AI held a news conference in Baghdad in May 2003 to publicize its concerns about the treatment of prisoners, and notified the Provisional Coalition Authority through several memos and meetings in 2003.	Apr./ May 2003	May 8/10, 2004
Pentagon-approved interrogation techniques for use at Guantanamo Bay prison	According to the *Post*, the classified list of twenty-four techniques "represents the first publicly known documentation of an official policy permitting interrogators to use physically and psychologically stressful methods during questioning"— techniques the document described as designed to "invoke feelings of futility." According to U.S. officials, those procedures, based in part upon the Justice Department memo of August 2002 (see below), "were less coercive than the ones that [Secretary Rumsfeld] had authorized" in 2002.	Dec. 2002; revised Apr. 2003	May 9, 2004
CIA General Counsel's Office: interrogation rules	Vetted by the Justice Department and approved by the National Security Council's general counsel, the rules required operatives to seek high-level approval to use "enhanced measures" that could cause temporary physical or mental pain.	After Sept. 11, 2001	May 11, 2004

Appendix A (*continued*)

Source of evidence	Description	Date produced/ released	Date first reported in the *Post*
Miller report: *Assessment of DoD Counterterrorism Interrogation and Detention Operations in Iraq*	Classified report by U.S. Army Major General Geoffrey D. Miller reviewing detention centers and intelligence operations in Iraq; the report argued that the military police at Abu Ghraib should be trained to set "the conditions for the successful interrogation and exploitation of internees/detainees," to "improve velocity and operational effectiveness of counterterrorism interrogation."	Sept. 9, 2003	May 11, 2004
Justice Department torture memos: *Decision Re Application of the Geneva Convention on Prisoners of War to the Conflict with al Qaeda and the Taliban* and *Standards of Conduct for Interrogation under 18 U.S.C §§ 2340–2340A*	The first memo, written by White House Counsel Alberto Gonzales, suggested that the president could suspend the Geneva Conventions' "quaint" protections for detainees. It also discussed the potential for the prosecution of U.S. operatives for violating U.S. and international law, and ways to avoid accountability by not classifying detainees in Afghanistan and at Guantanamo as prisoners of war. The second memo, from the Justice Department's Office of Legal Counsel to Gonzales, advised that the torture of captured terrorists held overseas "may be [legally] justified," and argued that U.S. interrogators may be exempt from international laws against torture under the president's authority as commander in chief. In fact, the memo argued that international laws against torture "may be unconstitutional if applied to interrogations" conducted in the U.S.-led War on Terror. It also attempted to specify a high threshold of pain in order for coercive tactics to be considered torture: "Physical pain amounting to torture must be equivalent in intensity to the pain accompanying serious physical injury, such as organ failure, impairment of bodily function or even death."	Jan. 25, 2002 and Aug. 1, 2002	First memo mentioned in passing Jan. 28, 2002; first reported substantively May 18, 2004; second memo reported June 8, 2004
Sanchez memoranda	Memos signed by Lieutenant General Ricardo S. Sanchez instructing interrogators to assume control over the "lighting, heating . . . food, clothing, and shelter" of those being questioned at Abu Ghraib, and telling intelligence officials at the prison to work more closely with military police to "manipulate an internee's emotions and weaknesses." The first memo allowed techniques such as the use of dogs without special approval, while the second memo restricted such tactics as requiring special approval.	Sept. 14 and Oct. 12, 2003	May 21, 2004

Appendix A (*continued*)

Source of evidence	Description	Date produced/ released	Date first reported in the *Post*
Pentagon Working Group: *Draft Report on Detainee Interrogations in the Global War on Terrorism*	Secretary Rumsfeld convened the Pentagon Working Group to review the Geneva Conventions and the 1994 Convention Against Torture and their applicability to U.S. Armed Forces detention policies. The report drew heavily on Justice Department memos (see above), providing a narrower definition of what constitutes torture. It concluded that "a defendant is guilty of torture only if he acts with the express purpose of inflicting severe pain or suffering on a person within his custody or physical control"—a definition different than that used in international law.	Mar. 6, 2003	June 8, 2004
Fay-Jones reports: *Investigation of Intelligence Activities at Abu Ghraib*	U.S. Army Lieutenant General Anthony R. Jones's and Major General George R. Fay's investigations of whether members of the 205th Military Intelligence Brigade were involved in detainee abuse at Abu Ghraib, and whether organizations or personnel higher up on the chain of command were involved directly or indirectly. They found that brigade leaders "failed properly to supervise the interrogation operations at Abu Ghraib" and "failed to react appropriately to those instances where detainee abuse was reported." The Fay-Jones reports concluded, "The primary causes of the violent and sexual abuses were relatively straightforward—individual criminal misconduct, clearly in violation of law, policy, and doctrine and contrary to Army values." They also concluded that the chain of command directly above the brigade was not directly involved in the abuses, but that policy memoranda promulgated by General Sanchez led indirectly to some of the nonviolent and nonsexual abuses. The Fay report also noted that many Iraqis had been detained through "cordon and capture" sweeps and had been subsequently released with no charges filed against them.	Aug. 23, 2004	Aug. 24, 2004

Appendix A (*continued*)

Source of evidence	Description	Date produced/ released	Date first reported in the *Post*
Schlesinger report: *Independent Panel to Review DoD Detention Operations*	The report, commissioned by Defense Secretary Rumsfeld, held top Pentagon civilian and military leadership "indirectly" responsible for inadequate oversight and allowing conditions such as overcrowding that led to the abuse of detainees in Iraq. The report did not find any U.S. "policy of abuse" or "approved procedures" that permitted torture or inhumane treatment of detainees, though it did find that interrogation policies devised between December 2002 and April 2003 for terrorism suspects at Guantanamo Bay "migrated to Afghanistan and Iraq where they were neither limited nor safeguarded." It also detailed how President Bush, according to the *Post*, "on the advice of his White House counsel and attorney general, decided in February 2002 that the Geneva Conventions would not apply" to detainees captured in the War on Terror.	Released Aug. 24, 2004	First mentioned Aug. 18, 2004; first reported substantively Aug. 24, 2004

APPENDIX B
Methods for Analyzing the News Framing of Abu Ghraib

The analysis of the news framing of Abu Ghraib presented in chapters 3 and 4 is based on news and editorial items published in the *Washington Post* between January 1 and August 31, 2004, that focused on the Abu Ghraib scandal; stories focused on Abu Ghraib that aired on the *CBS Evening News* between April and September of 2004; and a series of searches of a sample of ten national newspapers for the period between April 2004 and the first week of January 2005. All searches were conducted using the Nexis news database.

We began our analysis with the *Washington Post*, searching the Nexis database to gather all of that paper's news and editorial items that mentioned Abu Ghraib between January 1 and August 31, 2004. Prior to April 29, only two stories mentioning Abu Ghraib had appeared in the *Post*, on March 21 and 22, noting that criminal charges had been filed against soldiers for abusing or mistreating prisoners. The data show that such scattered reports of an investigation at Abu Ghraib were largely ignored by the news media in general until CBS broke the story of the photos on April 28.

The specific search term used was "Abu Ghraib or (Iraq and prison!)." This search garnered 609 items, including many articles that made only passing reference to Abu Ghraib or Iraqi prisons in the context of covering other topics about the war or the Bush administration. All letters to the editor were removed, since our focus is on journalistic framing. We then selected only those articles that focused substantially and directly on events at Abu Ghraib and/or U.S. policies related to the treatment of prisoners, prisons, interrogations, and related matters. Articles whose topic was tangential and in which Abu Ghraib was mentioned only once (for example, articles about domestic/electoral politics that only mentioned Abu Ghraib in passing) were deleted from the sample, as were articles not closely focused on Abu Ghraib events (for example, developments in the war in Iraq; kidnappings of Americans and others in Iraq; Supreme Court decisions regarding detainees). This left a sample of 294 items (242 news articles and 52 masthead editorials, columns, and op-ed pieces).

These 294 items were then coded by a graduate student trained for this task who was unfamiliar with the theoretical propositions of our study. We first asked the coder to identify the first label used in each item to describe the events at Abu Ghraib (which we call the "primary label") and, if present, the second as well (which we call the "secondary label"). The labels were chosen from a list previously identified by the authors through a close reading of news stories about Abu Ghraib, with the labels winnowed by automated word searches of news texts to eliminate infrequent terms. The final list from which the coder was instructed to choose included *abuse, mistreatment, scandal, torture,* or *none of the above.* The coder was also asked to determine whether a primary label appeared in the headline or lead paragraphs of the story (which we call "primary label placement"), along with other information about each article (see coding instrument in table B.1 below).

Coding reliability was assessed using a second coder and a subsample of 61 articles. Intercoder reliability scores were high, with intercoder percentage agreements of $p = .807$ for the primary label, .912 for the placement of the primary label in the headline or lead paragraph, and .754 for identification of the secondary label. Since percentage agreement is often too liberal a measure of reliability, we calculated both Cohen's kappa and Krippendorf's alpha measures, which also proved very strong, with primary label identification reliabilities of $alpha = .776$ and $kappa = .775$. Since error in the first label code magnified error in the second label code, we also merged the primary and secondary labels into a single, "prominent label" variable, which turned out to be the most generous measure of whether torture appeared as a counterframe (by counting it either in the first or the second position), while also producing strong intercoder reliability coefficients of $p = .917$, $alpha = .801$, and $kappa = .800$. The authors also conducted discussions of the remaining disagreements between the two coders, which revealed nuances such as several instances in which the *torture* label appeared as a denial rather than an affirmative description of events at Abu Ghraib.

A simplified version of this coding strategy was repeated on the full text of stories aired on the *CBS Evening News* (chosen because that network's 60 *Minutes II* first broke the Abu Ghraib photo story) between April and August of 2004 that focused on Abu Ghraib. The stories were gathered and culled using the same procedure as for the *Washington Post*, yielding a sample of 54 stories. The analysis was restricted to transcripts, and thus to the text and not the visual components of the CBS coverage (see coding instrument in appendix B.1 below). Intercoder reliability on the primary and secondary label data for the entire sample of *CBS Evening News* stories was high due to the shorter and simpler TV story format ($p = .98$ and .96, respectively).

Finally, we assessed the generalizability of our *Washington Post* and CBS findings for a national newspaper sample, with time period extended to include the Senate confirmation hearings for Alberto Gonzales (Gonzales had participated in drafting a White House policy memo justifying relaxed conventions against torture in the War on Terror, and thus his confirmation hearings brought Abu Ghraib into the news again). The national sample included news pieces and editorials from ten newspapers (the *Atlanta Journal Constitution, Boston Globe, Chicago Sun-Times, Los Angeles Times, New York Times, Cleveland Plain Dealer, San Francisco Chronicle, Seattle Times, St. Petersburg Times,* and *USA Today*) between April 2004 and mid-January 2005. For this sample, the search term used to establish the baseline of articles about Abu Ghraib in each newspaper was "hlead (Abu Ghraib or (prison and Iraq*))." We culled articles retrieved with this search to include only those focusing on Abu Ghraib and/or U.S. treatment of detainees, to yield a final sample of 895 news articles and editorials about Abu Ghraib from April 1, 2004, to January 15, 2005. We then machine coded the Nexis search results to ascertain the frequency of the labels *abuse, mistreat,* and *torture* in these articles; we omitted *scandal* from this stage of the analysis, since we had discovered it usually appeared in conjunction with *abuse* and thus tended to confound the findings.

In addition to the coding described above, we coded the descriptions of the Abu Ghraib detainees given in the *Washington Post* and on the *CBS Evening News*, material that is discussed in chapter 4. Appendix B.2 below provides the coding protocol for that analysis.

Appendix B.1: Coding instrument for *Washington Post* and *CBS Evening News* coverage of Abu Ghraib

The following coding protocol was followed for *Washington Post* news and editorial pieces; the same protocol was used for *CBS Evening News* items, the only difference being how the "lead" of each item was determined.

I. General story characteristics:

storynum   (assign a unique number to each story, using the number gen-
             erated by the Nexis search, located at the top of each story)
date   (publication date mm/dd/yy)
headline   (cut and paste primary headline from Nexis, or type verbatim)
reporter   (last name only, or "wire")
section/story type
             1 = front page section A
             2 = inside news pages
             3 = masthead/unsigned editorials
             4 = letter to the editor
             5 = regular column
             6 = guest editorial/op-ed
             7 = other, such as Magazine desk
             numwords (word count, per Nexis)

II. Primary Label ["label1"]: We are interested here in *the most prominent specific descriptive label* applied to what occurred at Abu Ghraib (please exclude labels that clearly are being applied *only* to incidents that occurred at *other* facilities). (When discussion of torture includes Abu Ghraib, or more generally "prisons in Iraq," it should be included, regardless of whether other prisons are mentioned as well). For each article, record the number corresponding to the term that is used *first* (including the headline).

   0 = none of the terms below used to describe Abu Ghraib
   1 = *abuse* (including *abusive, abused, abusing,* and *abuse scandal*)
   2 = *torture* (including *torturing, tortured*)
   3 = *mistreatment* (including *mistreat, mistreating*)
   4 = *scandal* (without any of the terms above)

III. Primary Label Placement ["label1pl"]: Code whether the label identified in the previous variable appeared in the headline and/or first paragraph of the article. (For print: If the first paragraph is only one sentence long, count the first two paragraphs as the "first" paragraph. For TV: The "lead" includes anchor's introduction of the story and first paragraph of the reporter's own words; for anchor-only stories, "lead" includes first paragraph).

   1 = appears in headline/lead
   0 = does not appear in headline/lead

IV. Sources of primary label ["labsrc1" and "labsrc2"]: With this variable, we are tracking *who* is applying the primary label to the situation at Abu Ghraib. On your coding sheet, you will see two columns marked "source1" and "source2." Enter the number from the list below corresponding to the type of source who uses the label you identified in the previous variable. If more than one source uses that label, record the *first two* sources in the story who use that term. If it appears that the journalist might be paraphrasing another source, choose "journalist" for "source1" and the possible original source as "source2." Note that if you chose "0" for "Primary Label" above—that is, if the primary label applied was *not* a term on the list above—then this variable should be left blank. In other words, if no one used one of the terms from the list above (*abuse, torture, mistreatment, scandal,* or *abuse scandal*), then no one should be coded for this variable.

   1 = Accused soldiers/enlisted soldiers—or their lawyers

2 = Military: Command structure within the prison (Karpinski, Pappas); Senior Military Commanders for Iraq (Ricardo Sanchez, Thomas Metz); Central Command (General Abazaid); top military leadership (e.g. Chair of Joint Chiefs Gen. Meyers); Gen. Taguba and other army investigators (including the Fay report)
3 = Civilian leadership of the military (Sec. of Defense Rumsfeld, Paul Wolfowitz) and the Schlesinger report (which was commissioned by the Defense Department); White House (President Bush, Dick Cheney, Justice Department/John Ashcroft, White House counsel Alberto Gonzales)
4 = Other government officials (e.g. members of Congress) and former government officials (e.g. Richard Clarke)
5 = Journalists on their own (includes columnists who appear regularly in the newspaper)
6 = Other: Independent, *nongovernmental* organizations (e.g. International Red Cross), experts, and think tanks; foreign news organizations; foreign officials; guest editorialists who don't fit in other categories.

V. Secondary Label ["label2"]: For each article, identify whether one of the labels below was *also* applied to the events at Abu Ghraib (again, please exclude labels that clearly are being applied *only* to incidents that occurred at *other* facilities).
0 = none of the terms below used to describe Abu Ghraib
1 = *abuse* (including *abusive, abused, abusing,* and *abuse scandal*)
2 = *torture* (including "torturing," "tortured")
3 = *mistreatment* (including "mistreat," "mistreating")
4 = *scandal* (without any of the terms above)

Appendix B.2: Coding protocol for descriptions of Abu Ghraib detainees in the *Washington Post* and *CBS Evening News*

I. "Victim" labels: Please cut and paste any labels other than *detainees* or *prisoners/inmates* that were applied to the people inside Abu Ghraib. Examples: *suspected Al Qaeda members, insurgents.*

II. Context1: Do we learn anything from this story about how people ended up in Abu Ghraib prison? (e.g. swept up in "cordon and capture" missions; already in prison under Saddam Hussein, etc.) Please highlight all relevant passages.
1 = contains context1 information
0 = does not contain context1 information

III. Context2: Do we learn anything from this story about the intelligence value of the people inside Abu Ghraib? This would include anything from claims that they had no intelligence value to claims that information extracted from them has saved American lives. Please highlight all relevant passages.
1 = contains context2 information
0 = does not contain context2 information

APPENDIX C

Further Findings from the Content Analysis

Table C1: Percentage of articles using prominent labels, by type, *Washington Post,* Apr. 1–Sept. 29, 2004*

	Abuse	*Torture*	*Mistreatment*	*Scandal*
News (*N* = 242)	91% (222)	11% (28)	16% (40)	33% (80)
Editorials (*N* = 52)	82% (43)	30% (16)	13% (7)	36% (19)

*Prominent labels were those that were used as either the first or the second label in each article (in contrast with the primary labels that were used first). Numbers in parentheses are the counts for each cell; percentages are not rounded.

Table C2: Articles in which journalists were the chief source of the primary label, by type, *Washington Post,* Apr. 1–Sept. 29, 2004*

Label	News items (*N* = 242)	Editorial items (*N* = 52)
Abuse	95% (179)	81% (26)
Torture	55% (5)	77% (7)
Mistreatment	85% (6)	100% (2)
Scandal	100% (29)	42% (3)

*Numbers in parentheses are the counts for each cell; percentages are not rounded.

Table C3: Frequency of labels, national newspaper sample, Jan. 1–Sept. 29, 2004*

#1	#2	#3	#4	#5	#6	#7	#8	#9
	Baseline News	Baseline Edits.	Torture Only News	Torture Only Edits.	No Torture News	No Torture Edits.	Other + Torture News	Other + Torture Edits.
AJC	55	17	0	0	39	11	15	6
BG	63	19	0	1	34	3	28	13
CST	50	18	0	0	29	10	21	8
LAT	164	31	0	0	105	14	58	14
NYT	195	32	1	4	136	8	51	19
PD	1	9	0	0	0	4	0	3
SFC	32	15	0	2	20	4	11	5
ST	99	9	0	0	65	5	32	3
STP	30	8	0	0	17	4	13	2
USA	78	13	1	1	55	8	19	4
Total	**767**	**171**	**2**	**8**	**500**	**71**	**248**	**77**

*Newspapers in the sample include the *Atlanta Journal Constitution* (AJC), *Boston Globe* (BG), *Chicago Sun-Times* (CST), *Los Angeles Times* (LAT), *New York Times* (NYT), *Cleveland Plain Dealer* (PD), *San Francisco Chronicle* (SFC), *Seattle Times* (ST), *St. Petersburg Times* (STP), and *USA Today* (USA).

Each column represents the number of items retrieved from the Nexis news database using a particular search term and parameter for inclusion or exclusion of articles:

• Column #2 = "Baseline" of all news articles focused on Abu Ghraib or other prisons in Iraq; search term "hlead (Abu Ghraib or (prison and Iraq*))." To ensure that these were items in fact focused on Iraq prisons, a trained coder retained only articles in which the lead paragraphs or substantial portions of the body of the story focus on Abu Ghraib events and/or U.S. policies related to torture, detentions, prisons, interrogations, etc.

• Column #3 = "Baseline" of all *editorial* page items (not including letters to the editor) retrieved with the search term described in #2 above.

• Column #4 = Number of news articles from the baseline using the term *torture* but not *abuse* or *mistreat* (search term "tortur! and not abus! or mistreat!").

• Column #5 = Number of editorial items from the baseline using the term *torture* but not *abuse* or mistreat (search term "tortur! and not abus! or mistreat!").

• Column #6 = Number of news articles from the baseline using the terms *abuse* or *mistreat* but not *torture* (search term "abus! or mistreat! and not tortur!").

• Column #7 = Number of editorial items from the baseline using the terms *abuse* or *mistreat* but not *torture* (search term "abus! or mistreat! and not tortur!").

• Column #8 = Number of news articles from the baseline using the term *torture* plus either *abuse* or *mistreat* (search term "abus! or mistreat! and tortur!").

• Column #9 = Number of editorial items from the baseline using the term *torture* plus either *abuse* or *mistreat* (search term "abus! or mistreat! and tortur!").

APPENDIX D
Interview Protocol

Some of the material in chapter 5 comes from interviews conducted by one of the authors. Interviews were structured around themes rather than a preset questionnaire. Each interviewee was presented with a description of the book project, including the following points:

- "We are trying to understand the Washington policy debate concerning the war in Iraq."
- "We are particularly interested in media and policy processes."
- "Among our case studies is the Abu Ghraib prison scandal."

The author-interviewer stated directly and unequivocally that the interview was on the record and for attribution. Each interviewee was then asked if he or she agreed to this condition. Nearly all agreed; no material was quoted from those that did not give their consent. Most interviews were tape-recorded unless such recording was impossible (true in only two cases) due to either ambient noise or an interview over the telephone.

Whether tape-recorded or recorded in handwritten notes, all quotations used in the book were reviewed for accuracy by the pertinent interviewee. For each interviewee quoted, an e-mail message was sent stating the following:

Dear X

As we discussed at the time of our meeting, I am one of three authors of a book that focuses on foreign policy and media coverage of the war in Iraq. The University of Chicago Press will publish the book. . . . My co-authors are W. Lance Bennett of the University of Washington and Regina Lawrence of Portland State University.

Your insights into the nature and development of the debate concerning the war and related events—such as the scandal concerning Abu Ghraib prison—have been invaluable to my colleagues and me.

We are in your debt. Thank you so much for your kind assistance. To help insure accuracy, I want to share with you several of the quotes taken from my recording/notes of our conversation. We plan to use these quotes in the finished book. Here are the quotes and a bit of the context:

QUOTES AND CONTEXT HERE

I also want you to review the assertions or conclusion we ascribe to you as a result of the interview. Here they are:

ASSERTIONS HERE

In receiving this e-mail from me, you have my only e-mail address. As you can see, it is sliv@gwu.edu. My two telephone numbers are listed below. Please contact me if you have the slightest concern about either the ascribed quotes, the context in which they are used, or assertions made. Thank you so much for helping us as we strive to get this right.

This letter was sent with an automatic e-mail message-reception confirmation request. Those who failed to confirm were e-mailed again. If a second e-mail was unacknowledged, the interviewee was contacted via telephone. If both e-mails and phone calls were unacknowledged, the interview material would not have been used, but in no case did this happen.

NOTES

1. *New York Times* (2004b, May 26).
2. See Bennett (2005c).
3. Milbank (2003, A24).
4. Stolberg (2004, A13).
5. Gellman and Pincus (2003, 6).
6. Massing (2004, 45).
7. *New York Times* (2002).
8. Purdum (2002, A1).
9. Ibid.
10. Risen (2004, A1).
11. Harris Interactive (2006). It is worth considering that the durability of this public belief—even after the media did report more on the absence of such a connection—may reflect the simple appeal of the Bush administration's original story of conspiracy between the nation's leading public enemies.
12. *New York Times* (2004b).
13. CBS News (2003).
14. Pincus (2003, 11).
15. See Feinstein (2002); Newport (2004); and Teixeira (2006).
16. Stevenson (2004a).
17. Stevenson and Jehl (2005).
18. Schiffer (2006, 3).
19. Ibid.
20. Ibid., 14.
21. Ibid., 12.
22. See Bennett (2005a, 2005b).
23. See Garrels (2003) and Shadid (2005).
24. Kurtz (2004b).
25. It is important to emphasize here that this theory applies mainly to news about policies and issues that are on government agendas. Other stories can generate more independent news judgments. For example, it seems clear that the flurry of stories in the international press in the fall of 2005 about the possibility of a flu pandemic spread quickly to the U.S. press, and led to a set of official reactions about whether government preparations were adequate.
26. See Bennett (1991, 103–25).

27. Massing (2004, 62).

28. Dowd (2005).

29. Hallin (1986).

30. See Cook (1998).

31. Taubman made these comments at Stanford University's McClatchey Symposium (2005, May 9). Technically, a "flywheel" is a rotating wheel used to regularize the workings of a piece of machinery, such as a clock. Following Taubman's metaphor, we use the phrase to indicate the institutional processes—congressional legislation writing and hearings, for example—that regularize for the press the operations of government.

32. Another example of journalists pegging coverage to what top officials do was provided by Karen deYoung, former assistant managing editor of the *Washington Post*, who spoke about President Bush and U.S. foreign policy at the Shorenstein Center for the Press, Politics, and Public Policy, in Cambridge, MA, in 2003. Regarding the lead-up to the war, deYoung claimed, "We [the media] really did a pretty okay job" covering the WMD story, but the stories didn't resonate in large part because congressional Democrats didn't respond. She predicted that soon, more political conflict would break out in Washington, and then "they'll be just like every other administration." Perfectly expressing the indexing mentality, she said, "We're in our element [when] people are fighting among themselves, people are leaking things, Congress is holding hearings."

33. See Ferree, Gamson, Gerhards, and Rucht (2002).

34. See Sparrow (1999).

35. As Sparrow (ibid.) argues, the media act more like "attack dogs" during political contests, such as elections and high-stakes, divisive policy debates, but more like "lap dogs" when they confront "policy monopolies."

36. See Entman (1993, 51–58).

37. See Entman (2004).

38. See Page (1996).

39. Between 2001 and 2004, a series of articles appeared in the *New Orleans Times-Picayune* documenting the vulnerabilities of the levees, and the reallocation of federal funds from the levee projects to other national initiatives, such as homeland security and the Iraq war. See Torres (2001, Oct. 13); Schleifstein (2004). For a more complete review of watchdog journalism on this, see the report in Annenberg Political Fact Check (2005).

40. Risen and Lichtblau (2005). In May of 2006, *USA Today* revealed that the NSA program included a massive database of millions of communications among Americans within the United States, not just their communications with points abroad.

41. See Bennett (1991, 103–25).

42. Zaller (1992).

43. Program on International Policy Attitudes (2003).

44. Ibid.

45. Cunningham (2003).

46. See Herbst (1998).

47. Janis (1972).

CHAPTER TWO

1. See Sigal (1973); Hallin (1986).

2. See Bennett (1991). The core idea is that *journalists index the range of viewpoints in the news to the divisions of power they perceive within various decision-making circles of government.*

3. For a general model of punctuated equilibrium in the policy-making process, see Baumgartner and Jones (1993).

4. Cappella and Jamieson (1997); Lawrence (2000a); Patterson (1993).

5. While this core news pattern has been demonstrated most clearly in studies of news coverage of foreign policy, some studies have found similar patterns in news coverage of domestic policy issues (see for example Lawrence [2000b]; Lawrence and Birkland [2005]; Sparrow [1999]). In part, this may reflect the greater ease of studying the former, in which episodes are more discretely bounded and the decision points are more limited and clear and therefore easier to measure. By contrast, domestic issues often involve multiple venues in which struggles play out simultaneously, such as state and local politics, citizen initiatives, and court cases, complicating reporters' ability simply to track relations between government power points as the basis for news coverage. There are also often elements of national security and patriotic considerations that further discourage prominent reporting of all available evidence and perspectives surrounding foreign policy stories, adding to the tendency of the mainstream press to emphasize perspectives anointed by a seal of official approval.

6. Entman's "cascading activation" model (2004) emphasizes this occasional ability of lower-level sources, such as congressional staffers, former officials, even journalists themselves, to trigger shifts in news coverage of foreign policy issues. Our model acknowledges the same possibility, but is less sanguine about how readily it occurs, given the strong journalistic norm of cleaving to the story lines of the most powerful—and given the news-management tactics that can discourage critical lower-level sources from stepping forward (see chapter 5).

7. Althaus (2003) finds the closest indexing of news to elite discourse with regard to "fundamental criticisms of U.S. policy"—that is, the "ends" of foreign policy—and somewhat more room for deviation when covering "means" questions. In elite press coverage of the first Gulf War, he finds that American citizens, not officials, were the most prominent source of criticisms of the administration's chosen means for dealing with Iraq. When discussing more fundamental questions, however, the predicted indexing pattern prevailed.

8. Althaus (ibid., 384) argues that because they interview many sources both on and off the record, Washington beat reporters sometimes are aware of greater levels of official debate than those officials are willing to reveal for the record. In those circumstances, "journalists may be emboldened to index according to the real [versus the public] level of latent criticism."

9. For example, Entman (2004, 42–43) describes how in 1983, *Newsweek* uncovered facts about the Soviet downing of Korean Air Lines Flight 007 that contradicted the Reagan administration's frame—and the magazine's own prior reporting—claiming that the USSR had intentionally committed "murder in the air." Despite reporting them for the record, *Newsweek* did not give those facts a prominent place in its subsequent reporting, or use those facts to refashion the framing of the incident.

10. As Sparrow (1999) observes of the disparaging news coverage of the few lone officials who stood up against the savings and loan debacle taking shape in the mid-1990s, and as the examples of coverage of the few Democrat-sponsored hearings discussed in this chapter and chapter 1 also reveal, even officials who can muster evidence of policy problems and instigate congressional hearings are not assured a prominent place in the news narrative. *Perceptions* of power matter; as Sparrow notes, "it was the perceptions of Washington journalists that mattered most" (159).

11. This phrase was used by a senior military investigator, James Schlesinger, when his report on Abu Ghraib was released to the news media. See chapter 3.

12. Althaus (2003, 381–414).

13. For discussions of how the news reports politics as an inside game and why it matters, see Patterson (1993). For the effects on citizens of this game framing of politics, see Cappella and Jamieson (1997).

14. The Pew Research Center reported in June of 2005 that "six-in-ten [respondents] see news organizations as politically biased, up from 53% two years ago. More than seven-in-ten (72%) say news organizations tend to favor one side, rather than treat all sides fairly; that is the largest number ever expressing that view." These perceptions may help to account for the popularity of recent books alleging systematic ideological bias in the media, such as Goldberg (2003) and McGowan (2003), who allege a liberal bias, and Alterman (2003), who alleges a conservative bias. Interestingly, the public may also have an inkling of the indexing dynamic we describe in this book, indicated by the Pew Center's finding that "by more than three-to-one (73%–21%), the public feels that news organizations are 'often influenced by powerful people and organizations,' rather than being 'pretty independent.'" See Pew (2005b).

15. Surveys of journalists show that they are more liberal in their social policy views than the average American, though not necessarily in their views about economic policy. What critics of "liberal bias" in the press typically miss, however, are the routines and norms that structure and constrain daily journalism—the forces we attempt to describe in this book. In other words, the news is not simply a product of individual journalists and their personal political views, but the product of organizations that are intricately linked to and frequently dependent on government actors and institutions.

16. See Domke (2004); Viguerie and Franke (2005).

17. McCombs and Shaw (1972); Iyengar (1991); Iyengar and Kinder (1987).

18. See, for example, Mermin (1999); Zaller and Chiu (1996).

19. Zaller and Chiu (1996, 389–91). The careful reader will note that despite these impressive statistical correlations, there is still some variance in news coverage not explained by indexing alone. In other words, despite the strength of the indexing norm, particularly in news about foreign policy, journalists still retain the discretion to construct the news differently—and apparently sometimes do. Indeed, no single theory of social behavior can hope to account for all variations in any data set. Nevertheless, these findings, which echo patterns discovered in other studies cited here, suggest that indexing is a prevailing news pattern. We explore further below some limitations to and extensions of the basic indexing hypothesis that may help to account for further variations in the news.

20. Ibid., 392.

21. Mermin (1999).

22. Hallin (1986).

23. For more extensive analysis of how this system works as a single political institution, see the special issue of *Political Communication* (vol. 23, no. 2 [Apr.–May 2006]), "New Institutionalism and the News," edited by David Michael Ryfe.

24. See Patterson (1992).

25. One irony of the brief flirtation of the mainstream press with Hersh's alternative version of events was a tongue-in-cheek consideration about whether Hersh should be admitted to their inner circle despite his aggressive reporting and adversarial relations with those in power. See Kurtz (2004a). Kurtz also notes that Hersh's earlier reports on the My Lai massacre in Vietnam, which eventually won a Pulitzer Prize, were turned down by the major newsmagazines. Rubien (2000) adds that those stories were finally published by a small news syndicate owned by a friend.

26. See Cook (1998); Sparrow (1999).

27. See Cohen (1963).

28. See Mindich (1998).

29. See Lawrence (2000b).

30. Entman (2004).

31. In many ways, as a theoretical proposition the CNN effect constitutes the null hypothesis to indexing. Whereas indexing argues that media debate is driven by official debate, the CNN effect claims that official debate and even policy decision making is driven by media operating independently of official sourcing and cuing, ultimately reorienting the trajectory of U.S. foreign policy. As a general proposition, this claim has received limited verification. Livingston and Eachus (1996) found that Washington politics (not media coverage) offered the best explanation for the U.S. intervention in Somalia, because the bulk of the coverage concerning Somalia *followed* key decisions made by the president and other principal offices, rather than preceded them, as the CNN effect would logically have it. Other subsequent studies have verified Livingston and Eachus's findings (see Mermin [1999]). More recent research has narrowed the parameters of the central claim of the CNN effect. Babak Bahador (2006) offers a convincing argument that media content galvanized top officials in the Clinton administration in their decision to launch the 1999 bombing campaign in Kosovo. But even here, Secretary

of State Madeleine Albright and special Balkans envoy Richard Holbrooke were inclined toward a tough military response to Serbia, so it is difficult to say precisely how much media coverage of Serbian atrocities played a role in the decision (see also Miller [2007]). It appears that the media may accelerate the pace of foreign policy processes, with important effects to policy-making institutions. Intelligence agencies and diplomats are left at the sidelines while the latest diplomatic exchange takes place on twenty-four-hour cable television; meanwhile, the perception that war casualties seen in news coverage undermine public resolve can itself reorient policy. In general, however, most research has demonstrated that the CNN effect— when understood as the media's ability to force decisions on policy makers—is unlikely, except in extraordinary circumstances. See Livingston (1996).

32. Livingston and Van Belle (2005); Livingston, Bennett, and Robinson (2005); Livingston (2000).

33. See Lawrence (2000b).

34. Kolhatar and Dana (2005).

35. Other examples of event-driven news that opened the news gates to large-scale policy criticism include the Rodney King beating (Lawrence [2000b]); the Exxon *Valdez* oil spill in Prince William Sound, Alaska (Lawrence and Bennett [2001]); and the shootings at Columbine High School (Lawrence and Birkland [2005]).

36. See Tuchman (1978).

37. Livingston and Bennett (2003), 363–80.

38. Even the paper's public editor was for months unable to get the *Times'* editors to explain for the record why they had opted to hold the story for a year (Calame [2006a]). When executive editor Bill Keller finally did agree to be interviewed by Byron Calame on the subject, his justification for withholding the story supports our propositions about journalistic assessments of power and credibility: Keller told Calame that the sources for the NSA story "hadn't been sufficiently 'well-placed and credible' to convince him that questions about the program's legality and oversight were serious enough to make it 'responsible to publish'" Calame (2006b).

39. Shane (2005); Toobin (2006).

40. Online NewsHour (2006).

41. See Bennett and Serrin (2005), 169–88.

42. For an overview of the literature on media and movements and an in-depth case study of how the nuclear freeze movement was covered by the press, see Rojecki (1999).

43. See Gitlin (2003); and Iyengar (1991).

44. Entman (2004).

45. See Fletcher (2005); and Swanson (2005).

CHAPTER THREE

An earlier version of portions of this chapter appeared under the title "None Dare Call It Torture: Indexing and the Limits of Press Independence in the Abu Ghraib Scandal" in the *Journal of Communication,* vol. 56 (2006): 476–85.

1. Higham and Stephens (2004, A1).
2. Danner (2004a); Higham, Stephens, and White (2004).
3. Malone (2004).
4. *Washington Post* (2004a, A12).
5. Molotch and Lester (1974, 1975); Bennett and Lawrence (1996); Lawrence (2000b).
6. Lawrence (2001); Lawrence and Birkland (2005).
7. Livingston and Eachus (1995); Livingston (1996, 2000); Potter (2002).
8. Livingston and Bennett (2003), Livingston, Bennett, and Robinson (2005); Livingston and Van Belle (2005).
9. Entman (2004).
10. Sontag (2004, 26).
11. Quoted in Meyer (2004).
12. Danner (2004a).
13. See Mueller (2005).
14. It bears mentioning here that no particularly "good" news came out of Iraq that would help to explain the rallying of opinion after the Abu Ghraib story broke; the Iraqi elections, for example, were still months away. Beyond the administration's management of the Abu Ghraib story, we might also point to its decision to raise the terror alert level at the time of the Democratic National Convention, which may again have primed public concerns about terror and the misplaced connection between Iraq and 9/11.
15. See Danner (2004a); Sikkink (2005); United Nations Commission on Human Rights (2006).
16. Perhaps this is why the term *torture light* was suggested by Lelyveld (2005).
17. Mayer (2006).
18. Ibid., 35.
19. Sikkink (2005, 22). Few Americans may realize the scope of alleged and documented American abuses of detainees. As of the end of April, 2006, more than 600 American military personnel had been accused of having been involved in abusing detainees in Iraq, Afghanistan, and Guantanamo Bay. Of those, 54 were found guilty, and more than 250 had been punished (Schmitt [2006d]).
20. Jehl and Schmitt (2004); White (2004a).
21. See Danner (2004a, 2004b); Judt (2005).
22. Sikkink (2005).
23. Program on International Policy Attitudes (2004).
24. See also Pew Research Center (2004).
25. The report included the following descriptions: "Breaking chemical lights and pouring the phosphoric liquid on detainees; pouring cold water on naked detainees; beating detainees with a broom handle and a chair; threatening male detainees with rape; allowing a military police guard to stitch the wound of a detainee who was injured after being slammed against the wall in his cell; sodomizing a detainee with a chemical light and perhaps a broom stick, and using military

222 NOTES TO PAGES 85–87

working dogs to frighten and intimidate detainees with threats of attack, and in one instance actually biting a detainee" (quoted in Hersh [2004b]). As Hersh further observed, "Such dehumanization is unacceptable in any culture, but it is especially so in the Arab world. Homosexual acts are against Islamic law and it is humiliating for men to be naked in front of other men, Bernard Haykel, a professor of Middle Eastern studies at New York University, explained. 'Being put on top of each other and forced to masturbate, being naked in front of each other—it's all a form of torture,' Haykel said."

26. Hersh (2004b).

27. In January 2006, Sanchez declined—or was encouraged to decline—Senate consideration of his promotion to a full four-star general, and elected instead to retire as a three-star general. The reason given by observers was that his hearing would "stir up too much political bad news in an election year." Quoted in Schmitt (2006a, 3).

28. Jehl and Schmitt (2004). Administration officials seized on the unclassified version of the Fay report, telling reporters before it was released that, as the *New York Times* reported, "senior officers in Baghdad . . . were found to have had no role in ordering or permitting the abuse, nor did senior Pentagon officials in Washington." Quoted in Shanker and Zernike (2004, 1). Somewhat incongruously, when asked by reporters whether the mistreatment of prisoners at Abu Ghraib amounted to torture, Major General Fay replied, "There were very few instances where in fact you could say that was torture. It's a harsh word, and in some instances, unfortunately, I think it was appropriate here. There were a few instances when torture was being used." Quoted in White (2004a, A1).

29. Jehl (2004). As explored further in chapter 4, the Schlesinger report also contended that Rumsfeld should not resign or be forced out of office for what were, in the panel's view, failures of omission rather than commission. Ironically, one of the report's several contradictions was its simultaneous assertion that the events *photographed* at Abu Ghraib—"acts of brutality and purposeless sadism," according to Schlesinger himself—had no connection with interrogation (see Danner 2004a); this assertion was then pushed further by Secretary Rumsfeld, who subsequently emphasized to reporters that *no* abuses at Abu Ghraib had anything to do with interrogation (Schmitt [2004]).

30. Quoted in Zernike (2004, WK7).

31. Kessler (2004). After these memos were leaked to the press, Gonzales told reporters that the president did not actually consider adopting those more aggressive measures and that "all interrogation techniques actually authorized have been carefully vetted, are lawful and do not constitute torture." The president, when asked, said what he continued to say, even when he was eventually forced politically to accept the McCain legislation banning cruel and inhumane treatment of prisoners: "We do not condone torture. I have never ordered torture. I will never order torture" (both quoted in Stevenson [2004b, A1]).

32. International Committee of the Red Cross (2004).

33. Ibid.

34. Amnesty International (2003); Human Rights Watch (2004).

35. Hersh (2004a, 2004b).

36. Danner (2004b); Hersh (2004c).

37. Danner (2004a, 44).

38. Entman (2004, 36–42).

39. Ibid., 17.

40. Bennett and Klockner (1996); Ferree et al. (2002).

41. The *Encyclopaedia Britannica*, for example, defines *torture* as "the inflic-
tion of excruciating physical or psychological pain for such reasons as punishment,
intimidation, coercion, the extraction of a confession, or the obtainment of information" (http://www.britannica.com/eb/article-9073000?query=torture&ct=,
accessed 18 October 2005). The International Convention against Torture includes
the purpose of gathering intelligence or extracting information as one element in its
definition of *torture*. See United Nations Commission on Human Rights (2006).

42. Priest and Stephens (2004).

43. Golden (2005).

44. *Washington Post* (2004b, A22).

45. Okrent (2004).

46. Downie (2004).

47. Bennett and Livingston (2003, 376).

48. Bennett and Klockner (1996); Ferree et al (2002).

49. Bennett and Klockner (1996); Entman and Page (1994); Hallin (1986);
Mermin (1999); Zaller and Chiu (1996).

50. Entman (2004).

51. Althaus (2003, 404).

52. Entman (2004).

53. Interestingly, Hersh himself used softened language to discuss Abu Ghraib
in some of his subsequent *New Yorker* pieces. See Jones (2006, 16–17).

54. VandeHei (2004). A broader search of the Nexis database for the terms
"abu ghraib and senate and torture" in close proximity yielded only three instances
between April and June of 2004 in which a senator used the term *torture* in conjunction with Abu Ghraib.

55. Shanker and Steinberg (2004).

56. VandeHei (2004).

57. *Washington Post* (2004b).

58. Kirkpatrick (2006).

59. Entman (2004); Jones and Rowling (2006).

60. Wolfsfeld et al. (2005, 5); see also Aday (2004); Fishman and Marvin
(2003).

61. Lawrence (2000b).

62. Bennett and Livingston (2003).

63. See for example Golden (2005) and Schmitt (2005). Almost two years
after the Abu Ghraib story broke, the extent of U.S. mistreatment of detainees in
many of its foreign detention centers had become clearer. In March of 2006, for

example, the *New York Times* described an infamous "black room" inside U.S. Camp Nama in Iraq in which members of one military unit violently mistreated prisoners for months before and after the Abu Ghraib story filled the headlines. "Placards posted by soldiers at the detention area advised, 'NO BLOOD, NO FOUL.' The slogan, as one Defense Department official explained, reflected an adage adopted by Task Force 6–26: 'If you don't make them bleed, they can't prosecute for it.'" According to the *Times*, the Camp Nama story helped to "belie the original Pentagon assertions that abuse was confined to a small number of rogue reservists at Abu Ghraib" (Schmitt and Marshall [2006, 1]).

64. See for example Lelyveld (2005).

CHAPTER FOUR

1. U.S. Department of State (2005, 11).

2. Armitage and Naim are quoted in Wright (2004, A26).

3. See the surveys conducted by the Pew Research Center (2004) and PIPA (2004).

4. As of June 2006, eleven U.S. soldiers had been convicted of crimes committed at Abu Ghraib. Lieutenant Colonel Steven L. Jordan, the former head of the interrogation center at the detention facility, was the highest-ranking officer at Abu Ghraib to have been criminally charged (Schmitt 2006d). Of the other U.S. personnel working for the CIA who were implicated in the deaths of at least four prisoners in Iraq and Afghanistan, only one was charged (Jehl and Golden 2005).

5. See Fay (2004, 72); International Committee of the Red Cross (2004).

6. See Danner (2004b); Fay (2004); White (2004a).

7. Quoted in Danner (2004a, 45).

8. Ricks (2006, 195).

9. White (2004a, A1).

10. A survey conducted by the Program on International Policy Attitudes (2004) after the Abu Ghraib story broke asked respondents for their views on torture given specific kinds of circumstances, such as having a high degree of certainty that a suspect held in U.S. custody had information about terrorist plots. In such circumstances, nearly half of the respondents supported using coercive tactics such as prolonged stress positions, but even in these cases, only small minorities supported more violent and humiliating measures, such as threatening detainees with dogs or guns; punching, kicking, or shocking them with electricity; making them go naked; or denying them food and water. Other surveys conducted by the Pew Research Center (2004) and Gallup (Carlson [2005]) similarly found widespread public disapproval of all but the mildest forms of coercion, such as sleep deprivation, even for prisoners suspected of having information about possible terrorist attacks against the United States. A Harris Interactive survey, conducted in December of 2005 as Congress debated the McCain amendment prohibiting torture by U.S. forces, found that "52 percent of all adults believe that the use of torture is justified either often (12%) or sometimes (40%)," but offered no specific scenarios to flesh out the conditions that would "sometimes" make torture allowable (Harris Interactive 2005).

11. Entman (2004, 32–33).

12. Note that we did not count labels that are cognates of *prisoner* or *detainee* (e.g., *captives; inmates*), including the phrase "ghost detainees" (which refers to those prisoners held incognito [their names were not registered with international authorities]). We did count the phrase "security detainees," since it implies people who somehow pose a threat to U.S. forces and/or have intelligence value. We did not count simple and widely reported adjectives such as *Iraqi* or *Muslim,* or adjectives such as *cowering* or *naked* that described the detainees' behavior in the photographs. In addition, we did not code any labels that referred to the detainees' behavior while in prison (such as *unruly*). We focused instead on markers of the detainees' identity and relationship to terrorism and the insurgency. Labels from different categories reported below were counted only once per article.

13. This was especially true in stories that also discussed the U.S. military detention facility at Guantanamo Bay. The identity of prisoners at Guantanamo might have been hard for the news audience to distinguish from those at Abu Ghraib, particularly since the point of these few stories was usually that techniques used at the former were then used at the latter.

14. Quoted in Andrews (2004).

15. Interestingly, the word *victim* itself was used only rarely by these news organizations, even though coverage generally took a critical tone toward the events at Abu Ghraib. We found only eleven stories in the *Washington Post* (one that used the term twice) and four on CBS that used *victim* to describe the abused detainees; the generic terms *detainee* and *prisoner* were far more prevalent, appearing in virtually every story. And when *victim* was used, it generally was by someone other than a reporter. Out of twelve appearances of *victim* in the *Washington Post* to describe the Abu Ghraib detainees, eight were direct quotations from sources (such as human rights activists, Iraqis, and others) or appeared in op-ed pieces. On CBS, however, all uses of *victim* were in the reporter's own words.

16. As one story noted, quoting an anonymous senior U.S. official in Baghdad, "We look like Saddam. . . . We pick up people and they disappear for a while. Wives, mothers, brothers—they try to find their relatives and they can't" (Slevin [2004, A19]).

17. Quoted in Spinner (2004, A20) and in Babington (2004, A18).

18. For example, an October 2003 Red Cross visit to another U.S. detention site in Iraq found prisoners routinely being stripped and humiliated—practices that were termed "part of the process" by the military intelligence officer in charge of interrogation. See Higham and Stevens (2004) and International Committee of the Red Cross (2004).

19. See Semetko and Kolmer (2005).

20. Jones (2006, 20).

21. For the data presented in figure 4.1, we ran a series of news database searches, repeating the same search criteria as described in the U.S. newspaper analysis in chapter 3. Assessing foreign news coverage presents several challenges, and it should be noted that the sources analyzed here are English-language ones that

could be obtained efficiently via the Nexis news database. Our search included the Nexis "UK Broadsheets" database, which contains an array of leading London newspapers, such as the *Daily/Sunday Telegraph*, the *Financial Times*, and the *Independent* and *Independent on Sunday*. We also consulted the broader array of foreign coverage found in the Nexis "BBC Worldwide Monitoring" database, a selective summary of broadcasts from 120 countries (not including the United States, Canada, or the UK) compiled by the Monitoring Service of the British Broadcasting Corporation. It should be noted that items in this BBC database are abstracts, not full news articles. Despite this limitation, it represents a rare opportunity to assess in at least a rough way the framing of the story in countries as diverse as Denmark, Poland, and Turkey. That these data are from abstracts and not the complete articles may increase the significance of our findings, because the labels found in abstracts most likely indicate the most prominent labeling of the Abu Ghraib story in these foreign news sources.

22. It should be noted that, as with figure 3.2 in chapter 3, the line graphs in figure 4.1 are based on both news and editorial items. And, as with figure 3.1, eliminating the editorials tends to reduce the percentages of articles mentioning *torture*.

23. Semetko and Kolmer (2005, 8–9).

24. Ibid. It is important to note here that "news reporting in the US appears to be more likely than in other countries to come with clear positive or negative evaluations of protagonists or actors. This emerges from the fact that the US news also devoted a larger share of its news to positive evaluations of the Iraqis, about twice as much as Al-Jazeera, the UK, Germany, the Czech Republic, and nearly three times as much as South African news."

25. Massing (2004, 12).

26. Program on International Policy Attitudes (2003, 17); emphasis added.

27. Ibid., 1. More recent surveys found that the percentage of Americans who believed that the war was not supported by world opinion eventually increased to 50% (Program on International Policy Attitudes [2004, 10–11]).

28. This dynamic in contemporary American journalism is explored by Fallows (1997) and Patterson (1993).

29. *New York Times* (2004a, A8).

30. See Risen (2006, 24). As he goes on to observe, "When reporters asked the White House whether President Bush had approved of torture or harsh interrogation practices, they were asking the wrong question. The right question was whether George W. Bush had been given plausible deniability by his own inner circle" (25).

31. This coding of claims about Rumsfeld's responsibility picked up two instances, on May 13 and then on May 23, in which the vice president was reported denying responsibility. Both occurred after Rumsfeld's May 9 apology to Congress in which he accepted responsibility (interestingly, neither article mentioned this), and both reported Rumsfeld's claims that his list of approved interrogation techniques did not violate the Geneva Conventions and/or had been adequately vetted by Pentagon lawyers.

32. Recall that in our coding we looked both for claims directly linking Rumsfeld to Abu Ghraib and for claims simply that he authorized techniques employed at Guantanamo and elsewhere that then made their way to Abu Ghraib via other military commanders—a much less direct allegation about the defense secretary's responsibility. It is noteworthy that only 9 out of 150 articles contained that less direct claim, with the remainder discussing more direct responsibility.

33. On the other hand, if the total number of Abu Ghraib articles in the *Post* (292) is used as the denominator, the percentage of articles with claims about Rumsfeld's direct responsibility is less impressive (though still not insignificant) at 15%.

34. Broder (2004, B7).

35. Graham and White (2004, A1).

36. *Washington Post* (2004b, A22).

37. Bumiller and Stevenson (2004).

38. Seelye (2004, A1).

39. Risen (2006, 24). Indeed, the CIA's Office of Inspector General found that "there was never any written form of presidential authorization covering the CIA's interrogation tactics used on detainees in its custody" (ibid.).

40. See Smith (2004) for one account. For an example of an op-ed piece that did assemble this causal chain cogently and concisely, see Applebaum (2004).

41. This charge was not as innocuous as it might sound. According to one account, "The prison barely had water. The food was foul. . . . electrical generators would go out, and with them the lights. . . . toilets overflowed. . . . MPs were in short supply. Detainees staged uprisings, weapons inside were plentiful, and the prison was under constant external attack." Midlevel officers requested more support, supplies, and equipment, but their requests were often denied. One sergeant stationed at Abu Ghraib simply said, "We were abandoned." See Wypijewski (2006, 44). But those appalling "conditions" were not described often in news accounts.

42. Former deputy secretary of defense John Hamre, quoted in Graham (2004, A14).

43. Eugene Fidell, quoted in Schmitt (2006b, A20).

44. This was considered a controversial action among some, who believed Miller had abdicated his responsibility to the military hierarchy by refusing to testify. See Lagouranis (2006).

45. Wypijewski (2006, 40). As this detailed account of the Abu Ghraib courts-martial observes, "The government's computer-forensics expert had reviewed twelve CDs acquired from soldiers containing 16,000 photographs, and had identified 281 individual pictures pertinent to the Abu Ghraib investigation. Those used in court were, for the most part, the two dozen or so that made the rounds of print and electronic media in 2004" (43).

46. Cappella and Jamieson (1997); Fallows (1997); Lawrence (2000a); Patterson (1993).

47. Quoted in Ricks (2004, A1).

48. Danner (2006).

49. Program on International Policy Attitudes (2004).

50. Cook (2005); Lawrence (2005).

CHAPTER FIVE

1. Quoted in Murray (2005, A6).

2. This question parallels E. E. Schattschneider's (1983) argument that debates were either privatized (walled off from the potentially disruptive influences of third-party participants) or socialized (given a broad public hearing) by a variety of strategic communication methods.

3. John MacArthur (publisher of *Harper's* magazine), quoted in Borjesson (2005, 98).

4. Robert Callahan, interview by Steven Livingston, Washington, DC, Feb. 9, 2006.

5. Entman (2004, 9).

6. Brock (2004); see also Massing (2005).

7. Suskind (2004).

8. Baudrillard (1981); Baudrillard and Patton (1995). Ron Suskind, one of the premier chroniclers of the George W. Bush administration, argues that the administration's governing philosophy is, "We don't feel there's an inherent value to public dialogue based on the pertinent facts. We don't. Strategically, there isn't much value to it in our minds and the question is: 'Will we be penalized for not engaging the way other White Houses have generally engaged? Let's see.'" Quoted in Borjesson (2005, 162).

9. NASA chief administrator Michael D. Griffin issued new rules in March 2006 that were intended to protect NASA scientists from such political pressure. See Leary (2006, 16).

10. Quoted in *Washington Post* (2006, A22).

11. Farrell (2006); see also Eilperin (2006).

12. Eilperin (2006).

13. Ironically, the AP article had relied on EPA data in making its case.

14. Kaufman (2005, A8).

15. Revkin (2005, 6).

16. Sanders (2005).

17. Jamie Wilson (2005).

18. Dean (2006, A16).

19. Pillar (2006), 19.

20. Livingston and Robinson (2006).

21. Pillar (2006, 24).

22. Victoria Clarke, interview by Steven Livingston, Washington, DC, Mar. 24, 2006.

23. Wilkerson (2005).

24. Risen (2006, 79).

25. Ibid., 109.

26. Ibid., 119.

27. Toppo (2005).
28. Carver (2002).
29. Mazzetti and Daragahi (2005).
30. Mazzetti (2006).
31. National Security Archive (2006).
32. Burns (2006).
33. The U.S. Information and Educational Exchange Act of 1948, generally called the Smith-Mundt Act, prohibits the U.S. domestic dissemination of information intended for a foreign audience. This prohibition has been strengthened by subsequent legislation. The Foreign Relations Authorization Act of 1972 reinforced the ban on disseminating within the United States any "information about the United States, its people, and its policies" prepared for dissemination abroad. If there has been, as the Pentagon "Roadmap" document describes, cases of Pentagon PSYOP operations making their way back to the United States, the Lincoln Group efforts might well have violated federal laws guarding against the domestic dissemination of propaganda.
34. McDermott (2004).
35. Connolly (2005).
36. *FreePress* (2006).
37. HometownLink (2006).
38. Taylor (2004).
39. This figure most likely underestimates the total. The GAO surveyed only seven of the fifteen cabinet-level departments, relied on self-reported data, and did not include subcontracts or public relations work done by government employees. See *California Chronicle* (2006).
40. MediaMatters for America (2005).
41. Keith Richburg, interview by Steven Livingston, Washington, DC, July 19, 2005.
42. Van Natta Jr. (2006).
43. Norton-Taylor (2006, 1); Sands (2005).
44. Van Natta Jr. (2006).
45. MediaMatters for America (2006).
46. President Bush Discusses Faith-Based Initiative in Tennessee (2003).
47. President George Bush Discusses Iraq in National Press Conference (2003).
48. This missing news coverage was first pointed out by *MediaMatters*, a liberal media watchdog organization. We followed up with a search of the Nexis news database for March 28 through March 31—the four days after the *Times* first published its story. According to our search, during that period none of these leading news organizations reported on "Bush and memo." Schiffer (2006) analyzed a broader swath of media coverage of the Downing Street Memo for a longer time period (April 30–July 5) and found that "over the entire period of analysis, the *CBS Evening News* mentioned the controversy once (June 7, after Bush's press conference), NBC's *Nightly News* did one segment and made one additional mention

(June 7), and ABC's *World News Tonight* ignored the story completely" (10). The *New York Times* mentioned the memo in only four stories, published in May and June, while the *Washington Post* mentioned it in nine news and editorial pieces, "though often from a dismissive or critical standpoint" (12).

49. John MacArthur, quoted in Borjesson (2005, 98).

50. See also Sparrow (1999, chap. 5).

51. Although the list is long, besides Al Gore, Boisfeuillet Jones, the publisher and chief executive officer of the *Washington Post*, and Don Graham, the chairman of the Post Company, attended St. Alban's in Washington before going on to Harvard, where they both wrote for the *Harvard Crimson*.

52. Addresses in the District of Columbia are divided among four quadrants. *NW* encompasses the pricey and prestigious northwest quadrant; *SE* is the poor southeastern quadrant of the city, inhabited mostly by black residents.

53. As veteran journalist David Broder told Sparrow (1999, 116), "It is hard for Washington journalists to maintain their distance. A lot of the problem revolves around eating. . . . The dinner [like the party] gives the reporters an opportunity to show off in front of their bosses, and the owners have a chance to hobnob with government officials."

54. Mike McCurry, interview by Steven Livingston, Washington, DC, Feb. 27, 2006.

55. Lawrence Wilkerson, interview by Steven Livingston, Washington, DC, Apr. 4, 2006. This rule of the Washington power game was learned by other former administration members who became its public critics, including John DiIulio, former head of the president's faith-based and community initiative, and former treasury secretary Paul O'Neill. DiIulio told independent journalist Ron Suskind on the record that "there is no precedent in any modern White House for what is going on in this one: a complete lack of policy apparatus. What you've got [in this administration] is everything—and I mean everything—being run by the political reign of the Mayberry Machiavellis." The day Suskind's *Esquire* magazine article containing DiIulio's statements appeared on the newsstands, DiIulio issued a public statement calling his own charges "baseless and groundless"—the very words White House spokesman Ari Fleischer had used earlier in the day to denounce the piece. According to Suskind, "This administration's desire, clearly, was to make an example of John, [who was] the first guy to leave the administration and speak with real frankness, so others would not exhibit similar temerity" (quoted in Borjesson [2005, 245–46]). Suskind and O'Neill then experienced that pressure firsthand when Suskind's book *The Price of Loyalty*, based on O'Neill's tenure as Treasury Secretary, was published (see ibid., 157–62). According to Suskind, the president's political adviser Karl Rove has played a central role in these intimidation campaigns: "That's an important thing that Karl does for the president. The president believes that people should understand that the choices they make will have consequences. . . . Karl, through surrogates, makes sure that the actual individuals know that they will face consequences for not doing what they're told" (quoted in ibid., 157).

56. Joseph Wilson (2004b, 9).

57. Novak (2004).

58. Joseph Wilson, interview by Steven Livingston, Washington, DC, June 13, 2006.

59. See for example Joseph Wilson (2002).

60. Joseph Wilson (2004a, 339).

61. Ibid., 334.

62. On the whole, former assistant defense secretary Victoria Clarke disagreed with our premise concerning a vindictive White House. But she concurred concerning its response to Joseph Wilson's criticisms. When asked if she could think of an example of a White House attack on critics in keeping with our premise, she said, "The only one that comes to mind . . . is Joe Wilson." Clarke, interview by Livingston, Mar. 24, 2006.

63. Wilson chose his cockroach metaphor deliberately, knowing that the interviewer had just returned from Rwanda, where the Hutu extremists who organized and executed the 1994 genocide referred to Tutsi as cockroaches in their radio exhortations to murder.

64. Waas (2006).

65. *Washington Post* (2003, A12).

66. Weintraub and Shanker (2003, A1).

67. For example, see Herman and Chomsky (2002).

68. Schmitt (2002).

69. V. Clarke, interview by Livingston, Mar. 24, 2006.

70. Richard Clarke, interview by Steven Livingston, Arlington, VA, Jan. 24, 2006.

71. Ibid.

72. The Washington press works in a constant calculus of motive when assessing sources ("Why is this person saying what he is saying?"), no doubt as a defense against spin. This is evident in the way Tim Russert questioned Clarke: "As you know, your motivation has been widely questioned both at the White House and by some on Capitol Hill" (*Meet the Press* [2004]).

73. The White House tried the same approach in its attack on Joseph Wilson. The logic of such attacks seems to be to create the impression that technocrats or other sorts of nonpartisan sources are simply playing partisan politics or "politics as usual." Anticipating this, we should recall that Joseph Wilson "dusted off" his pictures and notes from George H. W. Bush in anticipation of the attacks about to be leveled against him by the George W. Bush administration.

74. R. Clarke, interview by Livingston, Jan. 24, 2006.

75. Ibid.

76. *Meet the Press* (2004).

77. R. Clarke, interview by Livingston, Jan. 24, 2006.

78. Quoted in Milbank and Allen (2004, A1).

79. *Meet the Press* (2004).

80. Ibid.

81. Ibid.

82. Clarke responded by pointing out that White House staffers are often asked to present the best possible case for administration policies. What is more startling, he believes that the White House coached at least one Republican 9/11 Commission member in how to question Clarke. According to Clarke, James Thompson, the former governor of Illinois, took telephone calls from the White House during Clarke's testimony. Both in writing and by telephone, we requested a reply from Governor Thompson on this assertion. He declined comment. Besides Clarke, another source present at the hearing described Thompson's departures from the proceedings to take telephone calls. Unlike Clarke, our second source is unable to say whether someone from the White House was on the other end of the call.

83. R. Clarke, interview by Livingston, Jan. 24, 2006.

84. Fukuyama (2006, 7–8).

85. Risen (2006, 1).

86. See Entman (2004). Scowcroft's criticism of the Bush administration had consequences, even for him, George H. W. Bush's closest friend and confidant. His position as chairman of the President's Foreign Intelligence Advisory Board was not renewed when it expired at the end of 2004. See Blumenthal (2005).

87. Entman (2004, 109).

88. Wilkerson, interview by Livingston, Apr. 4, 2006.

89. Murray and Babington (2006).

CHAPTER SIX

1. Chertoff (2005).

2. Brown (2005).

3. For Williams's account and a link to this interview, see his blog posting of September 5, 2005: http://www.msnbc.msn.com/id/9216831/#050905.

4. To see the video, go to http://dir.salon.com/story/ent/feature/2005/09/07/reporters_gone_wild/index.html.

5. Bauder (2005).

6. The chapter epigraph exemplifies this challenge. See "Open Letter to President Bush" (2005).

7. This search of the Nexis database used the search term "Katrina and (Brown, FEMA, federal, or Bush)." We excluded editorials, opinion pieces, and letters to the editor.

8. Nagourney and Hulse (2005).

9. Bumiller (2004).

10. Herman and Chomsky (2002).

11. McChesney (2004, 74).

12. Entman (2004). An important contribution of Entman's "cascading activation" model of the news is its recognition that lower-level sources, even journalists themselves, may sometimes be able to kick off a cascade—some way of framing an issue that works its way up as well as down the power hierarchy. But his model depends on a combination of factors to enable bottom-up "cascades" to occur,

while the dominant pattern, acknowledged by his model and emphasized in ours, is one of top-down cascades of frames advanced by those at the top of the power ladder.

13. Hallin (1986).

14. See Sparrow (1999), chapter 6, for a detailed overview of several such press failures.

15. See the resolution at http://www.senate.gov/~feingold/releases/06/03/20060312.html.

16. Zogby International (2006). The wording of the Zogby poll question was, "If President Bush wiretapped American citizens without the approval of a judge, do you agree or disagree that Congress should consider holding him accountable through impeachment?"

17. For these and other polls, see www.pollingreport.com/iraq.htm.

18. On opinion trends during wars, see Mueller (2005).

19. Shanker (2006).

20. Packer (2006).

21. Entman (1989).

22. As the London *Guardian* reported in mid-June 2006, a Pew Center poll of 17,000 people in 15 countries found favorability ratings of the United States in decline (dropping from 83% favorable in the UK in 1999 to 56% in 2006, for example) and more apprehension about the U.S. presence in Iraq than about Iran's nuclear ambitions: "Only in the US and Germany is Iran seen as a greater danger than the US in Iraq. Public opinion in 12 of the other countries—Britain, France, Spain, Russia, Indonesia, Egypt, Jordan, Turkey, Pakistan, Nigeria, India and China—cite the US presence in Iraq as being the greater danger" (MacAskill [2006]).

23. Cook (1998); Sparrow (1999). For detailed elaboration of this point and its significance to governance, see the "New Institutionalism and the News," special issue, *Political Communication* 23, no. 2 (April–June 2006).

24. Kovach and Rosenstiel (2001, 12–13).

25. Quoted in Bates (1995).

26. Leigh (1947). Luce provided Hutchins with the budget to enlist twelve leading intellectuals who would meet in Chicago periodically over several years. They included Archibald MacLeish, Harold Lasswell, Arthur Schlesinger, William Hocking, Zechariah Chafee, and Reinhold Niebuhr, among others. Their investigations and deliberation focused on print media as well as broadcasting and film.

27. Pickard (2006). Though the Hutchins report was an elite project lacking a large base of popular support in the 1940s, its tenets would later reemerge and be referred to often during the 1970s, 1980s, and on into the public journalism movement of the 1990s.

28. Indeed, the Annenberg Policy Foundation and the Sunnylands Trust did convene such a discussion, and its general results are available in Overholser and Jamieson (2005).

29. For an overview of recent trends in public confidence in the media, see Cook and Gronke (2002).

30. Patterson (2000, 14).

31. Personal communication, based on forthcoming research.

32. McChesney (2004).

33. On media "uncertainties" that encourage cautious news coverage of political issues, see Sparrow (1999).

34. Personal communication.

35. See McQuail (2003).

36. Stewart (1975, 634). Though Stewart's description may have been historically inaccurate, he was articulating a powerful idea in American culture. See Cook (2005).

37. Napoli (1995); Prindle (2004).

38. See Lawrence (2005). The underlying ideal of free expression is well articulated by Emerson (1970).

39. See Bennett and Serrin (2005, 169–88).

40. Baker (2002).

41. For a fuller discussion of this dilemma, see McChesney (2004) and the essays in Cook (2005).

42. Sparrow (1999, 133).

43. Zaller (2003, 121–22).

44. See Bennett (2003).

45. Rosen (1999, 4).

46. Ibid., 187.

47. For an example of journalistic criticism of civic journalism, see Porter (2003).

48. It also bears mentioning here that much of the financial support for experiments in public journalism across the country came from the Pew Center for Civic Journalism. That funding has largely dried up, raising questions about public journalism's future.

49. Bennett and Serrin (2005), 169–88.

50. Keller (2006).

51. Lawrence (2000b).

52. See Bennett (2003); Bennett and Livingston (2003).

53. See Zaller (2003); Schudson (2005).

54. Lippman (1997).

55. Sparrow (1999, 193).

56. Tuchman (1978).

57. Quoted in Sparrow (1999, 194).

58. Quoted in Borjesson (2005, 31).

59. Quoted in ibid., 166.

60. Ibid., 163.

61. Entman (2004, 17).

62. Bennett and Klockner (1996); Ferree et al. (2002).

63. Rutenberg (2006).

REFERENCES

Aday, Sean. 2004. The real war will never get on television: An analysis of casualty imagery in American television coverage of the Iraq war. Paper presented at the annual meeting of the International Studies Association, Montreal, Mar. 17–20, 2004.

Alterman, Eric. 2003. *What liberal media? The truth about bias and the news.* New York: Basic Books.

Althaus, Scott L. 2003. When news norms collide, follow the lede: New evidence for press independence. *Political Communication* 20 (4): 381–414.

American Civil Liberties Union. 2005. *Torture FOIA.* Apr. 29. http://www.aclu.org/ International/International.cfm?ID=13962&c=36 (accessed May 2, 2005).

Amnesty International. 2003. Iraq: Amnesty International Digest. Apr. 25. http:// web.amnesty.org/library/Index/ENGMDE140982003?open&of=ENG-IRQ (accessed Dec. 3, 2005).

Andrews, Wyatt. 2004. Donald Rumsfeld visits Iraq. *CBS Evening News,* May 13.

Annenberg Political Fact Check. 2005 (Sept 2). http://www.factcheck.org/ article344.html (accessed Sept. 27, 2005).

Applebaum, Anne. 2004. So torture is legal? *Washington Post,* June 16, A27.

Babington, Charles. 2004. Senator critical of focus on prisoner abuse. *Washington Post,* May 12, A18.

Bahador, Babak. 2006. *The CNN effect in action: How the news media pushed the West towards war in Kosovo.* New York: Palgrave.

Baker, C. Edwin. 2002. *Media, markets, and democracy.* New York: Cambridge Univ. Press.

Bates, Stephen. 1995. Realigning journalism with democracy; The Hutchins Commission: Its times and ours. Annenberg Washington Program of Northwestern Univ. http://www.annenberg.northwestern.edu/pubs/hutchins/ (accessed June 14, 2006).

Bauder, David. 2005. NBC's Brian Williams: Katrina may be remembered as the time reporters took off gloves again. Associated Press, Sept. 11.

Baudrillard, Jean. 1981. *Simulacra and simulations.* Ann Arbor: Univ. of Michigan Press.

Baudrillard, Jean, and Paul Patton. 1995. *The Gulf War did not take place.* Bloomington: Indiana Univ. Press.

Baumgartner, Frank, and Bryan D. Jones. 1993. *Agendas and instability in American politics.* Chicago: Univ. of Chicago Press.

Bennett, W. Lance. 1991. Toward a theory of press-state relations. *Journal of Communication* 40 (2): 103–25.

———. 2003. The burglar alarm that just keeps ringing: A response to Zaller. *Political Communication* 20 (2): 131–38.

———. 2005a. Beyond pseudoevents: Election news as reality TV. *American Behavioral Scientist* 49 (3): 1–15.

———. 2005b. News as reality TV: Election coverage and the democratization of truth. *Critical Studies in Media Communication* 22 (2): 171–77.

———. 2005c. *News: The politics of illusion.* 6th ed. New York: Longman.

Bennett, W. Lance, and John D. Klockner. 1996. The psychology of mass-mediated publics. In *The psychology of political communication,* ed. Ann N. Crigler, 89–109. Ann Arbor: Univ. of Michigan Press.

Bennett, W. Lance, and Regina G. Lawrence. 1995. News icons and the mainstreaming of social change. *Journal of Communication* 45 (3): 20–39.

Bennett, W. Lance, Regina G. Lawrence, and Steven Livingston. 2005. In the camera's frame: The contest to define Abu Ghraib. Paper presented at the annual meeting of the International Studies Association, Honolulu, Mar. 2–5.

Bennett, W. Lance, and Steven Livingston. 2003. A semi-independent press: Government control and journalistic autonomy in the political construction of news. *Political Communication* 20 (4): 359–62.

Bennett, W. Lance, and William Serrin. 2005. The watchdog role. In *The press,* ed. Geneva Overholser and Kathleen Hall Jamieson, 169–88. New York: Oxford Univ. Press.

Blumenthal, Sidney. 2005. Happy talk. *Guardian* (London), Jan. 14. http://www.guardian.co.uk/usa/story/0,12271,1390294,00.htm.

Borjesson, Kristina. 2005. *Feet to the fire: The media after 9/11.* Amherst, NY: Prometheus Books.

Brock, David. 2004. *The Republican noise machine.* New York: Random House.

Broder, David S. 2004. McNamara moment. *Washington Post,* May 9, B7.

Brown, Michael. 2005. Interview by Ted Koppel. *Nightline,* ABC, Sept. 1.

Bumiller, Elizabeth. 2004. Interview by *Democracy Now,* Apr. 8. http://www.democracynow.org/article.pl?sid=04/04/08/1441248 (accessed June 14, 2006).

Bumiller, Elizabeth, and Richard W. Stevenson. 2004. Rumsfeld chastised by president for his handling of Iraq scandal. *New York Times,* May 6, A1.

Burns, Robert. 2006. Pentagon document shows "PSYOP" messages boomerang to U.S. *Editor & Publisher,* Jan. 27. http://www.editorandpublisher.com/eandp/news/article_display.jsp?vnu_content_id=1001919832.

Calame, Byron. 2006a. Behind the eavesdropping story, a loud silence. *New York Times,* Jan. 1, sec. 4, 8.

———. 2006b. Eavesdropping and the election: An answer on the question of timing. *New York Times,* Aug. 13, WK 10.

California Chronicle. 2006. Bush Administration spent over $1.6 billion on advertising and public relations contracts since 2003. Feb. 13. http://www.californiachronicle.com/articles/viewArticle.asp?articleID=5806.

Cappella, Joseph N., and Kathleen Hall Jamieson. 1997. *Spiral of cynicism: The press and the public good.* New York: Oxford Univ. Press.

Carlson, Darren K. 2005. Americans frown on interrogation techniques. http://www.gallup.com, Mar. 8 (accessed May 15, 2006).

Carver, Tom. 2002. Pentagon plans propaganda war. *BBC News,* Feb. 20. http://news.bbc.co.uk/1/hi/world/americas/1830500.stm.

CBS News. 2003. Bush knew Iraq info was dubious. July 10. http://www.cbsnews.com/ stories/2003/06/25/eveningnews/main560449.shtml?CMP=ILC-SearchStories.

Center for Media & Democracy. 2005. George C. Deutsch. SourceWatch: A project of the Center for Media & Democracy. http://www.sourcewatch.org/index.php?title=George_C._Deutsch.

Chertoff, Michael. 2005. Interview. *All Things Considered,* National Public Radio, Sept. 1.

Cohen, Bernard C. 1963. *The press and foreign policy.* Princeton, NJ: Princeton Univ. Press.

Connolly, Ceci. 2005. Drug control office faulted for issuing fake news tapes. *Washington Post,* Jan. 7, A17.

Cook, Timothy. 1996. Afterward: Political values and production values. *Political Communication* 13 (4): 469–81.

———. 1998. *Governing with the news: The news media as a political institution.* Chicago: Univ. of Chicago Press.

———. 2005. Freeing the presses: An introductory essay. In *Freeing the presses,* ed. Timothy Cook, 1–28. Baton Rouge: Louisiana State Univ. Press.

Cook, Timothy, and Paul Gronke. 2002. Trust and distrust, confidence and lack of confidence: New evidence of public opinion toward government and institutions from 2002. Paper presented at the Annual Meeting of the Southern Political Science Association, Savannah, GA, November. http://www.reed.edu/~gronkep/docs/SPSA02-version2.pdf.

Cunningham, Brent. 2003. Re-thinking objectivity. *Columbia Journalism Review* 4 (July–Aug.). http://www.cjr.org/issues/2003/4/objective-cunningham.asp (accessed Jan. 5, 2006).

Danner, Mark. 2004a. Abu Ghraib: The hidden story. *New York Review of Books,* Oct. 7, 44–50.

———. 2004b. *Torture and truth: America, Abu Ghraib, and the war on terror.* New York: New York Review of Books.

———. 2006. TomDispatch Interview: Mark Danner on Bush's state of exception. By Tom Engelhardt. TomDispatch.com, Feb. 26. http://www.tomdispatch.com/index.mhtml?pid=63903.

Dean, Cornelia. 2006. At a scientific gathering, U.S. policies are lamented. *New York Times,* Feb. 19, A16.

Domke, David. 2004. *God willing? Political fundamentalism in the White House, the war on terror, and the echoing press.* London: Pluto Press.

Dowd, Maureen. 2005. Woman of mass destruction. *New York Times,* Oct. 22, A17.

Downie, Leonard Jr. 2004. Iraq: New abuse details. *Washington Post,* May 21. http://www.washingtonpost.com/wp-dyn/articles/A44952–2004May21.html (accessed Feb. 2, 2005).

Eilperin, Juliet. 2006. Censorship is alleged at NOAA. *Washington Post,* Feb. 11, A7.

Emerson, Thomas. 1970. *The system of freedom of expression.* New York: Vintage.

Engelhardt, Tom. 2006. When facts fail. *Salon,* Feb. 28. http://www.salon .com/opinion/feature/2006/02/28/engelhardt/index.html (accessed May 3, 2006).

Entman, Robert M. 1989. *Democracy without citizens.* New York: Oxford Univ. Press.

———. 1993. Framing: Toward clarification of a fractured paradigm. *Journal of Communication* 43 (4): 51–58.

———. 2004. *Projections of power: Framing news, public opinion and U.S. foreign policy.* Chicago: Univ. of Chicago Press.

———. 2006. Punctuating the homogeneity of institutionalized news: Abusing prisoners at Abu Ghraib versus killing civilians at Fallujah. *Political Communication* 23 (2): 215–24.

Entman, Robert M., and Benjamin Page. 1994. The news before the storm: Limits to media autonomy in covering the Iraq war debate. In *Taken by storm: The media, public opinion, and U.S. foreign policy in the Gulf War,* ed. W. Lance Bennett and David L. Paletz, 82–101. Chicago: Univ. of Chicago Press.

Fairness and Accuracy in Reporting. 2004. Activism update: *NY Times* responds to FAIR alert on torture. *Extra!* June 10. http://www.fair.org/index .php?page=1578.

Fallows, James. 1997. *Breaking the news: How the media undermine American democracy.* New York: Vintage.

Farrell, Bryan. 2006. Political science. *Nation,* Feb. 13. http://www.thenation .com/doc/20060227/farrell.

Fay, Major General George R. n.d. *Investigation of the intelligence activities at Abu Ghraib.* http://www4.army.mil/ocpa/reports/ar15-6/AR15-6.pdf (accessed Oct. 20, 2006).

Feinstein, Lee. 2002. Commentary. In *Americans thinking about Iraq, but focused on the economy.* Pew Research Center for the People and the Press, Oct. 10. http:// people-ress.org/reports/display.php3?PageID=644 (accessed May 22, 2006).

Ferree, Myra Marx, William A. Gamson, Jurgen Gerhards, and Dieter Rucht. 2002. *Shaping abortion discourse: Democracy and the public sphere in Germany and the United States.* New York: Cambridge Univ. Press.

Fishman, Jessica M., and Carolyn Marvin. 2003. Portrayals of violence and group difference in newspaper photographs and media. *Journal of Communication* 53 (1): 32–44.

Fletcher, Michael A. 2005. Cindy Sheehan's pitched battle. *Washington Post,* Aug. 12, A01.

FreePress. n.d. Propagandists on the Pentagon payroll. http://www.freepress.net/ propaganda/=pentagon (accessed June 2, 2006).

Fukuyama, Francis. 2006. *America at the crossroads: Democracy, power, and the neoconservative legacy*. New Haven, CT: Yale Univ. Press.

Garrels, Anne. 2003. *Naked in Baghdad*. New York: Farrar, Straus, and Giroux.

Gellman, Barton, and Walter Pincus. 2003. Errors and exaggerations: Prewar depictions of Iraq's nuclear threat outweighed the evidence. *Washington Post National Weekly Edition*, Aug. 18–25, 6.

Gilson, Dave. 2004. Torture and truth: Tracing the origins—and aftermath—of what happened at Abu Ghraib. *Mother Jones*, Dec. 7. http://www.motherjones .com/news/qa/2004/12/12_401.html (accessed Jan. 15, 2005).

Gitlin, Todd. 2003. *The whole world is watching*. Paperback ed. Berkeley and Los Angeles: Univ. of California Press.

Goldberg, Bernard. 2003. *Bias: A CBS insider exposes how the media distort the news*. New York: HarperCollins.

Golden, Tim. 2005. In U.S. report, brutal details of 2 Afghan inmates' deaths. *New York Times*, May 20, A1.

———. 2006. U.S. should close prison in Cuba, U.N. panel says. *New York Times*, May 20, A1.

Graham, Bradley. 2004. Some seek broad, external inquiry on prisoner abuse. *Washington Post*, May 27, A14.

Graham, Bradley, and Josh White. 2004. Top Pentagon leaders faulted in prison abuse; oversight by Rumsfeld and others inadequate, panel says. *Washington Post*, Aug. 25, A1.

Gunther, Albert C., and Kathleen Schmitt. 2004. Mapping the boundaries of the hostile media effect. *Journal of Communication* 54 (1): 55–70.

Hallin, Daniel C. 1986. *The uncensored war: The media and Vietnam*. Berkeley and Los Angeles: Univ. of California Press.

Hanley, Charles J. 2003a. More than 5,000 detainees sit and wait behind U.S. razor wire, prison walls in Iraq. Associated Press, Oct. 8.

———. 2003b. Former Iraqi detainees tell of riots, punishment in the sun, good Americans and pitiless ones. Associated Press, Oct. 29.

Harris Interactive. 2005. Majorities of public believe that torture, "rendition" and the use of secret prison camps outside U.S. are sometimes justified. Dec. 21. http://www.harrisinteractive.com/harris_poll/index.asp?PID=621 (accessed May 15, 2006).

———. 2006. Poll 357, July 21. http://www.harrisinteractive.com/harris_poll/ index.asp?PID=684.

Herbst, Susan. 1998. *Reading public opinion: How political actors view the democratic process*. Chicago: Univ. of Chicago Press.

Herman, Edward S., and Noam Chomsky. 2002. *Manufacturing consent: The political economy of the mass media*, 2nd ed. New York: Pantheon Books.

Hersh, Seymour. 2004a. *Chain of command: The road from 9/11 to Abu Ghraib*. New York: HarperCollins.

———. 2004b. Torture at Abu Ghraib. *New Yorker*, May 10, 42. http://www. newyorker.com/fact/content/?040510fa_fact.

———. 2004c. The gray zone: How a secret Pentagon program came to Abu Ghraib. *New Yorker*, May 24, 38. http://www.newyorker.com/fact/content/?040524fa_fact

Higham, Scott, and Joseph Stephens. 2004. Punishment and amusement: Documents indicate 3 photos were not staged for interrogation. *Washington Post*, May 22, A1.

Higham, Scott, Joseph Stephens, and Josh White. 2004. Dates on prison photos show two phases of abuse. *Washington Post*, June 1, A01.

HometownLink. https://hn.afnews.af.mil/webpages/about.htm (accessed June 2, 2006).

Human Rights Watch. 2004. Enduring Freedom: Abuses by U.S. Forces in Afghanistan. Mar. 8, 2004. http://hrw.org/reports/2004/afghanistan0304/1.htm#_Toc64778166 (accessed Dec. 3, 2005).

International Committee of the Red Cross. 2004. Report of the International Committee of the Red Cross (ICRC) on the treatment by the Coalition Forces of prisoners of war and other protected persons by the Geneva Conventions in Iraq during arrest, internment and interrogation. Feb. 2004. http://www.globalsecurity.org/military/library/report/2004/icrc_report_iraq_feb2004.htm (accessed Feb. 20, 2005).

Iyengar, Shanto. 1991. *Is anyone responsible?* Chicago: Univ. of Chicago Press.

Iyengar, Shanto, and Donald Kinder. 1987. *News that matters*. Chicago: Univ. of Chicago Press.

Janis, Irving. 1972. *Victims of groupthink*. Boston: Houghton Mifflin.

Jehl, Douglas. 2004. A trail leads to Rumsfeld. *New York Times*, Aug. 25, A1.

Jehl, Douglas, and Tim Golden. 2005. C.I.A. is likely to avoid charges in most prisoner deaths. *New York Times*, Oct. 25, 6.

Jehl, Douglas, and Eric Schmitt. 2004. Army's report faults general in prison abuse. *New York Times*, Aug. 27, A1.

Jones, Timothy M. 2006. Framing and social identity: A cross-national news analysis of the Abu Ghraib prison scandal. Paper presented at the annual meeting of the International Studies Association, San Diego, CA, Mar. 2–5.

Jones, Timothy M., and Charles Rowling. 2006. Abuse vs. torture: How social identity, strategic framing, and indexing explain U.S. media coverage of Abu Ghraib. Paper presented at the Southern Political Science Association Conference, Atlanta, Jan. 5.

Judt, Tony. 2005. The new world order. *New York Review of Books* 52 (12). http://www.nybooks.com/articles/article-preview?article_id=18113 (accessed Feb. 25, 2006).

Kaufman, Marc. 2005. FDA official quits over delay on Plan B. *Washington Post*, Sept. 1, A8.

Keller, Bill. 2006. Letter from Bill Keller on the *Times'* banking records report. *New York Times*, June 25. http://www.nytimes.com/glogin?URI=http://www.nytimes.com/2006/06/25/business/media/25keller-letter.html (accessed Oct. 20, 2006).

Kessler, Glen. 2004. U.S. releases human rights report delayed after abuse scandal. *Washington Post*, May 18, A15.

Kirkpatrick, David D. 2006. He's battered, but his agenda isn't beaten. *New York Times*, Mar. 5, sec. 4, 1.

Kolhatkar, Sheelah, and Rebecca Dana. 2005. The story of the hurricane: After a period of self suppression, the horrific story spurs the press. *New York Observer*, Sept. 12, 1. http://observer.sbsisp.com/printpage.asp?iid=11413&ic=News+Story+ (accessed June 15, 2006).

Kovach, Bill, and Tom Rosenstiel. 2001. *The elements of journalism: What news-people should know and the public should expect.* New York: Three Rivers Press.

Kurtz, Howard. 2004a. Seymour Hersh: At the front lines on war scandals. *Washington Post*, May 19, C1.

———. 2004b. The *Post* on WMDs: An inside story; prewar articles questioning threat often didn't make front. *Washington Post*, Aug. 12, A1.

Lagouranis, Anthony. 2006. Tortured logic. *New York Times*, Feb. 28, A19.

Lawrence, Regina G. 2000a. Game-framing the issues: Tracking the strategy frame in public policy news. *Political Communication* 17 (2): 93–114.

———. 2000b. *The politics of force.* Berkeley and Los Angeles: Univ. of California Press.

———. 2001. Defining events: Problem definition in the media arena. In *Politics, discourse and American society,* ed. Roderick P. Hart and Bartholomew H. Sparrow, 91–110. Lanham, MA: Rowman & Littlefield Publishers, Inc.

———. 2005. Daily news and first amendment ideals. In *Freeing the presses: The first amendment in action,* ed. Timothy Cook, 87–108. Baton Rouge: Louisiana State Univ. Press.

Lawrence, Regina G., and W. Lance Bennett. 2000. Civic engagement in the era of big stories. *Political Communication* 17 (4): 377–81.

———. 2001. The Exxon *Valdez* and Alaska in the American imagination. In *American Disasters: A Reader,* ed. Stephen Biel, 382–402. New York: New York Univ. Press.

Lawrence, Regina G., and Thomas A. Birkland. 2005. Guns, Hollywood, and criminal justice: Defining the school shootings problem across public arenas. *Social Science Quarterly* 85 (5): 1193–1207.

Leary, Warren E. 2006. New NASA policy backs free discussion by scientists. *New York Times*, Mar. 31, A16.

Leigh, Robert D., ed. 1947. *A free and responsible press.* Chicago: Univ. of Chicago Press.

Lelyveld, Joseph. 2005. Interrogating ourselves. *New York Times Magazine*, June 12, 36–69.

Lewis, Neil A. 2004. U.S. spells out new definition curbing torture. *New York Times*, Dec. 30, A1.

Lippman, Walter. 1997 [1922]. *Public opinion.* Reissue ed. New York: Free Press.

Livingston, Steven. 1996. *Beyond the CNN effect: An examination of media effects according to type of intervention.* Cambridge, MA: Shorenstein Center on

Press, Politics and Public Policy, Kennedy School of Government, Harvard University.

———. 2000. Transparency and the news media. In *Power and conflict in the age of transparency*, ed. Bernard I. Finel and Kristin M. Lord, 257–85. New York: St. Martins Press.

———. 2002. The new information environment and diplomacy. In *Cyber-diplomacy in the 21st century*, ed. Evan Potter, 110–27. Montreal, Quebec: McGill Univ. Press.

Livingston, Steven, and W. Lance Bennett. 2003. Gatekeeping, indexing, and live event news: Is technology altering the construction of news? *Political Communication* 20:363–80.

Livingston, Steven, W. Lance Bennett, and W. Lucas Robinson. 2005. International news and advanced information technology: Changing the institutional domination paradigm? In *Media and conflict in the 21st century*, ed. Philip Seib, 33–55. New York: Palgrave.

Livingston, Steven, and Todd Eachus. 1995–96. Humanitarian crises and U.S. foreign policy: Somalia and the CNN effect reconsidered. *Political Communication* 12 (14): 413–29.

Livingston, Steven, and Lucas Robinson. 2006. Strange bedfellows: The emergence of the Al Qaeda–Baathist news frame prior to the 2003 invasion of Iraq. In *Leading to the 2003 Iraq war: The global media debate*, ed. Alexander G. Nikolaev and Ernest A. Hakanen, 21–37. New York: Palgrave.

Livingston, Steven, and Douglas A. Van Belle. 2005. The effects of new satellite newsgathering technology on newsgathering from remote locations. *Political Communication* 22 (1): 45–62.

MacAskill, Ewan. 2006. US seen as a bigger threat to peace than Iran, worldwide poll suggests. *Guardian* (London), June 15. http://www.guardian.co.uk/.

Malone, William Scott. 2004. The general and the journalists. MediaChannel.org, Apr. 30. http://www.mediachannel.org/views/dissector/affalert189.shtml, accessed Sept. 27, 2005.

Martin, David. 2004. Ongoing calls for Rumsfeld to resign or be fired over Iraqi prisoner scandal. *CBS Evening News*, May 6.

Massing, Michael. 2004. *Now they tell us*. New York: New York Review of Books.

———. 2005. The end of news? *New York Review of Books* 52 (19), Dec. 1. http://www.nybooks.com/articles/18516.

Mayer, Jane. 2006. The memo. *New Yorker*, Feb. 27, 32–41.

Mazzetti, Mark. 2006. Military will keep planting articles in Iraq. *Los Angeles Times*, Mar. 4, A3.

Mazzetti, Mark, and Borzou Daragahi. 2005. U.S. military covertly pays to run stories in Iraqi press. *Los Angeles Times*, Nov. 30. http://www.latimes.com/news/nationworld/world/la-fg-infowar30nov30,0,5638790.story?page=1&coll=la-home-headlines.

McChesney, Robert. 2004. *The problem of the media: U.S. communication politics in the 21st century*. New York: Monthly Review Press.

McCombs, Maxwell E., and Dennis Shaw. 1972. The agenda-setting function of the mass media. *Public Opinion Quarterly* 36:176–87.

McDermott, Bill. 2004. Bring us the heads of "Karen Ryan" and "Alberto Garcia." *CJR Daily Development,* Mar. 15. http://www.cjrdaily.org/spin_buster/ bring_us_the_heads_of_karen_ry.php

McGowan, William. 2003. *Coloring the news: How political correctness has corrupted American journalism.* San Francisco: Encounter Books.

McQuail, Denis. 2003. *Media accountability and freedom of publication.* New York: Oxford Univ. Press.

MediaMatters for America. 2005. Hannity on Gannon: A terrific Washington bureau chief and White House correspondent for Talon News. Feb. 9. http:// mediamatters.org/items/200502100001.

———. 2006. Media ignored, underreported *NY Times* disclosure of explosive Bush-Blair memo. Mar. 28. http://mediamatters.org/items/200603280013.

Meet the Press. 2004. MSNBC, Mar. 28. http://msnbc.msn.com/id/4608698/.

Mermin, Jonathan. 1999. *Debating war and peace: Media coverage of U.S. intervention in the post-Vietnam era.* Princeton, NJ: Princeton Univ. Press.

Meyer, Dick. 2004. Rush: MPs "Just blowing off steam." CBS News.com, May 6. http://www.cbsnews.com/stories/2004/05/06/opinion/meyer/main 616021 .shtml (accessed Feb. 2, 2005).

Milbank, Dana. 2003. The military is the message: Triumphant president casts strong image for the '04 election. *Washington Post,* May 2, A24.

———. 2005. Colonel finally saw whites of their eyes. *Washington Post,* Oct. 20, A04.

Milbank, Dana, and Mike Allen. 2004. White House counters exaide; advisers call Clarke disgruntled, partisan. *Washington Post,* Mar. 23, A1.

Miller, Derek. 2007. *Media pressure on foreign policy.* New York: Palgrave.

Mindich, David T. Z. 1998. *Just the facts: How "objectivity" came to define American journalism.* New York: New York Univ. Press.

Molotch, Harvey, and Marilyn Lester. 1974. News as purposive behavior: On the strategic use of routine events, accidents, and scandals. *American Sociological Review* 39:101–12.

———. 1975. Accidental news: The great oil spill as local occurrence and national event. *American Journal of Sociology* 81 (2): 235–59.

Morin, Richard. 2006. Majority in U.S. fear Iraq civil war. *Washington Post,* Mar. 7, A3.

Mueller, John. 2005. The Iraq syndrome. *Foreign Affairs* Nov.–Dec., 44–54.

Murray, Shailagh. 2005. Durbin apologizes for remarks on abuse. *Washington Post,* June 22, A6.

Murray, Shailagh, and Charles Babington. 2006. Democrats struggle to seize opportunity: Amid GOP troubles, no unifying message. *Washington Post,* Mar. 7, A1.

Nagourney, Adam, and Carl Hulse. 2005. Democrats intensify criticism of White House response to crisis. *New York Times,* Sept. 8, A21.

Napoli, Philip M. 1995. The marketplace of ideas metaphor in communications regulation. *Journal of Communication* 49:151–69.

National Security Archive. 2006. Rumsfeld's roadmap to propaganda. Jan. 26. http://www.gwu.edu/~nsarchiv/NSAEBB/NSAEBB177/index.htm.

Newport, Frank. 2004. Iraq and Al Qaeda. Gallup Organization, June 22. http:// poll.gallup.com (accessed May 22, 2006).

New York Times. 2002. Threats and responses; with few variations, top administration advisors present their case. Sept. 9, A8.

———. 2004a. "My deepest apology" from Rumsfeld. May 8, A8.

———. 2004b. The *Times* and Iraq. From the editors. May 26. http://www .nytimes.com/2004/05/26/international/middleeast/26FTE_NOTE.html?ex =1400990400&en=94c17fcffad92ca9&ei=5007&partner=USERLAND (accessed Apr. 12, 2006).

———. 2004c. Report card on the occupation. June 29.

Norton-Taylor, Richard. 2006. Blair-Bush deal before Iraq war revealed in secret memo. *Guardian* (London), Feb. 3, 1.

Novak, Robert. 2004. Mission to Niger. *Washington Post,* July 14, A21.

Okrent, Daniel. 2004. "Torture" vs. "abuse" in the *Times*'s coverage of Iraqi prisons.*New York Times,* June 1. http://forums.nytimes.com/top/opinion/ readersopinions/forums/thepubliceditor/danielokrent/index.html?offset=31 (accessed Feb. 24, 2005).

Online NewsHour. 2006. CIA leaks. PBS, Apr. 25. http://www.pbs.org/newshour/ bb/media/jan-june06/leaks_4-25.html

Open letter to President Bush. 2005. *New Orleans Times-Picayune,* Sept. 4, A 15.

Overholser, Geneva, and Kathleen Hall Jamieson, eds. 2005. *The Press.* New York: Oxford Univ. Press.

Packer, George. 2006. The lesson from Tal Afar. *New Yorker,* Apr. 10, 48–65.

Page, Benjamin I. 1996. *Who deliberates? Mass media in modern democracy.* Chicago: Univ. of Chicago Press.

Patterson, Thomas. 1992. Irony of the free press: Professional journalism and news diversity. Paper presented at the annual meeting of the American Political Science Association, Chicago, Sept. 3–6.

———. 1993. *Out of order: How the decline of political parties and the growing power of the news media undermine the American way of electing presidents.* New York: Knopf.

———. 2000. Doing well and doing good: How soft news and critical journalism are shrinking the news audience and weakening democracy—and what news outlets can do about it. Cambridge, MA: Shorenstein Center on the Press, Politics, and Public Policy, Kennedy School of Government, Harvard University.

Pew Research Center. 2004. Foreign policy attitudes now driven by 9/11 and Iraq. Aug. 18. http://people-press.org/reports/print.php3?PageID=871 (accessed Feb. 16, 2005).

———. 2005a. Bush approval falls to 33%, Congress earns rare praise. Mar. 15. http://people-press.org/reports/display.php3?ReportID=271 (accessed Mar. 22, 2006).

————. 2005b. Commentary: The public's complicated views of press point to solutions. June 26. http://people-press.org/reports/display.php3?PageID=971 (accessed Nov. 15, 2005).

Pickard, Victor. 2006. Media democracy deferred: The rise and fall of progressive communication policy, 1945–1948. Paper presented at the Union for Democratic Communications Conference, Boca Raton, FL, May 18–26.

Pillar, Paul R. 2006. Intelligence, policy, and the war in Iraq. *Foreign Affairs*, Mar.–Apr., 15–27.

Pincus, Walter. 2003. Little words, big implications: "Strategic Coordination" may have led to an allegation about Iraq being repeated. *Washington Post National Weekly Edition*, Apr. 11–17, 11.

Porter, Tim. 2003. An uncivil eulogy to civic journalism. Apr. 18. http://www.timporter.com/firstdraft/archives/000105.html.

Potter, Evan H. 2002. The new information environment and diplomacy. In *Cyber-Diplomacy: Managing foreign policy in the 21st Century*, ed. Evan H. Potter, 110–27. Georgetown, ON: McGill-Queen's Univ. Press.

President Bush discusses faith-based initiative in Tennessee. 2003. Feb. 10. http://www.whitehouse.gov/news/releases/2003/02/20030210–1.html (accessed June 2, 2006).

President George Bush discusses Iraq in national press conference. 2003. Mar. 6. http://www.whitehouse.gov/news/releases/2003/03/20030306–8.html (accessed June 2, 2006).

Priest, Dana, and Joe Stephens. 2004. Pentagon approved tougher interrogations. *Washington Post*, May 9, A1.

Prindle, David F. 2004. The idea of a marketplace of ideas. Paper presented at the annual meeting of the Western Political Science Association, Portland, OR, Mar. 11–13.

Program on International Policy Attitude/Knowledge Networks Poll. 2003. Misperceptions, the media, and the Iraq War. Program on International Policy Attitudes (Center for International and Security Studies at Univ. of Maryland) and Knowledge Networks (Menlo Park, CA). Oct. 2. http://65.109.167.118/pipa/pdf/oct03/IraqMedia_Oct03_rpt.pdf

————. 2004. Americans on detention, torture, and the war on terrorism. Program on International Policy Attitudes (Center for International and Security Studies at Univ. of Maryland) and Knowledge Networks (Menlo Park, CA). July 22. http://www.pipa.org/OnlineReports/Terrorism/Torture_Ju104/Torture_Ju104_rpt.pdf

Purdum, Todd S. 2002. Bush officials say time has come for action in Iraq. *New York Times*, Sept. 9, A1.

Revkin, Andrew C. 2005. White House official altered climate data. *International Herald Tribune*, June 9, 6.

Ricks, Thomas E. 2004. Rumsfeld's war plan shares the blame. *Washington Post*, Aug. 25, A1.

————. 2006. *Fiasco: The American military adventure in Iraq*. New York: Penguin Press.

Risen, James. 2004. Hussein warned Iraqis to beware outside fighters, document says. *New York Times,* Jan. 14, A1.

———. 2006. *State of war: The secret history of the CIA and the Bush administration.* New York: Free Press.

Risen, James, and Eric Lichtblau. 2005. Bush lets U.S. spy on callers without courts. *New York Times,* Dec. 16, A1.

Rojecki, Andrew. 1999. *Silencing the opposition.* Chicago: Univ. of Chicago Press.

Rosen, Jay. 1999. *What are journalists for?* New Haven, CT: Yale Univ. Press.

Rubien, David. 2000. Seymour Hersh: The man who broke the story of Vietnam's My Lai massacre is still the hardest working muckraker in the newspaper business. *Salon,* Jan. 18. http://dir.salon.com/story/people/bc/2000/01/18/hersh/ (accessed Sept. 27, 2005).

Rutenberg, Jim. 2006. "Civil war" is uttered, and White House's Iraq strategy is dealt a blow. *New York Times,* Aug. 6, A4.

Sanders, Lisa. 2005. Exxon hires Bush energy aide. CBS MarketWatch.com, June 14. http://www.marketwatch.com/News/Story/Story.aspx?dist=newsfin der&siteid=mktw&guid=%7B03CA702F%2D7BB4%2D46C5%2DADB8%2 DCF5D44E3063A%7D&link=&keyword=exxon%20and%20bush.

Sands, Philippe. 2005. *Lawless world: America and the making and breaking of global rules.* New York: Viking.

Schattschneider, E. E. 1983 [1960]. *The semi-sovereign people.* Fort Worth, TX: Holt, Rinehart, and Winston.

Schiffer, Adam. 2006. Blogswarms and press norms: News coverage of the Downing Street memos. Paper presented at the 2005 meetings of the American Political Science Association, Washington, DC, Aug. 31–Sept. 3.

Schleifstein, Mark. 2004. Corp sees its resources siphoned off; wetlands restoration officials sent to Iraq. *New Orleans Times-Picayune,* Apr. 24, 2.

Schlesinger, James R. 2004. Final report of the independent panel to review DOD detention operations. Independent Panel to Review DOD Detention Operations. August. http://f11.findlaw.com/news.findlaw.com/wp/docs/dod/ abughraibrpt.pdf.

Schmitt, Eric. 2002. Three retired generals warn of peril in attacking Iraq without backing of U.N. *New York Times,* Sept. 24, 16.

———. 2004. Rumsfeld denies details of abuses at interrogations. *New York Times,* Aug. 28, A1.

———. 2005. Three in 82nd Airborne say beating Iraqi prisoners was routine. *New York Times,* Sept. 24, A1.

———. 2006a. Career of general in charge during Abu Ghraib may end. *New York Times,* Jan. 5, A3.

———. 2006b. Iraq abuse trial is again limited to lower ranks. *New York Times,* Mar. 23, A20.

———. 2006c. Abuse charge set for U.S. colonel. *New York Times,* Apr. 25, 1.

———. 2006d. Few punished in abuse cases. *New York Times,* Apr. 27, 24.

Schmitt, Eric, and Carolyn Marshall. 2006. In secret unit's "Black Room," a grim portrait of U.S. abuse. *New York Times*, Mar. 19, 1.

Schudson, Michael. 2005. Why democracies need an unlovable press. In *Freeing the presses*, ed. Timothy Cook, 73–86. Baton Rouge: Louisiana State Univ. Press.

Seelye, Katharine Q. 2004. For six hours onstage, the Rumsfeld survival rules displayed, by the man himself. *New York Times*, May 8, A1.

Semetko, Holli, and Christian Kolmer. 2005. The news media as political institution: Reporting Iraq in comparative perspective. Paper presented at the annual meeting of the American Political Science Association, Washington, DC, Aug. 31–Sept. 3.

Shadid, Anthony. 2005. *Night draws near*. New York: Henry Holt and Co.

Shane, Scott. 2005. Criminal inquiry opens into leak in eavesdropping. *New York Times*, Dec. 31, A1.

Shanker, Thom. 2006. U.S. general says Iraq could slide into a civil war. *New York Times*, Aug. 4, 1.

Shanker, Thom, and Jacques Steinberg. 2004. Bush voices "disgust" at abuse of Iraqi prisoners. *New York Times*, May 1, A1.

Shanker, Thom, and Kate Zernike. 2004. Abuse inquiry faults officers on leadership. *New York Times*, Aug. 19, A1.

Sigal, Leon V. 1973. *Reporters and officials: The organization and politics of newsmaking*. Lexington, MA: D. C. Heath and Company.

Sikkink, Kathryn. 2005. U.S. compliance with international human rights law. Paper presented at the annual meeting of the International Studies Association, Honolulu, Mar. 1–5.

60 Minutes. 2004a. Clarke's take on terror. CBS, Mar. 21. http://www.cbsnews .com/stories/2004/03/19/60minutes/main607356.shtml.

———. 2004b. Rice leads counterattack. CBS, Mar. 28. http://www.cbsnews.com/ stories/2004/03/28/60minutes/main609074.shtml.

Slevin, Peter. 2004. System failures cited for delayed action on abuses. *Washington Post*, May 20, A19.

Smith, R. Jeffrey. 2004. General is said to have urged use of dogs. *Washington Post*, May 26, A1.

Sontag, Susan. 2004. Regarding the torture of others. *New York Times Magazine*, May 23, 25–42.

Sparrow, Bartholomew H. 1999. *Uncertain guardians: The news media as a political institution*. Baltimore: Johns Hopkins Univ. Press.

Spinner, Jackie. 2004. U.S. general says Iraqi security will run Abu Ghraib by August. *Washington Post*, May 27, A20.

Stevenson, Richard W. 2004a. Bush disputes ex-official's claim that war with Iraq was early administration goal. *New York Times*, Jan, 13, A22.

———. 2004b. Orders by Bush about prisoners set humane tone. *New York Times*, June 23, A1.

Stevenson, Richard W., and Douglas Jehl. 2005. Leak case renews questions on war's rationale. *New York Times,* Oct. 23, 1.

Stewart, Potter. 1975. Or of the press. *Hastings Law Journal* 26:634.

Stolberg, Sheryl Gay. 2004. Kennedy says war in Iraq was choice, not necessity. *New York Times,* Jan. 15, A13.

Suskind, Ron. 2004. Faith, certainty and the presidency of George W. Bush. *New York Times,* Oct. 17. http://www.nytimes.com/2004/10/17/magazine/17BUSH .html?ex=1255665600&en=890a96189e162076&ei=5090&partner=rssuse rland.

Swanson, David. 2005. How Cindy Sheehan is waking the media up. Mediachannel.org, Aug. 22. http://www.mediachannel.org/blog/node/713.

Taylor, Guy. 2004. Pentagon Channel targets troops. *Washington Times,* Dec. 27, A04.

Teixeira, Ruy. 2006. The Iraq War: Three years on. Center for American Progress, Mar. 22. http://www.americanprogress.org/site/pp.asp?c=biJRJ8oVF&b=15 00197 (accessed May 22, 2006).

Toobin, Jeffrey. 2006. Name that source. *New Yorker,* Jan. 9. http://www. newyorker.com/fact/content/articles/060116fa_fact.

Toppo, Greg. 2005. Education Department paid commentator to promote law. *USA Today,* Jan. 7. http://www.usatoday.com/news/washington/ 2005-01-06-williams-whitehouse_x.htm.

Torres, Manuel. 2001. Flood work to slow down; corps delay new projects. *New Orleans Times-Picayune,* Oct. 13, 1.

Tuchman, Gaye. 1978. *Making news: A study in the construction of reality.* New York: Free Press.

United Nations Commission on Human Rights. 2006. Situation of detainees at Guantanamo Bay. http://www.ohchr.org/english/bodies/chr/docs/62chr/ E.CN.4.2006.120_.pdf (accessed Feb. 16, 2006).

U.S. Department of State. Advisory Committee on Public Diplomacy. 2005. *Cultural diplomacy: The linchpin of public diplomacy.* http://www.state.gov/ documents/organization/54374.pdf (accessed Apr. 21, 2006).

VandeHei, Jim. 2004. Kerry assails Bush on Iraq. *Washington Post,* May 13, A1.

———. 2006. Bush says U.S. troops will stay in Iraq past '08. *Washington Post,* Mar. 22, A01.

Van Natta Jr., Don. 2006. Bush was set on path to war, British memo says. *New York Times,* Mar. 27, 1.

Viguerie, Richard A., and David Franke. 2005. *America's right turn: How conservatives used new and alternative media to take power.* New York: Bonus Books.

Waas, Murray. 2006. Iraq, Niger, and the CIA. *National Journal,* Feb. 4. http://www .informationclearinghouse.info/article11778.htm.

Washington Post. 2003. Shinseki repeats estimate of a large postwar force. Mar. 13, A12.

———. 2004a. This will be a decisive blow to terrorism. May 25, A12.

———. 2004b. Closer to the truth. Aug. 22, A22.

———. 2006. The politics of science. Feb. 9, A22.

Weintraub, Bernard, and Thomas Shanker. 2003. Rumsfeld's design for war criticized on the battlefield. *New York Times*, Apr. 1, A1.

White, Josh. 2004a. Generals point to contractors, Military Intelligence soldiers. *Washington Post*, Aug. 26, A1.

———. 2004b. U.S. generals in Iraq were told of abuse early, inquiry finds. *Washington Post*, Dec. 1, A1.

Wilkerson, Lawrence. 2005. Remarks to the New American Foundation, Washington, DC. http://www.thewashingtonnote.com/archives/Wilkerson%20 Speech%20—%20WEB.htm.

Wilson, Jamie. 2005. Bush's climate row aide joins oil giant. *Guardian* (London), June 16. http://www.guardian.co.uk/usa/story/0,12271,1507554,00.html.

Wilson, Joseph C. 2002. How Saddam thinks. *San Jose (CA) Mercury News*, Oct. 13. http://www.politicsoftruth.com/editorials/saddam.html.

———. 2004a. The politics of truth: A diplomat's memoir; Inside the lies that led to war and betrayed my wife's CIA identity. New York: Carroll & Graf Publishers.

———. 2004b. What I didn't find in Africa. *New York Times*, July 6, 9.

Wolfsfeld, Gadi. 1997. Media and political conflict: News from the Middle East. Cambridge: Cambridge Univ. Press.

Wolfsfeld, Gadi, Paul Frosh, and Maurice T. Awabdy. 2005. Journalistic mechanisms for covering death in violent conflicts: News about the second Intifada on Israeli, Palestinian, and Al-Jazeera television. Paper presented at the annual meeting of the International Communication Association, New York, May 26–30.

Wright, Robin. 2004. U.S. faces lasting damage abroad; moral high ground lost, experts say. *Washington Post*, May 7, A26.

Wypijewski, JoAnn. 2006. Judgment days: Lessons from the Abu Ghraib courts-martial. *Harper's* (Feb.): 39–50.

Zaller, John. 1992. *The nature and origins of mass opinion.* New York: Cambridge Univ. Press.

———. 2003. A new standard of news quality: Burglar alarms for the monitorial citizen. *Political Communication* 20:109–30.

Zaller, John, and Dennis Chiu. 1996. Government's little helper: U.S. press coverage of foreign policy crises, 1945–1991. *Political Communication* 13:385–405.

Zernike, Kate. 2004. Defining torture: Russian roulette, yes. Mind-altering drugs, maybe. *New York Times*, June 27, WK7.

Zogby International. 2006. Zogby poll: Majority supports impeaching Bush for wiretapping. Jan. 16. http://www.zogby.com/Soundbites/ReadClips.dbm? ID=12528.

INDEX

ABC: on British memo on Bush's preference for war, 148, 229n48; and Bush
administration rationales for Iraq war, 43;
Nightline, 167; public opinion polls on Iraq
war, 174
Abizaid, John P., 175, 197
abortion, 4, 39–40, 90, 100, 176, 195
Abu Ghraib, 72–107
  as boon for terrorists, 108–9
  Bush administration and: "Animal House
  on the night shift," 52, 78, 88; Bush apologizes for humiliation of Iraqi prisoners,
  126; Bush's plausible deniability for, 123,
  226n30; on Durbin's criticism of, 131–32;
  as "low-level abuse" problem, 6–7, 9, 84,
  88, 98, 102–3, 106, 116; news management of, 78, 79, 81, 101–3, 105, 222n28;
  Rumsfeld and, 82, 86, 102, 104, 110, 122–
  29, 201, 222n29; Rumsfeld's visit to, 103
  conditions at, 227n41
  controversy over abuses at: documentary
  evidence for torture at, 84–90, 199–204;
  as institutional policy not human error,
  83, 87; as international scandal, 109–10;
  Justice Department memo on exempting
  U.S. from legal restraints on torture, 86,
  202; McCain and, 6–7, 10, 47, 52, 74,
  99, 105, 106, 222n31, 224n10; Pentagon
  memo on interrogation techniques,
  86; Senate Armed Services Committee
  hearings on, 103, 201; whether *torture* is
  correct label for abuses at, 81–84
  detainee abuse after, 223n63
  the detainees, 111–16, 225n12, 225n15;
  ghost detainees, 123, 225n12
  as intelligence-gathering site, 115
  and Iraq war: increasing unease about
  the war as context of, 78, 88; public approval of war drops after publication of
  photographs of, 78–81, 79; rebound in war
  support after, 81, 104, 221n14

low-level offenders punished for, 106, 110,
  122, 127–28, 224n4
military trials of soldiers involved in,
  127–28, 227n45
official reports on: Fay report, 85, 87, 96,
  109, 124, 203, 222n28; Ryder report, 200;
  Schlesinger report, 78, 85, 86, 87, 96,
  109, 111–12, 114, 124–25, 127, 128, 204,
  222n29; Taguba report, 85, 87, 102, 199,
  221n25
press coverage of: *abuse* applied to, 90,
  92, 92, 93, 94, 95–97, 99, 102, 103, 105,
  106, 107, 130; in alternative press, 75, 81,
  101; in arc of news from Iraq invasion to
  Hurricane Katrina, 70, 71; on CBS, 6, 61,
  72, 73, 91, 95, 102, 106, 113–14, 225n15;
  consequences of news reality filter
  regarding, 108–30; Democrats and press
  limits regarding, 103–4; foreign news
  coverage of, 116–19, 225n21; gap between
  world opinion and U.S. news on, 110, 111,
  115–21; Hersh's reporting on, 57, 62, 73,
  85, 87, 101, 219n25, 221n25; on higher
  responsibility for, 121–29; high-level
  dissent to Bush administration missing in,
  100, 109; indexing and, 51–53, 75; labels
  applied to events at, 90, 92; and limits of
  press independence, 99–106; *mistreatment*
  applied to, 90, 92, 92, 95, 97, 103, 105;
  and narrowed of range of debate about,
  109; news framing of, 89–98, 205–11;
  in *New York Times*, 88, 91, 94, 96, 99,
  104, 106, 119, 128, 148, 175; as one-sided,
  top-down story, 81; pattern and volume
  of press perspectives on, 92–94; press
  buying Bush administration version of,
  137–38; press failing to challenge Bush
  administration over, 6–7, 9–10, 47, 74–75,
  99; press independence demonstrated in
  breaking story of, 61, 106, 174–75; press
  lacking "flywheel" to advance story on,